SECURITY OFFICERS AND POLICING

T0347929

This book is dedicated to Emma and Conrad

Security Officers and Policing

Powers, Culture and Control in the
Governance of Private Space

MARK BUTTON
Institute of Criminal Justice Studies,
University of Portsmouth, UK

LONDON AND NEW YORK

First published 2007 by Ashgate Publishing

2 Park Square, Milton Park, Abingdon, Oxon OX14 4RN
711 Third Avenue, New York, NY 10017, USA

Routledge is an imprint of the Taylor & Francis Group, an informa business

First issued in paperback 2016

British Library Cataloguing in Publication Data
Button, Mark
    Security officers and policing : powers, culture and
    control in the governance of private space
    1. Police, Private - Legal status, laws, etc. - England
    2. Police, Private - Legal status, laws, etc. - Wales
    3. Police, Private - England 4. Police, Private - Wales
    I. Title
    344.4'205289

Library of Congress Cataloging-in-Publication Data
Button, Mark.
    Security officers and policing : powers, culture and control in the governance of private space / by Mark Button.
       p. cm.
    Includes bibliographical references and index.
    ISBN-13: 978-0-7546-4797-3
    ISBN-10: 0-7546-4797-8
  1. Police, Private--England. 2. Private security services--Law and legislation--England. 3. Police, Private--Wales. 4. Private security services--Law and legislation--Wales. 5. Police. I. Title.

  KD4839.B88 2006
  342.42'0418--dc22

                         2006021137

ISBN 978-0-7546-4797-3 (hbk)
ISBN 978-1-138-26458-8 (pbk)

Contents

List of Figures		*vii*
List of Tables		*ix*
Table of Legislation and Cases		*xi*
Foreword		*xiii*
Acknowledgements		*xv*
List of Abbreviations		*xvii*

Introduction — 1

1   Power, Authority and the Security Officer: Under-researched and Under-estimated? — 5

2   Researching Security Officers — 21

3   The Legal Tools of Security Officers in England and Wales — 31

4   Nodes of Governance: Pleasure Southquay and Armed Industries — 45

5   'Knowledge is Power?': Security Officers' Understanding of their Legal Tools — 65

6   Universal Legal Tools: Consent, Coercion and Commonsense — 87

7   Select Legal Tools: Compliance, Consent and Commonsense — 111

8   Occupational Hazards: Too Many Masters, Isolation and Abuse — 133

9   'I'm a Security Guard Get Me Out of Here!' The Cultural Characteristics of Security Officers — 151

10   'Big Fish in Little Ponds', Security Officers and the Policing of Private and Hybrid Space — 177

Bibliography — *189*
Index — *201*

List of Figures

Figure 3.1   Models of security officer power   43

Figure 7.1   The Armed Industries system for prosecuting breaches
              of the speed limit   122

Figure 7.2   Lukes' three dimensional model of power applied to
              security officers achieving outcome situations   128

Figure 9.1   Watchmen – Parapolice Continuum   173

Figure 9.2   The cultural characteristics of security officers   174

Figure 10. 1 Security officer orientation applied to models of security
              officer power   185

List of Tables

Table 2.1   Structured interviews conducted at each case study   23

Table 2.2   Semi-structured interviews conducted   24

Table 2.3   Documentary sources used during research   27

Table 4.1   Recorded crime in Pleasure Southquay compared to the city's main shopping area 1 January 2001–31 December 2001   53

Table 4.2   Personal characteristics of security officers interviewed at Pleasure Southquay and Armed Industries (%)   59

Table 4.3   Educational achievement of security officers interviewed (%)   60

Table 4.4   Training received by officers interviewed (%)   61

Table 4.5   Attitude towards the suitability and quality of training for current job at Pleasure Southquay (%)   62

Table 4.6   Attitude towards the suitability and quality of training for current job at Armed Industries (%)   62

Table 5.1   How well security officers think they know their legal tools   66

Table 5.2   How well security officers rated the quality and quantity of their training in their legal tools (%)   68

Table 5.3   All security officers knowledge of their legal power to arrest compared to other occupations (%)   69

Table 5.4   Pleasure Southquay officers' knowledge of their legal power to arrest compared to other occupations (%)   70

Table 5.5   Armed Industries officers' knowledge of their legal power to arrest compared to other occupations (%)   70

Table 5.6   Security officers' answers to Question 22 (%)   71

Table 5.7   Security officers' answers to Question 23 (%)   73

Table 5.8   Security officers' answers to Question 24 (%)   76

Table 5.9   Security officers' answers to Question 25 (%)   78

Table 5.10   Security officers' answers to Question 26 (%)   79

Table 5.11   Security officers' answers to Question 27 (%)   82

Table 5.12   Mean number of answers per security officer which were satisfactory *minor* and **major** errors   83

Table 5.13   Mean number of answers per security officer according to level of training which were satisfactory, *minor* or **major** errors   84

Table 6.1   Number of 'arrests' security officers have claimed to have made (%)   89

Table 6.2   Number of times security officers have used force (%)   95

Table 6.3   Should security officers be granted additional special
             legal powers (%)   101
Table 6.4   Should private security officers be allowed to carry
             non-lethal weapons such as truncheons, cs gas, pepper sprays
             etc to to defend themselves (%)   105
Table 7.1   Number of searches security officers have made (%)   116
Table 7.2   Recorded traffic offences at Armed Industries during 2002   123
Table 8.1   Pleasure Southquay security officers' perception of police
             attitude when they visit (%)   136
Table 8.2   Pleasure Southquay security officers' perception of police
             attitude towards them (%)   137
Table 8.3   Pleasure Southquay security officers' perception of public
             attitude towards them at night and day (%)   139
Table 8.4   Armed Industries security officers' perception of Armed
             Industries staff attitude towards them (%)   139
Table 8.5   Security officers' experience of verbal abuse (%)   141
Table 8.6   Security officers' experience of threats of violence (%)   143
Table 8.7   Security officers' experience of assault
             (slight bruising/bleeding) (%)   145
Table 9.1   Reasons for entering current employment (%)   158
Table 9.2   The number of security officers actively seeking
             alternative employment (%)   159

Table of Legislation and Cases

Legislation

Anti-Terrorism, Crime and Security Act 2001   35
Aviation Security Act 1982   35
Commonwealth Immigrants Act 1962   11
Constables Act 1750   7
Courts Act 2003   36
Criminal Justice Act 1991   11, 36
Criminal Justice and Public Order Act 1994   11
Criminal Law Act 1967   35, 80, 91
Immigration Act 1971   11
Immigration and Asylum Act 1999   11
Nationality, Immigration and Asylum Act 2002   11
Police and Criminal Evidence Act (PACE) 1984   32, 34–5, 71, 91
Police Reform Act 2002   11, 36, 101
Private Security Industry Act 2001   18, 41
Protection of Aircraft Act 1973   35
Railways Act 1993   36
Road Traffic Act 1972   11
Serious Organised Crime and Police Act 2005   32, 33, 65
Vagrancy Act 1824   32

Regulations and Statutory Instruments

Channel Tunnel under the Channel Tunnel (Security) Order 1994   36
Serious Organised Crime and Police Act 2005 (Commencement No. 4 and
Transitory Provision) Order 2005.   33

Cases

Appleby and Others v United Kingdom [2003] ALL ER (D) 39   37
BL Cars Ltd v Brown [1983] IRLR 193   40
CIN Properties v Rawlings [1995] 2 EGLR 130   37
Entick v Carrington [1765] 19 St. Tr. 1030   7
Laselles Stanley v Ajab Singh Benning (T/A Temptation Clothing and Charlie

Brown Menswear) [1998] LTL 14/7/98 Extempore (Unreported elsewhere)   34

Porter v Commissioner of Police of Metropolis [1999] WL 852129   37

R v Jackson (Kenneth) [1984] Crim LR 674   34

R v Howell [1981] All ER 383   34

R v Self [1992] Cr App R 42   34

Showboat Entertainment Ltd v Owens [1984] ICR 65   40

Weathersfield Ltd (t/a Van and Truck Rentals) v Sargent [1999] IRLR 99   40

Foreword

It is an enormous pleasure to have been invited to write the Foreword to Mark Button's latest book on the Private Security Industry.

When I first began to take an interest in the private security industry as a relatively new Member of Parliament in the mid 1970s, the security industry was in its early stages of development and there were only a handful of academics studying, publishing and lecturing on the subject. There were far more researchers involved in policing subjects, but this academic attention was at that time not well advanced, though certainly far more developed than interest in private security. It was ironic that although what we now call the private security industry and 'profession' had a very long history, the literature devoted to it was sparse, with a few exceptions in the USA and Canada. There were some researchers that took a brief interest, but who soon disappeared to pursue their academic endeavours in other areas of public policy. The Home Office was similarly disinterested, tolerating, indeed endorsing an unregulated industry relying upon what can only be described as grossly imperfect and partial self-regulation. The media was sporadically excited but almost invariably after some major or minor scandal. All this began to change albeit slowly. Parliament began to pay attention, a Labour Government committed to regulation was elected and more inside and outside the industry were converted to the cause of a regulated and transforming industry. A handful of those academics that developed an early interest stayed the course and there were very few newcomers entering the field. It is only in the last decade or so that a new generation of academics have realised this to be an important subject worthy of study and persistence. Mark Button represents one of this new generation, with nearly 10 years commitment to researching the industry.

This excellent book is a very welcome addition to the still limited though growing area. I am delighted to write that the serious literature available both emanating from the UK and abroad is burgeoning and some University departments and policy institutes are taking this subject seriously and I might add the Home Office is at last a major and serious player. Relations with the police are improving, in contrast to previous decades and the industry is perceived by them to be part of 'the wider police family'. The events in New York and Washington on 11 September 2001 and elsewhere has afforded a great opportunity for security in all of its dimensions to play a bigger role in protection.

This book is groundbreaking for a number of reasons. First it is one of only a handful of published studies across the world that provides an empirical study of security officers in their working environments. Second, it provides a snapshot of the private security industry on the eve of regulation illustrating many examples of poor standards that still regrettably blights much of the industry. Indeed, Mark's study is of some of the better quality companies, albeit a small minority who meet British Standards and were members of the British Security Industry Association. I suspect that if Mark had conducted his research across the entire spectrum of the guarding sector, the picture of the industry would have been far bleaker.

The Security Industry Act 2001 is already helping to transform the industry in a broader sense, something Mark and I campaigned very long and hard on together to help secure. It is not the only factor that is contributing to positive change in the industry, but is possibly the most significant. This excellent book explores principally the manned guarding sector of this growing industry at that point of transition from the old, pre Security Industry Authority period. It shows security guards working for low pay, working very long hours, in often trying conditions and desperate to leave. Turnover of staff was incredibly high, reflecting public perception of their job and their own frustration. Morale was low and many felt themselves alienated from their fellow workers and the public. It portrays security officers as the butt of verbal abuse, threats of violence and for some, assault is a regular occurrence. Despite these conditions, however, it also shows how some security officers were and are extremely brave, dealing with drunken yobs and sometimes drug crazed and infected shoplifters. It also highlights a new breed committed to their role as well as enhancing the standing of their occupation.

The new regulatory system that Mark and I campaigned for is not a panacea, it will not metamorphosize the industry and many of its old and bad practices will take time to be eliminated. The legislation, which was rushed through Parliament just in time before the General Election of 2001, is far from perfect. There are those who opposed statutory regulation who still persist with this view, and those who were convinced realise the complexities and problems of regulating this vitally important growing industry. However, I am confident that there are already strong signs that the legislation is already having a positive impact and the snapshot of the industry Mark presents here, will begin to change as the impact of regulation begins to transform the culture and practices of the industry.

I hope this empirical study will stimulate further research in the UK and abroad, so we can begin to compare the impact of regulation. Mark has provided an original and fascinating account of security officers in the UK and this should be required reading for practitioners, policy-makers and academics with an interest in this subject.

Rt Hon Bruce George MP

Acknowledgements

I must first thank Professor Robert Reiner who proved a very patient and invaluable source of advice over the long gestation of this project and without whom this research would never have reached this stage. Additionally the staff and students in seminars at the LSE and University of Portsmouth have also provided a challenging environment in which to present early findings as well as offer advice. There are many other people who have helped me while undertaking this research and it will not be possible to name them all. I will, however, try and name most, but apologies if you have not been mentioned! First of all I would like to thank Barry Loveday for his comments on the original research proposal and comments on the final draft. Once I began the research there were a number of people who helped me in securing access and information that was required for this project. Raymond Clarke of SITO must be thanked for allowing me to spend time in their offices reviewing their many manuals and training courses. Bob Ralph, Lance Ayres, Chris Northy-Baker, Andrew Merret and Gill Poulter must also be thanked in their roles in securing me access to the two case studies. The many security officers who allowed me to interview them and observe them must also be thanked, this study would not have been possible without them. I would also like to thank Professor Steve Savage, Professor Les Johnston, Professor Nigel South and Dr Philip Rawlings for providing detailed comments on drafts of this book. Linked to this I must also thank the University of Portsmouth for providing financial support as well as the time and resources to conduct this study. I would also like to thank Dr Alison Wakefield and Dr Deborah Michael who have also helped through providing useful information and articles. Finally I would also like to thank the Rt Hon Bruce George MP who has always been a source of inspiration for ideas and issues relating to the private security industry and for finding the time in his busy schedule to read a draft of this book and write a foreword.

List of Abbreviations

AI   Armed Industries
BRC   British Retail Consortium
BS   British Standard
BSIA   British Security Industry Association
CSO   Customer Service Officer (security officer at Pleasure Southquay)
HAC   Home Affairs Committee
IPSA   International Professional Security Association
ISI   Inspectorate of the Security Industry
MB   Mark Button
NAHS   National Association of Healthcare Security
NTE   Night Time Economy
PACE   Police and Criminal Evidence Act
PS   Pleasure Southquay
SIA   Security Industry Authority
SITO   Security Industry Training Organisation
SO   Security Officer (security officer at Armed Industries)

Introduction

Over the last 30 years, the provision of policing has changed considerably, with a marked increase in private security agents and organisations employed in a wide variety of roles (Bayley and Shearing 1996; Johnston 2000; Reiner 2000a; Rawlings 2002; and Crawford and Lister 2004a and b). Loader (2000, 323) described this shift thus, '…the sovereign state – hitherto considered the focal point to both provision and accountability in this field – [has been] reconfigured as but one node of a broader, more diverse "network of power"'. Today, policing, security and governance occur at a number of inter-twined levels which have been described as 'nodes' and 'bubbles' of governance (Loader 2000; Johnston and Shearing 2003; Rigakos and Greener 1999).

In most industrial countries, the private security industry now employs more people than the public police (Jones and Newburn 1995; and De Waard 1999). More significantly than manpower, however, the private security industry increasingly undertakes many roles that were traditionally those of the state police. There is, indeed, hardly a function that the police perform that is not now also carried out by the private security industry (Jones and Newburn 1998).

The growth in private security naturally raises many research questions, most notably about security officers. There have been several empirical studies of this subject, by South (1985), McManus (1995), Flynn (1997), Noaks (2000), Rigakos (2002), Michael (2002), Wakefield (2001 and 2003), Crawford and Lister (2004a) and Joh (2005). Research is still lacking, however, into the extent of private security officers' powers and how they make use of them, if at all. Most security officers do not have any special statutory powers, yet to many they are seen as authoritative figures and derive other legal powers from a complex range of legal sources (Stenning and Shearing 1979, Sarre 1994; South 1997; and Stenning 2000).

As Sarre and Prenzler (1999, 24) have argued,

> Private security personnel are a formidable force for good or ill in modern society. In many countries they substantially outnumber the police. As agents of property owners they possess considerable powers, and their authority, while on private property, more often than not exceeds that of conventional police. It is therefore somewhat anomalous that questions regarding public police accountability continue to receive far more attention from academics, civil libertarians and policy makers than private operations do.

Security officers' legal powers can include being able to search people and property, forcibly eject people from private property, undertake intrusive surveillance and enforce rules which may involve the ability to apply sanctions (such as financial penalties for unauthorised parking). Some routinely use their citizen's right of arrest, which most members of the public do not. Despite popular misconceptions about their ineptitude and incompetence (Livingstone and Hart 2003), in their own little 'ponds', security officers often have considerable power.

Therefore the view that security officers are little more than ordinary employees or citizens with the addition of a uniform will be challenged in this book (Home Office 1979; and Murray 1996). As South (1988, 127) has argued, 'Private security personnel do not act like ordinary citizens, indeed their commercial raison d'etre is that they should not.'

This study is also important because the growth of private security raises significant questions concerning divisions emerging in society (Johnston and Shearing 2003). This can be identified in the access given to different groups to policing services and the exclusion of certain groups from places of shopping and entertainment. Increasingly social divisions are emerging between the rich and corporate clients on the one side and the poor on the other. The former have been able to supplement limited state provision with private policing, while the latter have been left with reduced public services (Davis 1990; and Johnston and Shearing 2003). Fears have also arisen as to how landowners can arbitrarily exclude certain groups from places of entertainment and shopping, which located on private space could lead to what Charles Reich has called an 'internal exile' (cited in Gray 1994). This study will seek to investigate whether these concerns have any validity based upon the two case study sites.

The book is based upon two stages of research that sought to address a series of questions. The first stage seeks to answer, what are the legal tools of security officers in England and Wales? The second part of the research answers a much wider range of research questions. These include what is the role of security officers within their workplace and what other strategies are used alongside them to achieve their objectives? How good is their knowledge and how confident are security officers of their legal tools? To what extent do security officers actually use their legal tools and when they do, how do they use them? How does the use of tools vary in different spatial contexts? What hazards do security officers face in undertaking their duties, particularly making use of their legal tools? Do security officers possess an occupational culture and if so how does that affect their use of their legal tools? How important are security officers in the governing structures of their place of work? These are some of the main research questions this book attempts to answer.

This study will commence in Chapter 1 with an examination of some of the research that has been conducted on security officers and their legal powers. It also explores what power is, as well as examining research on police powers, which has parallels and additionally provides clues to researching security officers. Chapter 2 outlines the challenges of researching security officers and briefly outlines the two-stage methodology used for this research. The results of the first stage of the research are presented in Chapter 3. This sets out the two types of legal powers security officers can draw upon. These include universal legal tools that all security officers possess no matter where they work and select legal tools, which depend upon the spatial context of where the officer is working. From the analysis of the types of legal tools available the chapter identifies different models of security officer based upon the legal powers available to them.

Chapter 4 provides the first of 6 chapters on the data drawn from the second stage of the research. This chapter examines the two case study sites utilised for this research: Pleasure Southquay and Armed Industries. It sets out the characteristics of the two locations, the security arrangements and a brief examination of the systems of governance. It explores these two places within the context of Johnston and Shearing's (2003) tools for analysing nodes of governance. The chapter also provides an analysis of the personal characteristics of the security officers at the two locations and how representative these might be of the broader occupation of security officer in England and Wales.

Chapter 5 draws upon the knowledge test security officers undertook. The quality of their knowledge of their legal tools is explored. It shows that although they were prone to make at least one mistake in the test, they generally had a good understanding, although their confidence of their knowledge did not always reflect their ability. Chapters 6 and 7 explore respectively the universal and select legal powers used by security officers. The chapters offer an examination of the range of legal tools used and also provides quantitative data on their extent of use. Drawing upon observational and interview data the chapters also examine examples of how these legal tools are used in practice and the types of strategies security officers pursue to secure compliance. Chapter 7 concludes by utilising Lukes' (1974) three dimensional model of power to illustrate how security officers are part of a broader range of strategies to secure outcomes in their place of operation.

A significant finding in this research was some of the occupational hazards faced by security officers in conducting their role. In Chapter 8 these hazards are explored. These include the difficulties of working in an environment where there are multiple structures of management, often with conflicting agendas. It also comprises the problem of isolation faced by security officers, as well as abuse in the form of verbal insults, threats of violence and assault. There has been much research on police culture and how that influences the use of their powers and the controls placed upon them. In Chapter 9 the cultural characteristics of security officers are examined. In doing so the chapter identifies the core characteristics and some of the other facets that distinguish different models of officer.

Finally the book concludes by drawing together the findings and arguing that although in society as a whole security officers are not generally considered as important or powerful, in the context of their working environment and as part of a broader security system they are significant agents and hence 'big fish in little ponds'.

Chapter 1

Power, Authority and the Security Officer: Under-researched and Under-estimated?

Introduction

Changing structures of governance, policing and security have meant that the primary human protective resource in many places has shifted from the police to security officers (as well as other non-police personnel) (Johnston and Shearing 2003; and Crawford and Lister 2004a). In undertaking these functions security officers can draw on a wide range of resources (or tools as Mopas and Stenning call them) to secure the outcomes necessary for their role, that include legal rights, uniforms and weapons amongst others (Mopas and Stenning 2001). These 'tools' potentially provide security officers with significant power, although relatively little is known about how security officers use them, if at all. This chapter will explore the research and scholarship on security officers and their powers, examining the sources of power, the extent of their use and abuse, amongst other issues. This chapter will also briefly examine the much more extensive literature on police powers, because this provides clues for researching security officers. Before embarking upon this, however, it is necessary to briefly explore what is meant by power as this will aid an understanding of the legal powers of security officers.

What is power?

Power has been the subject of much debate. At the base level it seems a relatively simple concept: the ability of A to get B to do something they otherwise would not do. This is only part of the picture, however, and this first dimension, as Lukes (1974) would call it, forms the foundations of less visible forms of power. For Lukes there are another two dimensions to power, the second of which, involves a critique of the first and is where A prevents an issue of conflict from emerging so that B still pursues a course of action that if that issue had arisen B might have pursued differently. As Lukes (1974, 20) writes,

> ...the two dimensional view of power involves a qualified critique of the *behavioural focus* of the first view and it allows for consideration of the ways in which *decisions* are

prevented from being taken on potential issues over which there is an observable *conflict of interests*, seen as embodied in express policy preferences and sub-political grievances.

Such power was also recognised by Foucault (1977) in Bentham's panopticon, where a prison constructed to enable the surveillance of prisoners without them knowing if they were been watched meant conformity was the only option for them. The third dimension provides a further critique of the earlier two views and is a consideration of ways in which potential issues are kept out of decision-making so as to influence the decision-making of an actor, without them even realising it. In this case it would be a scenario where A pursues a course of action because B has created an environment which means A will follow that course of action without realising B wanted that to occur. In short it is the creation of social structures that encourage a course of action that the subjects are not observably aware of. Such social control measures that exist are extensive and have been explored by Cohen (1985) in broader society.

To put these in a security context if a security officer asks a 'youth' to leave a shop when they do not wish to and they do, that could be considered as an example of the first dimension of power. An example of the second, might be where a security officer's mere presence leads a 'youth' not to enter the shop when they want to. The third dimension could be illustrated by a 'youth' not even wanting to enter the shop because sub-consciously they have been influenced not to do so, hence the behaviour of the 'youth' had been influenced without there been any observable conflict.

Another analysis of power that distinguishes the more opaque side is Dowding's (1996) distinction between 'outcome power' and 'power over' or 'social power'. Dowding defines them as,

> Outcome power = the ability of an actor to bring about or help to bring about outcomes.
> Social power = the ability of an actor deliberately to change the incentive structure of another actor or actors to bring about or help to bring about outcomes (Dowding 1996, 5).

Thus a security officer has the power to make a citizen's arrest in certain circumstances – an outcome power. They also possess a wide range of social powers varying according to their skill and the social environment they work within. Social power is recognised as being an important concept, as it reflects the ability of an individual to make x happen by manipulating the social environment. This might be at one extreme the threat of coercion to more subtle tactics of influencing the incentive structures of an individual. For example a security officer who wants to make a trespasser leave private property could at one extreme threaten to physically remove them if they refuse to leave. Alternatively the officer could persuade the trespasser to leave by threatening legal action or to call the police.

By its very nature, then, social power is a much more complex concept and also more difficult to measure than outcome power. In the case of security officers an analysis of their legal powers can be undertaken to list their outcome powers. With social power it varies between individuals and according to the social environment. The types of resources that determine the degree of social power include factors such as knowledge, legitimate authority, incentives available to offer and reputation

(Harsanyi 1976a and b, cited in Dowding 1996). These could also be reapplied as potential sources of power for security officers.

This brief overview of power has illustrated the complexities of power and in-particular the more opaque sides. These help in understanding the power of security officers because they show that one has to do more than identify what legal tools they have available to them. It is important to examine the security officer in the social environment in which they work and how they achieve outcomes. Indeed as the next section reveals, studies of police powers have also delved into the more opaque side in-order to secure the fuller picture of the power of the police.

Police powers

There is an extensive literature on police powers. Broadly it can be divided into legalistic works describing what police (and other state officials) powers are (such as Feldman, 1996; Zander, 2003; and Jason-Lloyd 2005) and studies into their use (see, Dixon 1997 for overview). Such is the wide range and amount of literature on police powers it would not be possible to provide a comprehensive overview in the space available in this book. However, some of the research conducted on police powers provides important insights for a study of security officers.

Attitudes to police powers have also changed over time. Up until the eighteenth century the legal powers of constables were very complex and their power stemmed more from the office of constable rather than legal powers. By the eighteenth century, however, with the changing nature of the state, society and policing, changes in this conception emerged. In response to challenges to the authority of constables, the Constables Act 1750 was passed which gave legal immunity to constables acting under a magistrate's warrant. In the famous judgement of Lord Chief Justice Camden in 1765 in *Entick v Carrington* he stated, '[i]f it is law, it will be found in our books. If it is not to be found there, it is not law' (cited in Dixon 1997, 55).

This marked the beginning of putting police powers into the law books. However, even by the formation of the 'new police' in 1829 there were few special powers given to the police. Five years previously the Vagrancy Act had created a wide range of deviant acts, which had a power of arrest attached that could be used by any citizen; such powers, however, would be of much greater use to a constable. Thus the view of police officers as nothing more than ordinary men doing what any good citizen would do had a strong basis at this time. By the 1960s, however, this view – which still prevailed even in the 1962 Royal Commission – did not reflect the growth of special police powers and what in reality the police actually did vis-à-vis ordinary citizens in terms of policing. As Choongh (1997) has argued where the police have not possessed a legal power they have simply assumed them when necessary. He argues,

...the police tightened their grip over the suspect by simply assuming powers which the law denied them. This process of expanding their powers by engaging in unauthorized practices was accompanied by a co-ordinated police effort to legitimate and authenticate their actions by persuading judges, politicians and the public that what they were doing was necessary in order to curb crime. They did this by denigrating rules designed to protect suspects, claiming that they only knew what had to be done to apprehend and convict criminals, and by putting themselves forward as a professional body who could be trusted to respect the freedoms and liberties of law abiding citizens (Choongh 1997, 12).

Thus for many hundreds of years formal legal powers were not what gave the constable power to achieve objectives, it was holding the office of constable that gave him the authority to achieve them. It is only with the changes in state society relations that it became necessary to begin to write down and then gradually extend the powers a constable possessed. An important issue that arises from history is the importance of the 'office of constable' in securing compliance and consent. This authority that the office of constable provides still exists today. The police are able to secure compliance and consent through a wide range of strategies one of which is merely being a constable. This consent is extremely important in the relationships between police and society as will shortly be discussed.

The legal powers of police officers do not present the whole picture, as securing consent is also widely used to secure objectives. As soon as consent is achieved by a police officer the legal relationship also changes. No longer is it a relationship between an official of the state and a citizen, rather *prima facie* between two citizens (Dixon 1997, 90). This also means that many of the obligations that are required of a police officer exercising legal powers are not required when consent is gained. This means in many situations the rights of suspects disappear, records do not have to be kept, to name some examples.[1] Consent is therefore very important as it gives not only power to the police, but also in many cases a much less regulated power. As Dixon (1997, 90) has noted,

> Some of the consequences of 'consensual' encounters are that statutory requirements for the exercise of powers do not apply (so that, for example, a suspect can be searched without reasonable grounds for suspicion), record-making is unnecessary (rendering supervision more difficult), and the rights of the suspect do not have the protections which are corollaries of the exercise of legal power.

By their very nature it is also possible for police officers to secure consent through a number of strategies. Police officers are frequently viewed by members of the public as authoritative figures who possess power (Loader 1997). The fact that constables were able to exercise powers up until 1750 with little legal clarity on what their powers actually were, is testament to the long history of the authority of the office of constable. The perception of constables as authoritative and powerful still continues today. It is interesting that a study of the Wandsworth Parks Police (who are constables but only in the context of local authority bye-laws) found that of 40 arrests during 1994 only 4 related to the bye-laws. It was concluded that most of the other arrests (90 per cent)

---

1   Although the Police and Criminal Evidence Act 1984 did include the regulation of some specific activities undertaken by consent.

were unlawful (Goodwin 1996). The fact that constables were able to undertake these arrests can largely be explained by their image as police constables. It is unlikely that 'park wardens' would have been able to achieve the same results.

The use of language is another important strategy used by the police. Often police officers will ask 'What have you got in your bag?' rather than 'Open your bag so I can search it'. Thus they are asking a question rather than forcing them to do something. Dixon (1997) describes examples from New South Wales in Australia where officers have never had to say 'You are under arrest'. Instead they say 'You are going to have to come back to the station'.

The threat of use of legal powers, arrest, search warrant etc is yet another strategy used by police officers. One of the most common areas in which this occurs is related to searches of premises. Often police officers will threaten to come back later with a search warrant if they aren't allowed in. These same strategies are also often used in relation to searches and asking suspects to come to the police station to help them with their enquiries.

Another common strategy of police officers in securing consent is to exploit the suspect's ignorance. In a survey of 2,000 officers, 79 per cent claimed suspects rarely knew their rights. Of those that claimed they knew their rights, officers would then often resort to 'bamboozling' the suspect by claiming they have the authority to do something or threatening arrest. In a study by Lidstone and Bevan (u.d.) they found that 32 per cent of recorded searches in two force areas were undertaken through consent and that in most cases this 'consent' was gained in situations of duress, when the suspect was unlikely to be aware that they could refuse.

Perhaps one of the most significant issues that enables police officers to secure consent is the implied guilt of the suspect if they don't agree to their requests. Thus if they are asked to empty their pockets, if their house can be searched or if they will come to the police station to 'help with enquiries', in many cases suspects will, for fear of appearing guilty if they don't .

Overall what the extensive research on police powers reveals is the ability of police officers to exercise considerable power without using their legal powers simply by securing consent. If power can be achieved without recourse to legal powers then for those occupations engaged in policing who do not have any or as many special legal tools, they could potentially exercise power through securing consent. Thus not only will it be necessary to assess the legal powers of private security officers it will also be essential to examine the relationship between private security officer and those they police in various situations.

Security officers' powers

There has been relatively little research into the legal powers of private security officers internationally and virtually none in England and Wales.[2] The research

---

2   England and Wales is used as the legal systems are different in Scotland and Northern Ireland.

which does exist has mainly focused upon what legal powers security personnel possess (Braun and Lee 1971; Stenning and Shearing 1980; Sarre 1994; Jason-Lloyd 2003; and Sarre and Prenzler, 2005), public perceptions of private security officers' powers (Mopas and Stenning 1999), the regulation of their powers and accountability mechanisms (Scott and McPherson 1971; and Button 1998; and Stenning 2000), and security officers' knowledge of their legal powers (Kakalik and Wildhorn 1971d).

The literature on the legal powers of private security officers generally shows no special powers given to them through legislation (although there are a few exceptions to this that will shortly be discussed). Much of the research, however, does suggest that private security personnel do derive power from a variety of other sources. These include various legal sources (most commonly from property law, contract law and employment law), through the wearing of uniforms and carrying weapons to name some. Mopas and Stenning (1999) describe the various sources of power as 'tools of the trade'. This term will be used to examine some of the many sources of power for security officers.

Legal tools

There are a wide variety of legal sources that give powers to private security officers. First there are some security officers working in specialist locations who have been given special legal powers to search, as in courts in England and Wales. Second there are powers that all citizens possess which security officers make greater use of, such as the right to make a 'citizen's arrest'. Finally security officers working on private space or policing those in employment relationships can often derive powers from property, contract and employment law. As South (1997, 107) has argued,

> Ordinary citizens are in fact routinely in positions where private security personnel may search them (airport security), exclude them (shopping malls), place them under surveillance (CCTV), evict them (nightclubs) and so on.

Some of these 'legal' tools used by security officers will now be explored.

Special legal powers

There are some security officers that possess special statutory powers, although this is relatively rare. For instance research in the USA has illustrated many private security personnel who are deputised by the local police (Braun and Lee 1971). In Canada Stenning and Shearing (1979) have shown the many private security staff possess 'peace officer' status, which gives them additional powers. In some countries security personnel are given special powers that do not amount to 'police powers'. For instance in Finland private security officers have the right to remove from property they are guarding someone who does not have the right to be there (Allen 1991). There is also a protection of the security officer of an offence of 'violent behaviour towards a security officer'.

There are also some a-typical security personnel that have been given special legal powers. Prison custody officers working in private prisons and prison escorts in England and Wales possess similar powers to public sector prison officers under the Criminal Justice Act 1991 and Criminal Justice and Public Order Act 1994 (Jason-Lloyd 2003). Security officers working in courts also possess special powers of search and the Police Reform Act 2002 has provisions to give security staff working for accredited community safety schemes a range of special powers (some of the powers of these type of officers will be examined briefly in Chapter 3). Some security officers also possess special powers under private/hybrid legislation and local bye-laws. For instance the New Covent Garden market security force have powers to enforce the provisions of the Road Traffic Act 1972 – although they were found to hardly use these powers (Jones and Newburn 1998).

The legal powers of private security officers working at Immigration Detention Centres has also raised some interesting debates. When detention centres were first contracted out to the private sector in 1970 some critics asked under what basis immigration and asylum seekers could be detained, given that private security officers possessed no special legal powers and at the time there had been no legislation enabling the contracting out. Initially officials cited the 1962 Commonwealth Immigrants Act, which stated, 'Any person required or authorized under this Act may be detained in such places as the Secretary of State may direct' (South 1988). Until the 1999 Immigration and Asylum Act, as amended by the Nationality, Immigration and Asylum Act 2002, the 1971 Immigration Act had been cited (Jason-Lloyd 2003). This legislation gives private security staff similar legal powers and responsibilities as prison custody officers in private prisons.

In some jurisdictions the legal rights of citizens, private property owners and employers have been challenged in the courts on a variety of issues. In some jurisdictions this has led to the extension of these rights beyond what legislators may have originally intended. In a study of the legal powers of private security officers in Canada, Rigakos and Greener (1999) found that although the legal grounds for arrest by a private citizen or security officer were narrower than for a peace officer, courts in cases of wrongful imprisonment and arrest had loosened these greater constraints effectively expanding a security officer's arrest powers.

A common right in some countries is for security personnel to carry arms or a non-lethal weapon. As Mao Zedong once said, '…political power grows out of the barrel of a gun' (Ransley 1991, 331). In many countries private security officers are frequently armed. In the USA, Australia and in some countries in Europe this occurs either through special legislation that allows them to be armed or using general citizen rights to carry weapons. The carrying of arms by private security officers provides a basis for power in signalling authority and ultimately in forcing compliance – which has often been used illegally (Kakalik and Wildhorn 1971b and d). In the UK private security officers are never officially armed, although up until 1966 a limited number of security officers were authorised to carry firearms to protect bullion and cash in transit (South 1989). It was also common up until the 1970s for some private security officers to carry lesser weapons such as truncheons. In 1973, however, three security officers were convicted under the 1953 Prevention of Crime Act for carrying batons. There was an appeal to the Court of Appeal, which failed and since then most reputable companies have agreed that private security officers should not be armed (Draper 1978). There are also a growing number of security staff who are been given defensive weapons such as handcuffs (Ralph, 2004).

General citizen legal powers

In most countries citizens possess rights of arrest and self-defence in specific circumstances. The exact nature and extent of such legal powers varies between countries. The general powers of arrest in England and Wales will be considered in more depth in Chapter 3. These legal powers are different from some of the other legal powers private security officers possess, that will shortly be considered, as they cannot be withdrawn by the employer (Stenning and Shearing 1979). Thus all citizens, including private security personnel, possess these rights, which cannot be removed by anyone else (such as an employer), although influence can be exerted from employers on how and if security personnel use them.

Rights of property owners

In the twentieth century there has been what Stenning and Shearing (1980) describe as a growth in 'mass private property'. These include large shopping malls, leisure facilities, office complexes, industrial locations. In many of these settings large numbers of people work and pursue leisure activities. They do so often as a member of the public entering private property. This mass private property has emerged in England with little recognition in law of the changes that have taken place in the nature of private property that is open to the public (Gray and Gray 1999a, b and c). There has been a movement from small private properties generally restricted to the owner and his/her guests to larger properties open to members of the public as guests or paying customers. These same private property owners generally possess a wide range of rights on their property as if it was their own private home. These include restrictions on who has access, setting conditions on those that enter, rights to remove trespassers to name a few. Most of these rights can and are delegated to agents of the owner. In many cases this is private security personnel who when properly trained in the use of these legal tools can secure significant power. As Rigakos (2002, 77) noted when observing new Intelligarde security officers being trained in these tools,

> The talk of private powers captivates the candidates. Many of them can hardly believe how much authority they will be able to exert on private property. They are told, 'As long as you can justify it, make the arrest.'

Thus a situation has emerged where private property that is open to the public is policed by private security personnel who possess a wide range of legal tools in their workplace which are analogous, if not more impressive, than those of the public police in a public area. Thus some of the legal tools that private security personnel might derive by operating on private property include, inter alia, powers of denial of entrance, forcible ejection, to search and to conduct surveillance (Stenning and Shearing 1979; Sarre 1994; and Button 1998).

Employment and generic contracts

The majority of citizens work for an employer in an employment relationship that involves an employment contract. These contracts are often extensive documents that are frequently linked to codes of conduct and the rules of the workplace. These often allow the employer to undertake various practices with regard to their employees, which if refused by the latter could result in disciplinary action leading to termination of employment. The most common requirement is for employees to agree to undergo searches of their personal belongings (Stenning and Shearing 1979). There are other requirements that are frequently set in their contracts of employments either directly or indirectly which include credit reference checks, surveillance, and drug tests (Sarre 1994; and Button 1998). Again some of these tools will be explored in more depth later in this book.

Many citizens ordinarily enter into contracts with another individual or organisation for a wide variety of reasons. Often these contracts give the parties certain rights in particular situations (Sarre 1994). One of the most common contracts relates to contractors working for a company on a specific project. Often the company will seek to extend the same – if not more – powers over contractors as they would their own staff concerning search, surveillance, checks etc.

Physical tools

It has been argued by Loader (1997) that the police derive significant authority from symbolic images based upon uniforms, equipment, rituals etc. Similarly private security personnel also derive varying degrees of authority by the images they present (Stenning and Shearing 1979). There has been much research that has illustrated how an individual wearing a uniform can secure a greater degree of compliance than someone not wearing one. Bickman (1974) undertaking experiments using a civilian, milkman and guard was able to show the latter – through the uniform worn – secured much greater compliance than the others vis-à-vis the public. Further research on this subject by Bushman (1984) also found that compliance increased as the perceived authority did, where a person dressed as a fireman was able to secure greater success in requests made to the public than a man dressed in a business suit or as a 'bum'. Most private security personnel wearing police/military style uniforms, drive in officially marked vehicles, carry 'official' identity badges, and in some countries carry weapons (De Waard 1993). Nearly all security personnel in some form represent a corporate body or organisation that is seen by some to have power and authority which private security staff as agents of, also derive. These all combine to give private security staff a degree of authority. As Davis (1957, 22, cited in Becker 1974) states,

> The mere presence of a uniformed individual contributes a psychological condition of great significance to the average mind. Over the period of many years, the wearer of the uniform has represented a leader, designated and recognised by government bodies. This association has been attached to the form of distinctive wearing apparel.

Indeed in Great Britain one of the frequent arguments that has been used against statutory regulation of the private security industry has been the authority such regulation might give to the industry (see Button 1998; and George and Button 1998). In many ways, however, security personnel already possess that authority without statutory regulation. As Scott and McPherson (1971, 272) argue,

> ...it is probably true that most individuals when confronted by a uniformed guard or a man stating that he is a 'detective' or 'investigator' naturally assume he has some kind of legal authority.

Linguistic tools

Earlier in this chapter it was illustrated how police officers frequently prefer to persuade a person to do something through the language they use to secure consent, rather than exercise their legal powers (Dixon 1997). This often enables a police officer to circumvent some of the many legal controls that often regulate their powers. These observations also apply to security officers. For even if they have no formal powers to ask an individual to do something, if that individual consents they can. Moreover because of their authoritative nature it could be argued that they are also more likely to secure consent than an ordinary citizen. Many of the powers of the legal tools of private security officers rest on the consent of the individual. Without it – even in situations where there might be a legal right – security officers are often reluctant to pursue action for fear of litigation. As Braun and Lee (1971, 566) have argued, 'In the absence of consent, however, it appears that there is little legal authority for most forms of private search'.

Knowledge tools

It was also revealed earlier in this chapter how police officers use their superior knowledge of their legal tools to secure outcomes. Knowledge also gives confidence to officers to use their tools. As one extract from a trainer's comments to new security officers at Intelligarde noted by Rigakos (2002, 81) illustrates, 'The law is your tool – like a mechanic. If you know the law, you can better do your job. If I don't have him under this section, I'll use another... I'll place a guy under arrest for littering so that I can get his name.' There has, however, been very little research into the quality of security officers' knowledge of their legal tools. The only research that has been conducted was in the USA in the early 1970s (Kakalik and Wildhorn 1971d). Obviously the relevance of these findings to England and Wales over 30 years later is limited. They do, however, represent a base to build a comparable study for the UK.

In their study they surveyed 275 private security officers on a range of issues including: employee and job description; how they would act in hypothetical situations; their knowledge and attitudes towards their job, supervisor, regular police, and public; and their views on how the company and public see themselves. The study raised some very interesting – and often disturbing findings – on the attitudes and knowledge of private security officers. For instance 18 per cent of respondents said they did not know what their legal powers were and a further 23 per cent were unsure of them. Less than 50 per cent of respondents knew their arrest powers were the same as an ordinary citizen and 6 per cent thought they held the same powers as a police officer. Only 22 per cent knew under what conditions an arrest for a felony was legal. The study even found that 31 per cent of respondents thought it was a crime if someone called them a 'pig'! Six per cent of respondents would have been prepared to use deadly force to protect private property and 19 per cent thought as long as an arrest was made in good faith the security officer could not be subject to civil action.

The questionnaire presented to security officers also gave them hypothetical examples where they were asked to provide the lawful action they should pursue. In these questions 97 per cent of respondents made at least one mistake. The following example is typical of a number of the hypothetical situations that were presented (Kakalik and Wildhorn 1971d, 217):

> Suppose you are a security officer working in a retail store and you SUSPECT someone has concealed an article on his person without paying for it. What would you do?

> A. 2%   Approach him immediately and arrest him for shoplifting.
> B. 24%   Arrest him after he leaves the building.
> C. 56%   After the person leaves the store, ask him if he has forgotten to pay for something.
> D. 6%   Nothing.
> E. 5%   Take the person to the backroom and search them.
> F. 0%   Other (Specify)

Answers A and B were major errors as 'suspicion' would not justify an arrest, nor would it justify E in taking them to be searched. Based upon their research into the knowledge of their authority by security officers Kakalik and Wildhorn (1971d, 202) concluded, 'they (private security officers) do not know their legal authority, they exhibit faulty judgement in the stress situations we posed, and they surely need training'. Given the lack of knowledge of their powers and the fears over litigation it is also of no surprise to find that half the respondents had been told by their employer never to arrest anyone and a third had been told never to search anyone. The knowledge tool was therefore clearly under-utilised in the American context.

Cultural context

Even with access to all the tools identified above, if the philosophy and/or culture of the organisation and/or occupation is not to use them then they make very little difference. On the other hand if you combine the above tools with a culture of active use then the result is a potentially powerful security officer. There is little research in the UK on this cultural aspect of security officers. In Canada, however, amongst Intelligarde security officers Rigakos (2002, 49) found a culture of encouragement and active use of legal tools. He wrote,

> It will quickly become obvious that Intelligarde staff do not have special powers. What they do have is an organisational philosophy, and willingness to 'push the envelope' with the powers they do have.

This compares with the evidence from Kakalik and Wildhorn (1971d) cited above of the active discouragement of the use of legal tools. Therefore it is also important to consider the culture of an occupation and organisation to consider what values are placed on the use of legal tools.

Obedience to authority

There is also much evidence illustrating how ordinary citizens are obedient to authority. The most notable are the experiments of Milgram, which illustrated how individuals under the direction of authoritative figures in white coats were capable of administering potentially lethal shocks of electricity to a person who had failed to answer a question correctly (Milgram 1975). Research in Canada into public perceptions of the power of private security officers, however, suggests they might not be as obedient towards security officers' requests. Mopas and Stenning (1999) administered a survey to 200 individuals in Metropolitan Toronto over a three week period who were asked a range of questions including: what they would do in hypothetical situations with private security officers. Based upon their findings they suggested that the perception that members of the public were willing to comply with the requests of private security officers was perhaps overstated. For instance, amongst many other findings, their survey discovered that 43 per cent would not be willing to comply with a request by a security officer to search their bag. Furthermore they found that only 36.5 per cent thought they had the authority to make such a request.

The extent of use of powers by security officers

So far we have considered some of the research that illustrates what tools security officers can draw upon to undertake their policing functions, as well as how the public may be obedient to authority figures such as security officers. The next question that arises from this is do security officers make use of their legal tools and, if so, how do they do so and how frequently? Again there is limited research on these issues but some that has been published will be explored here.

The British Retail Consortium (BRC) annually publishes statistics on the number and cost of criminal incidents against retailers. For many of the early reports detailed statistics were presented on the number of apprehensions. For instance in 1997, 1.217 million shoppers and 17,000 staff were apprehended for theft of which 0.85 million and 7,000 were handed over to the police respectively (British Retail Consortium 1998). Unfortunately the BRC presents these findings differently now as the number of suspects detained per 100 outlets, rather than the absolute number of detentions. Given most of the surveys in the 1990s, using the old form of presentation, usually had between 1 and 1.5 million shoppers being detained it would be reasonable to assume that around 1 million people are detained every year by retailers. The vast majority of these apprehensions are carried out by either security officers or store detectives, so they provide some indication of the number of detentions carried out by security staff in this sector.

Rigakos (2002) in his study of Intelligarde presented a range of quantitative data on the use of different legal tools and involvement in incidents by security officers. He found Intelligarde officers were much more likely to be dealing with dangerous incidents than Metropolitan Toronto police officers. He also illustrated their use of verbal warnings, banning notices, photographing of suspects and use of search.

Another legal tool used by security officers is exclusion of undesirable people from private property. There have been two empirical studies that have offered quantitative data on the extent of use of this tool. Wakefield (2003, 177–179) in her study of three leisure/shopping facilities on quasi-public space undertook detailed analysis of the number and type of exclusions. She found during her observations (20 days at each) 34 people excluded from the 'Arts Plaza', 578 from the 'Quayside Centre' and 63 from the City Mall. In a study of the surveillance system of shopping malls in a northern city McCahill (2002, 135) also found security officers regularly ejecting shoppers for inappropriate behaviour. He found that of a total 52 incidents (no period of time specified) where security officers were deployed, that if teenagers were targeted 43 per cent were ejected, of those in their twenties only 18 per cent ejected, and those in their thirties none were ejected.

The abuse of power

There is limited evidence illustrating the abuse of authority by security officers in the UK and in other countries. In the survey of private security officers in the USA conducted by Kakalik and Wildhorn (1971d) in the early 1970s, discussed earlier, they found 22 per cent of respondents had witnessed a case of a private security officer using excessive authority. When asked to explain, 40 per cent described a case where excessive force was used, 30 per cent described improper arrest, detention, search etc. It was also discovered 12 per cent of respondents had had someone threaten to complain but not sue, while 3 per cent had been threatened with legal action which had been pursued in 25 per cent of cases. The Rand report provides a series of examples of the abuse of authority by private security officers (Kakalik and Wildhorn 1971b and d). The examples of the misuse of firearms are particularly disturbing. However, as they amount to anecdotal evidence from the USA some 30 years ago they do not warrant detailed consideration here. In the absence of empirical data, however, some anecdotal examples from England and Wales will be used to illustrate some of the abuses of authority that take place by private security officers.

In evidence to the HAC inquiry into the private security industry there was substantial evidence of security personnel using excessive force and violence when undertaking enforcement roles. At road construction sites there were numerous allegations of the use of excessive force and violence by security officers. The case of Paul Gill who was dragged from the protest site by security officers, punched in the face and also allegedly had musical instruments worth £800 smashed, is one example (Liberty 1995). At hunts there have also been numerous allegations of the use of excessive force and violence detailed by the Hunt Saboteurs Association (HSA) (1994) and Liberty (1995). The HSA also illustrated many examples where they had suffered excessive violence from security officers/stewards guarding hunts. Allegations included being whipped, kicked, beaten and threatened with knives, spades, coshes and even stun-guns. In one of the most graphic examples a woman protester was allegedly attacked and forced to eat sheep dung by two security staff (Hunt Saboteurs Association 1994). Senior managers from reputable firms have also been alleged to encourage the use of excessive violence. For instance a security manager at the Newbury by-pass demonstrations was alleged to have told his security officers at a briefing, 'Anything in the trees today you whack it, right? Thwack it with your helmet. Anything. And don't get caught' (*The Guardian*, 25 January, 1996). There has also been much anecdotal evidence of 'heavy handed' tactics used by wheel clampers. For instance during the debates over the Private Security Industry Act 2001 in Parliament in one illustrative case a lone woman whose car had been clamped and then towed away had been forced to travel 20 miles to a dump to pick up her car in exchange for £240 in cash (*Hansard* 28 March 2001: 1002). The extent to which the abuse of power might occur amongst security officers was shown by Adu-Boakye (2002) in his covert study as a security officer. On catching a notorious shop-lifter in the supermarket where he was working he was asked by senior managers to lie in his statement, to say the culprit had also been racist and violent, in the hope he would receive a tougher sentence – he refused, but many officers under such pressure would probably not.

Regulation and accountability of security officers

The regulation of powers used by private security personnel is generally not as systematically controlled in comparison to police officers. Indeed Scott and McPherson (1971) argued that without special arrest powers private security personnel often had greater latitude in investigations than public police. This was illustrated by statements from some private security personnel interviewed,

We can rough a guy up if we want to.
We can get a confession in cases where the police can't because we don't have to worry so much about a guy's rights.
We can use every means possible to secure information (Scott and McPherson, 1971, 272).

Similarly it was illustrated earlier in this chapter that in England and Wales the police often prefer to exercise power through 'consent' rather than through the use of statutory powers because this often means less regulation (Dixon 1997). The mechanisms that do exist can be divided into licence revocation, criminal prosecution and tort liability (Braun and Lee 1971). In Great Britain the possibility for licence revocation for security officers was introduced only in 2006 with the implementation of the 2001 Private Security Industry Act, although in-house security officers are still exempt (Button 2003). For criminal prosecution there has to be a breach of law and there has to be sufficient evidence to bring a successful prosecution. Therefore in minor and indeed some major breaches this is not a realistic option. The use of Tort law can be more effective and it is probably the biggest fear for private security organisations, particularly in the USA. Many people, however, would be put off by the costs of launching such action in the UK.

Conclusion

The limited research that has been conducted on security officers and their powers suggests these are under-estimated and they are more than ordinary citizens in uniform. Braun and Lee (1971, 582) have argued that private security personnel possess powers analogous to the police, stating, 'Private police enjoy extensive powers which enable them to perform functions analogous to public police activity'. Others have argued that private security personnel could be even more powerful than the public police (Becker 1974; and Scott and McPherson 1971). With the introduction of legislation to regulate private security, combined with the 2002 Police Reform Act which will enhance the role of private security in policing it is essential that more research is conducted on security officers and their powers. This book will contribute to this growing debate. As Becker (1974, 452) wrote nearly 30 years ago regarding the private security industry in the USA,

> Research directed towards understanding the effects of widespread use of private police on various interrelationships and attitudes within a community, including the citizen public police relationship, is needed in order to structure effective regulation concerning private police use.

Yet over 30 years later there has been relatively little research into the legal powers of security personnel in the USA, let alone the rest of the world. This book will contribute to that debate and hopefully stimulate further research in this under-researched field.

Chapter 2

Researching Security Officers

Introduction

The previous chapter revealed some of the most significant empirical studies of private security officers. The most common methods of researching security staff have been questionnaires and interviews (for example Flynn 1997; and Michael 2002), sometimes supported by observation where the researcher is known (for example Rigakos 2002 and Wakefield 2003) and very rarely covert observation (see South 1985; and Adu-Boakye 2002). As the study required the security officers to be interviewed it was not possible to pursue covert observation. Nevertheless observation, structured and semi-structured interviews as well as documentary research were pursued for this book in a two stage process. The next two sections will examine the two stages of the research outlining the methods used. The chapter will then identify the strategies for data analysis and then finally some of the ethical considerations in this research.

Stage 1: Establishing the legal tools of security officers

Chapter 1 illustrated the complex range of sources that provide private security officers with their legal tools. These come from citizens' rights, the rights of property owners as well as employment and contract law. There is no readily available codified document that outlines the full range of legal tools available to a security officer. This largely reflects the diverse nature of private security officers and the environments they operate in.

There are, however, numerous training manuals and guides that contain sections on the legal tools of private security officers. The first task was therefore to review some of the many manuals and guides that exist for their explanations of what legal tools private security officers possess. For instance the Security Industry Training Organisation (SITO), which sets the minimum standards of training for private security officers, have produced a number of training manuals which touch upon this issue. They include the industry basic training, and the Professional Security Officer and Advanced Security Officer training courses. Second, there were a number of codes of practice that provided information on what legal tools private security officers possess. For instance the Institute of Personnel and Development library had codes of practice from a number of organisations and associations related to the use of legal tools. The following are some of the guides that were consulted: Midlands

Co-operative Society, Right of Search; J Sainsbury, Searches; Tesco, Security Searches. There is even a Crime Prevention Agency publication, *Making Arrests – A Good Practice Guide for Retailers*. Third there were a number of books, primarily on police powers and civil rights, which provided useful information (Stone 1994; Jason-Lloyd 2003; and Zander 2003). Finally case law relating to the use of legal tools by private security officers was examined using the database *Lawtel*. The results from this research are presented in Chapter 3.

Stage 2: Security officers in their nodal context

The only other study that has specifically set out to explore the knowledge and use of legal tools by private security officers undertook a survey of them from a range of different companies (Kakalik and Wildhorn 1971d). It was decided that this would also be pursued for this study. However, the different nature of legal tools available to private security officers according to the environment they work in suggested a more focused approach based upon case study sites of different types of space where security officers predominate. As Dixon (1997, 73) has argued in researching police powers, 'Powers cannot be considered in isolation from other features of the criminal justice system.' Crawford (2002) has also noted the importance of the locality and how the 'place' has been ignored or underplayed in the context of debates concerning globalisation. Therefore with private security officers it was necessary to understand the 'place' or 'node of governance' where they operated, as well as their use of legal tools in relation to their own private justice system (as well as the criminal justice system). This could only be achieved by researching private security officers working at a specific 'place' or 'node' of governance. Thus the study required detailed case studies of private security officers operating in specific locations of governance, rather than a range of security officers working for a private security company for a multiplicity of different clients in different spatial environments. For this study two case studies were selected. The first was given the pseudonym Pleasure Southquay and was a retail leisure facility based upon quasi-public space with a team of 32 security officers. The second was a manufacturer of defence equipment based upon private space with 22 security officers. More information on these two sites will be provided in Chapter 4.

Methods used at the two case study sites

Given the wide range of research questions this study sought to answer it was necessary to utilise a variety of research methods. This is often referred to as 'triangulation' (Hagan 1993) or 'methodological pluralism' (Walklate 2000). The use of a wider range of methodologies would also provide more balanced and reliable results. In this study structured and semi-structured interviews, were combined with observation as well as analysis of documentary sources. The tools used will now be examined in more depth.

Interviews

Interviews are one of the most popular and effective means to secure information in research. They do, however, require careful planning and skill to conduct effectively. As Cohen (1976, 82) advocates, 'like fishing, interviewing is an activity requiring careful preparation, much patience, and considerable practice if the eventual reward is to be a worthwhile catch.' The first decision required was whether to use structured, semi-structured or unstructured interviews (Bell 1993). It was decided for this study to use a mixture of structured and semi-structured interviews.

Given the aims of the research the primary research tool used was structured interviews with the security officers. The questions relating to knowledge in these interviews were inspired by the questionnaires used for the Kakalik and Wildhorn (1971d) study of American security officers. Additional questions were also applied to cover a range of other issues, other than testing the knowledge of security officers. Their aim was to provide information on the following issues: personal information and background; employment conditions; education and training; knowledge of legal powers; attitude to legal powers and other important issues; attitude to relationship with other agencies (police, client etc); and attitudes to supervisors and managers. As the questions tested the security officers' knowledge it was important that they were administered in an interview and not as a postal questionnaire as the latter would enable them to cheat to find the answers. The structured interview did enable security officers to open up to certain questions and if they did, diversions from the questionnaire frequently occurred. The structured questions have provided a great deal of data that is comparable and this will be illustrated in subsequent chapters. Table 2.1 below outlines the structured interviews conducted during the research and the high percentage of officers at each site interviewed. The interviews generally lasted around one hour, although some were as short as 30 minutes and one lasted over 2 hours. Throughout the rest of this book when an extract from an interview with one of these officers is presented Pleasure Southquay officers will be identified CSO 1 to 29 and Armed Industries officers SO 1 to 20 (CSO is customer service officer and the rationale for this will be discussed in Chapter 4, SO is security officer).

Table 2.1 Structured interviews conducted at each case study

	Male		Female		Total	
	N	%	N	%	N	%
Pleasure Southquay	24	96	5	83	29	94
Armed Industries	18	90	2	100	20	91

In addition to the structured interviews with security officers semi-structured interviews were also pursued with key personnel involved in the policing of these assignments. As the data sought was not as focused this enabled the interviews scope to cover a wide range of issues. General themes in the interviews were identified and then depending upon the response a range of supplementary questions pursued. Table 2.2 identifies those who were interviewed using the semi-structured interview.

Table 2.2 Semi-structured interviews conducted

Name of job function interviewed	Case study
Security Supervisor	Pleasure Southquay
Operations Manager	Pleasure Southquay
Contract Manager (Security contractor)	Pleasure Southquay
Police Sergeant	Pleasure Southquay
Marketing Director	Pleasure Southquay
Security Controller	Armed Industries
Contract Manager (Security contractor)	Armed Industries

There is much debate over the merits of tape recording interviews versus taking notes. Maguire (2000, 133) in relation to researching offenders has argued against tape recording, stating, '…I decided early on never to use a tape-recorder, even in prison interviews, as it could damage the crucial trust I had built up with those I spoke to.' Clearly a tape recorder allows all the information to be recorded and then an accurate transcript to be produced. However, some interviewees are often put off by the tape recorder and do not open up to the same extent, although interviewees' fears can often be allayed by promising to turn off the tape recorder on the request of the interviewee (Reiner 2000b). Once the interview begins, Reiner (2000b, 224) argues, 'This seldom happens because of the momentum generated by the interview once it has begun, but when it does it is of interest in itself to note the points that arouse particular concern.' Not recording interviews, however, means it is often difficult for the interviewer to record all the information given and the interviewer will have to rely on the quality of his/her memory. On balance, however, it was decided to try and record all interviews, subject to the consent of the participant. In the case of Pleasure Southquay 25 of the structured interviews were recorded and all the semi-structured except the police sergeant interview. At Armed Industries all the semi-structured interviews were recorded, but none of the structured interviews. This was decided because the interviews took place largely in their gatehouses which meant they were frequently interrupted and there also seemed a much more suspicious culture, that tape recording might provoke a much less open interview. The interviews that were recorded were transcribed in relation to the open questions, but because it was the researcher undertaking this task it was felt pointless to type up answers relating to closed questions such as personal information, educational achievement, training undertaken etc.

Observation

Structured and semi-structured interviews were only likely to secure a limited amount of information on security officers' knowledge of their legal tools, attitudes and how and if they use them. As Agnew and Pyke (1982, 129) have argued, 'On a questionnaire we only have to move the pencil a few inches to shift our scores from being a bigot to being a humanitarian.' Observation can reveal data that is invaluable as Bell (1993, 109) has argued, '(observation) once mastered, is a technique that can reveal characteristics of groups or individuals which would have been impossible to discover by other means.' Therefore to assess how security officers actually made use of their legal tools in practice rather than how they talked about it was also necessary to undertake observation. As Foster (2003, 206) has argued,

> Where researchers observe policing in practice, they are often present at the time accounts are constructed and are, therefore, in a position to differentiate between officers' accounts of events and their own observation of those events. Furthermore, where interviews and observations are combined researchers can link what officers say with what they do (authors emphasis).

Gold (1969) has identified four ideal types of observation. First there is the complete observer, who does not take part in the activity and whose status as a researcher is unknown to participants. Second, there is the observer-as-participant who does not take part in the activity but whose status as a researcher is known. Third there is participant as observer who takes part in the activities and whose status is known. Finally there is the complete participant who takes part in the activities and whose status is unknown. During the research for this study the observer-as-participant was pursued as it was unlikely that the status of myself as a researcher could be kept secret when the officers were also going to be interviewed. As with interviews when your status is known to those you are researching there is a danger of the interviewer effect ie that those you are observing changing their behaviour because of your presence.

Indeed my presence on the first few night shifts at Pleasure Southquay did arouse the suspicions of some security officers. When leaving site on one night a group of 5 CSOs congregating by the entrance called me over. One CSO, who I had not yet interviewed, said to me, 'What the fuck are you really doing here?' After a brief conversation it transpired he thought – and probably others – that I was some kind of management spy. I reassured them at this point that I wasn't a spy and that all the data gathered would be treated anonymously. Clearly it was an issue I would have to do more about in order to reassure the security officers that I wasn't a spy. As the observation proceeded these barriers were gradually broken down. Indeed on another night this same security officer took me off with a colleague to play marbles in an empty office when they were suppose to be patrolling the site, illustrating the trust I had secured with him and others. At Armed Industries because of the shorter period on site a lower level of trust was secured and there did seem to be a much more suspicious culture towards me amongst most of the officers.

When conducting observation researchers can pursue either a structured or unstructured approach (Bell 1993). In this study it was decided to pursue an unstructured approach because of the diversity of what was going on. At Pleasure Southquay day and night shifts were observed where I would randomly attach myself to a security officer and follow them around. In addition I also attended a team leaders meeting and tenants meetings for day and night tenants. In doing the observation I tried to secure a feel for all aspects of their work. In total just under 50 hours observation were pursued at this site. At Armed Industries I also went to both the day and night shifts and sought to observe activities at all the main gates and functions. There were no group meetings to attend and over 40 hours observation was pursued. At Pleasure Southquay the observation took place over a three month period and 12 separate visits to site ranging from 1 hour to 8 hours. Where as at Armed Industries most of the observation took place during one week. The longer 'engagement' at Pleasure Southquay probably explains why officers were far more open towards me.

One of the most difficult tasks is writing up the field notes. As I was known as a researcher it did not matter that I was seen to be taken notes, they were expecting it. However, one wants to blend in and taking notes in front of them could be off putting. Therefore whenever possible I would go for a break in the canteen or go to the toilet and write rough notes and reminders. I would then when the shift was complete write up the notes in greater depth.

Documents

Another important source of information for research are documents. Scott (1990, 12) has defined documents as '…accounts, returns, statutes, and proclamations that individuals and groups produce in the course of their everyday practice and that are geared to their immediate and practical needs.' Scott divides documents based upon their authorship and their level of access. Authorship is distinguished between personal, private and official and access by closed, restricted, open archival and open published. While undertaking this research a wide range of documentary sources became available. Using Scott's classification of documentary sources Table 2.3 illustrates some of the information that was used for this study.

Stage 3. Data analysis and writing up

The research produced a significant amount of quantitative and qualitative data that required very different means of analysis. The quantitative data from the structured interviews was coded and then entered and analysed using the statistical software SPSS. This package enables complex statistical tests to be applied. However, the relatively small number of security officers interviewed and the reliance on categorical data rendered many statistical tests too complex and/or insignificant. SPSS, does nevertheless, enable data once entered to be analysed relatively quickly.

As the results are presented in subsequent chapters some of these issues will be explored in greater depth. Almost all results will be presented in tables as percentages (which were rounded up so may not add up to 100 per cent) to enable relatively easy interpretation of them. It must be said, however, that in using this approach there is the danger in using percentages for relatively low numbers of officers of giving an impression of much large numbers participating in the project than there were. Ten per cent of armed industry officers was only two people after all. This caveat must be borne in mind when considering the tables throughout this book.

Table 2.3 Documentary sources used during research

Access	Authorship		
	Personal	**Private**	**Public**
Closed		PS – Selected Memos and Letters	
Restricted	PS – Security Supervisor's CV	PS – Agendas and minute to selected meetings PS – Training manuals AI and PS – Assignment instructions AI and PS – Incident reports AI – Staff handbooks AI and PS –Relevant forms	PS – Police report on impact of crime at PS on surrounding area
Open archival			PS – Police crime statistics
Open Published		PS –Promotional literature of PS and contract security companies at PS and AI AI – Guidance to contractors and visitors	PS –Local authority report on area
PS = Pleasure Southquay AI = Armed Industries			

The qualitative data was analysed in a very different way. There are software packages available such as NUDIST that enable the analysis of this type of data. This package was investigated and a sample of data was added to it to assess whether it was worth using. A number of researchers who have used this package were also contacted and their views sought on its applicability. After these considerations it was decided that it would be too time consuming to enter this data for the benefits such a package would secure. Instead the following strategy was pursued. First of all a list of themes and subjects were identified such as: access control, arrest and detention, culture, discretion, to name some. All observation notes, semi-structured interviews and documents were then analysed and appropriate items of information added under each of the headings identifying the source. Some information found itself in several different sections because of its nature. When this was complete it produced over 70 pages (A4) of information. For the structured interviews all the data from different interviews were placed under each question to enable comparison of the different answers from security officers. The data was then assessed against the themes from the other analysis and where appropriate this information was marked with the appropriate theme. This approach enabled analysis of a number of themes to be pursued. As will be seen in subsequent chapters the themes explored draw upon the full range of research tools pursued for this research.

When the coding was completed the data was analysed and ideas and themes began to emerge. This enabled a rough plan of the book to be identified and then the process of writing up the results was pursued.

Ethical considerations

There are two major ethical considerations when conducting research (Walliman 2001). First there are issues relating to honesty and frankness of the researcher and second there are the responsibilities towards the subjects of research relating to privacy, confidentiality and courtesy. It is the latter that poses the most dangers as the actions of the researcher can impact upon those being researched. Indeed during the research I was faced with several dilemmas. One example that illustrates this was a discussion with the management at Armed Industries about the performance of the officers in the knowledge test as they were very keen to find out which officer had answered number 4 (search without consent) to question 24. Only one security officer had answered this and it was clearly a question that was very relevant to the work of security officers at Armed Industries. I was pressed to offer some form of expression (a nudge or a wink) to identify the officer as candidates were identified. Clearly if I had acknowledged the officer concerned this would have put him/her at risk of sanction from management because of my research. This was something I was not prepared to do and I offered no indication – although it was clear from management they had a clear indication of who they thought gave this answer (an illustration of 'profiling' which was actually wrong!). The observations of security officers also revealed behaviour that management would clearly be concerned about.

These included the issues of competence, abuse of position, time wasting to name a few. It was therefore essential to do all that was possible to protect the identities of the subjects.

A major principle of any research study should be informed consent. The 1964 World Medical Assembly adopted the Declaration of Helsinki. This sets out that adequate information should be provided to research participants, participation must be volunteered, the subject can withdraw at any time and informed consent must be given. These principles are applied to many academic disciplines' ethical principles (Wolfgang 1976). In terms of this study the aims and purpose of the research was explained in depth to the 'gatekeepers' to the two case studies sites. A brief outline was also provided before each of the interviews were conducted and interviewees were told they were free to leave at any point or refuse to answer a question. The officers were also sent a letter from me outlining the purpose of the research before I arrived on site to further enlighten them. They were also asked if they consented to the interview being taped and were told they could ask me to stop the recording at any point. They were also assured that all tape recordings would be destroyed at a suitable point after the completion of the research. As the example above illustrates it was very important to ensure the identity of the security officers were kept confidential. All security officers were assured their identity would not be revealed and that all references to their comments in any publications would be portrayed anonymously through numbers – which could not be traced to them. This also applied in the observation of them at work. With the semi-structured interviews this was more difficult, but the use of a pseudonym for the case study sites protects these interviewees to an extent. Such principles are not only ethically 'right' but they also allow subjects to be more open in their answers and actions as they have the guarantee of anonymity. Thus this was also used as a selling point to subjects to take part in the research.

Conclusion

This chapter has outlined the research methods used for this book. It has set out the two stages of the research. The first set out largely a documentary approach to identify the legal tools available to security officers in England and Wales. The second stage was then set out describing how and why the research sites were selected and the 'methodological pluralism' pursued to undertake this part of the study drawing upon interviews, observation and documentary sources. Finally this chapter examined some of the ethical considerations that emerged when conducting this research.

Chapter 3

The Legal Tools of Security Officers in England and Wales

Introduction

In Chapter 1 some of the many sources of power for security officers were illustrated. In this chapter the aim is to identify what legal tools an ordinary security officer generally has available to them in England and Wales. This chapter will consider the legal tools available to security officers under two broad headings. First there are 'universal legal tools', which are legal powers that all security officers possess no matter what type of space they are operating within. These are based upon citizens' rights or 'any person' powers in legislation and include such powers as the right to undertake a citizen's arrest. The second section will consider 'select legal tools', which are legal tools based upon property, employment, contract or special statute that security officers possess according to where they work. The chapter will end by identifying models of security officer based upon the types of legal tools available to them.

Universal legal tools

There are a number of legal tools that are available to all security officers because they are *any person* powers in legislation. Before these are examined, however, the importance of the right of a security officer (or any person) to ask someone to do something will be illustrated.

The right to ask

Underpinning many legal tools of private security officers is the requirement for consent to undertake an action. By asking – and if consent is given – the security officer can undertake a very wide range of functions. Freedom of speech is available to us all so if a security officer makes a reasonable request and the person agrees, then so long as it does not breach some other legal provision that is a legitimate tool for a security officer. As was illustrated in Chapter 1 the police often prefer to undertake many of their intrusive functions through consent rather than exercising their powers. Indeed many people – including myself – have had their baggage searched when leaving a shop because the alarm system has activated, simply because the officer asked to look in the bag. They have no grounds to force such a search and the alarm activation on itself would not warrant grounds for a citizen's arrest. If I had wanted to I could have ignored the request and walked out of the store. What makes this significant is that a security officers in uniform is often seen as an authoritative figure. As the Advanced Security Officer course states (SITO 1999a, 127),

> The security officer's uniform makes him/her a symbol of authority. Whenever something happens we always turn to the person wearing a uniform and expect them to cope... The uniform is a symbol of authority. It is the way that we have been conditioned since childhood...

This and the public's often poor knowledge of their rights means that a well trained security officer could make requests to a member of the public that many would comply with. Indeed at the Advanced Security Officer level the course encourages security officers to make use of questions and requests, rather than exercise statutory rights. While the Store detective course encourages them to stop and ask questions and requests rather than arrest. Thus it is important to stress this general right because of the way it underpins many of the other legal tools as it is also encouraged, and because of the authoritative nature of many security officers in securing consent.

The power to arrest

Since the completion of this research the *any person* powers of arrest have been amended with the Serious Organised Crime and Police Act 2005. The impact of these changes remain the subject of much debate. Some argue it represents an extension (Maxwell, 2006), while others a diminution (see for example, Whitehead, 2006) of powers. It is – as yet – too early to make objective observations upon these changes. Clearly research maybe required to investigate the impact of these amendments. The research relating to arrest powers in this book is therefore based upon the old powers and so this section will set these out. It will, however, also indicate how they have been changed at the appropriate point. It should also be noted that in some subsequent sections of this book some of the discussion of security officers' actions and knowledge relates to the old powers and reference will not be made to the new. This is entirely appropriate as the research took place when those powers were in force.

There are certain legal tools that all citizens possess that security officers can make potentially greater use of. At the time of the research the most salient example was the citizens' right of arrest under section 24 (4) and (5) of the Police and Criminal Evidence Act (PACE) 1984 (subsequently amended by the Serious Organised Crime and Police Act 2005)[1] where,

---

1   In 2005 after the completion of the research the *any person* powers of arrest were changed under Section 110 of the Serious Organised Crime and Police Act 2005. This changes 'arrestable offence' to 'indictable offence' throughout. It introduces a new code of practice and

Any person may arrest without warrant -

(a) anyone who is in the act of committing an arrestable offence;
(b) anyone whom he has reasonable grounds for suspecting to be committing such an offence.

Where an arrestable offence has been committed, *any person* may arrest without warrant -
(a) anyone who is guilty of the offence;
(b) anyone whom he has reasonable grounds for suspecting to be guilty of it. (Authors Emphasis)

There was also a power of arrest for *any person* under the Vagrancy Act 1824. Under this legislation section 4 states,

A person commits an offence who is found in or upon any dwelling-house, warehouse, coach house stable or outhouse or in an enclosed yard, garden or area for any unlawful purpose.

Section 6 of this Act went on to state (and which has been deleted)[2],

Any person may arrest without warrant a person found committing an offence under this Act.

This was old legislation, but previously a warehouse was taken to cover most modern buildings. However, this legislation in more simple terms gave citizens and therefore security officers the right to arrest someone found on premises or in an enclosed area who was there for a criminal purpose. Deciding what is an 'unlawful purpose' did pose some challenges, however. This was considered only in any depth from the Professional Security Officer level and above and it was only in the Advanced Security Officer course that decision-making guides were given to the security officer in undertaking such an arrest under this legislation.

At common law *any person* may also arrest anyone committing a Breach of the Peace while it is happening and if he/she has reasonable grounds for believing that it will continue (This has been unaffected by the recent changes, Whitehead, 2006). This usually means behaviour that is or is likely to cause violence, such as a fight between two people. As the distance learning materials for the SITO course for store

---

most significantly introduces a 'necessity test'. Under the latter arrest is only exercisable if it is not reasonably practical for a constable to undertake the arrest and the arrest is necessary at the time to prevent physical injury to themselves, another person or the suspect; or to prevent damage to property; or to prevent the person making off before a constable can assume responsibility for them.

2   Section 6 has been deleted by Schedule 17 Part 2 of the Serious Organised Crime and Police Act 2005 which came into force on the 1st January 2006 with the Serious Organised Crime and Police Act 2005 (Commencement No. 4 and Transitory Provision) Order 2005. SI 2005 No. 3495 (C. 146).

detectives state, 'Generally speaking, the breach in whatever way it happens, would normally involve a threat of serious injury for an arrest to be justified' (SITO 1993, 38).

These rights give a citizen – and therefore a security officer – a wide range of circumstances where they can make use of them. Arrestable offences included: those where the penalty is fixed by law, such as murder and treason; offences that carry a penalty of five or more years imprisonment; and a range of offences listed in section 24 (2) of PACE (Zander 2003). More specifically the type of offences included are theft, criminal damage, arson, burglary, robbery and more serious types of assault occasioning actual or grievous bodily harm. As the manual of the National Association of Healthcare Security (1997, Unit 12) states, 'A security officer will therefore usually find powers under this Act are adequate to cover most situations where an arrest is justified and necessary'. These rights have been tested on a number of occasions in the courts in varying circumstances for both security staff and ordinary citizens. In *R v Howell* [1981] All ER 383, the right of constables and citizens to arrest an offender without warrant where they honestly and reasonably believe that a breach of the peace is in imminent danger of being committed was held. A breach of the peace includes whenever harm is or likely to be committed against a person or in his presence to his property or whenever a person is in fear of being harmed through an assault, affray, riot, unlawful assembly or other disturbance (National Association of Healthcare Security 1997, Unit 12).

In *R v Jackson (Kenneth)* [1984] Crim LR 674, A after hitting B's car gave a false name and address and refused to wait for the police. M a passenger in B's car tried to stop A leaving by grabbing the ignition key and was subsequently dragged 70 yards with his arm trapped in A's car suffering a serious injury. It was held that because A had contravened section 25 of the 1972 Road Traffic Act, which is not an arrestable offence, he was entitled to restrain M, but the force used in resisting M was wholly excessive and unreasonable.

The arrest for 'arrestable offences' has also been tested in the courts on a number of occasions. In *R v Self* [1992] Cr App R 42, D ran away from a store detective after been accused of shoplifting. A passer by then arrested D after a chase and D was charged with theft and assault with intent to resist arrest. In his trial he was acquitted of theft. The Court of Appeal subsequently held that he could not be found guilty of assault with intent to resist arrest as the precondition for the application of section 24 (5) had not been met (cited in Zander 1995, 66–7). More recently this has been further tested in *Laselles Stanley v Ajab Singh Benning* (T/A Temptation Clothing and Charlie Brown Menswear) [1998] LTL 14/7/98. In this case Stanley's employer suspected him of stealing a pair of trousers and attempted to stop him. Stanley pushed past, but was chased by the employer leading to a scuffle on the ground. Stanley was acquitted of the charge of theft but convicted of assault by the jury. Consequently Stanley then sought damages for assault on the grounds that as he had been acquitted of theft and the arrest had been unjustifiable. This claim was dismissed by the judge, but was then appealed on a number of grounds, but also dismissed. Central to this decision was the view that section 24 (4) of PACE gives a power to citizens to make an arrest if they have reasonable cause that an offence is being committed. So if an individual saw someone stealing trousers and making off without paying they could rely on section 24 (4) of PACE to arrest them.

If a person is arrested by a police officer they can often be expected to be searched, transported to a police station and then interviewed. With private citizens and therefore security officers there are no rights to pursue these activities. There is no right to search the arrested without their consent and ignoring their refusal could result in them pursuing litigation for assault (see later in this chapter).

The power to use force

Any person and therefore security officers have also been given the right to use force in certain circumstances. Under the Criminal Law Act 1967 section 3 (1),

> Any person may use such force as is reasonable in the circumstances, in the prevention of crime, or in assisting or affecting in the lawful arrest of offenders, suspected offenders or of persons at large.

Thus if a security officer saw an individual stood outside a shop window with a hammer raised about to be smashed into the window the officer could use what force is necessary and reasonable (ie proportionate) to prevent him smashing the window. The other occasions when security officers are likely to use force are in arresting someone or evicting them for trespassing. In all these occasions force may only used that is reasonable in the circumstances.

Select legal tools

These powers only apply to selected private security officers because they are based upon property, employment, contract law or some other source. Before these select legal tools are considered, however, it would be useful to briefly examine some of the powers that have been given to security officers working in specific contexts.

The legal tools of 'a-typical' security officers

Over the last 30 years security officers operating in some specialised areas have been given special legal tools under specific legislation in England and Wales. As they are generally very specialised areas with only small numbers of officers concerned they will not be considered in any depth (for a more detailed consideration and review see Jason-Lloyd 2003). However, it is worth briefly setting out some of the powers that have been given to these a-typical security officers and where they can be found.

One of the first and most significant areas where this has occurred was in airports and ports where security officers were given special rights to conduct searches. Originally under the Protection of Aircraft Act 1973 these powers have been refined with further legislation including the Aviation Security Act 1982 and the Anti-

Terrorism, Crime and Security Act 2001 (Jason-Lloyd 2003). Powers of search also exist for security officers working on the Channel Tunnel under the Channel Tunnel (Security) Order 1994 and on railways under the Railways Act 1993 (Button and George 2001). In Magistrates courts under the Criminal Justice Act 1991 security officers were given powers of search; powers to remove, exclude or restrain persons; and powers to retain seized or surrendered articles. Under the Courts Act 2003 these powers were also extended to security officers in Crown courts. The potential for security officers to be given special powers in public areas was also realised under the Police Reform Act 2002 which gives the Chief Constable the ability to give powers to accredited community safety schemes.[3] These powers include to issue fixed penalty notices, to require the giving of a name and address, to stop someone consuming alcohol in a designated public place, to confiscate alcohol and tobacco, to remove abandoned vehicles, to stop vehicles for testing, and to direct traffic for the purposes of escorting a load of exceptional dimensions. Private prisons, secure training centres and immigration removal centres where the private sector operate them also have staff with special powers equivalent to prison officers. It is questionable, however, whether these can be considered as security officers.

The legal right to remove someone from private property

A security officer (or any agent of the landowner) working on private property generally has the legal right to remove a person who is trespassing. Trespass is a pre-condition for some criminal offences, such as burglary, but ultimately it is a civil wrong. There are also some actions that constitute 'criminal trespass' but generally most instances a security officer deal with are related to the civil form. Hence the popular sign on private property that 'trespassers will be prosecuted' is generally meaningless. Trespass takes a number of forms: trespass to the person, which includes false imprisonment; trespass to goods, interference with another's goods without lawful authority; and trespass to land, which is entry to land or premises which is possessed by another. It is the latter case, which is of most relevance to security officers, as many operating on private property frequently confront this issue. The landowner or a security officer as an agent of the landowner has the right to refuse admission or withdraw permission to remain on the property. If they refuse to leave after been asked the owner or his/her agent has the right to use the reasonable force necessary to eject the trespasser (Card et al. 1998). If the trespass continues or is repetitive the plaintiff could sue for damages, although the losses are usually minimal so damages likely to be achieved would be too, making it an uneconomical strategy. Alternatively the landowner could seek an injunction to compel the defendant to cease the offending behaviour. Further breach of this would then become contempt of court and could result in fining or imprisonment for the defendant. Where trespass involves claims of squatting the legal situation changes significantly. As this is a

---

3   These schemes largely cover wardens as well as security officers contracted to local authorities.

specialist area that most security officers do not confront the legality relating to this will not be considered. The training manuals also generally stress that if there is a risk of violence security staff should call the police.

The rights of property owners (and therefore their security staff) relating to the removal or exclusion of people from their property, however, have become much more blurred in recent years with the growth of shopping centres open to the public built upon private space, which have been referred to as 'hybrid' or 'quasi-public' space (Jones and Newburn 1998; and Gray and Gray 1999a). Permission to enter most private property is based upon a *bare licence,* which can be express or implied. Most businesses, including shopping centre developments, are subject to an implied licence permitting entrance to members of the public for commercial or consumer purposes (therefore not for 'busking', skateboarding etc). The *bare licence* can be revoked by the landowner (or his agents), with words or conduct, which sufficiently illustrate that the authorisation to be on the land has been removed. The person then has a reasonable time to leave the premises in accordance with the particular circumstances of the case. A person who then refuses to leave becomes a trespasser (Gray and Gray 1999b).

It is generally held that landowners have a right of arbitrary exclusion where they can decide for whatever reason they like who enters or remains on their land. This has been tested in the English courts with a number of cases. The most prominent was *CIN Properties v Rawlings* [1995] 2 EGLR 130. In this case CIN, the leaseholder of a shopping centre, sought to indefinitely ban a group of unemployed youths from the precincts of the centre after unsubstantiated allegations of misbehaviour. The ban was subsequently re-enforced with a court injunction. CIN argued that as they were the owners of the property they did not have to show any good cause for denying them entry. The Court of Appeal upheld this decision and European Commission of Human Rights was unable to intervene because the UK – at the time – had not ratified the guarantee of liberty of movement. This decision has effectively given property owners unprecedented power to regulate citizens' freedom of movement, assembly, association and speech. However, the implementation of the Human Rights Act 1998 Gray and Gray argue,

> will result in a significant curtailment of the estate owner's right in respect of quasi-public property. The incorporation of Convention freedoms will effectively impose on landowners a duty to demonstrate that any exclusion from privately owned areas of quasi-public space is justified on reasonable grounds which do not contravene the guaranteed liberties of the citizen (1999a, 50).

These changes will effectively create a new category of space. Wakefield (2003) cites two further recent cases that support Gray and Gray's claims of a movement from arbitrary to reasonable exclusion, in *Porter v Commissioner of Police for Metropolis* and *Appleby and Others v United Kingdom* where the principle of reasonable access was usefully raised. In the latter, where the case surrounded a group of protesters' right to set up a stall in a local shopping centre, the European Court of Human Rights hinted that if there were not alternative venues for youths to congregate or protesters to protest, property rights could be regulated by the protection of human rights. Nevertheless although arbitrary exclusion may disappear on such 'hybrid' space, landowners and therefore their agents will still be able to deny access and exclude so long as they have reasonable grounds. While on private space that is closed to the public this is unlikely to apply as entrance to this kind of property is based upon a *contractual licence*.

The legal tool to search (with consent)

One of the most common legal tools private security staff exercise is that of search. Many people on condition of entrance to a private place such as a nightclub, pop concert, museum etc have to submit to a search of their personal belongings and outer clothes as a condition of entrance. Similarly many employees have clauses inserted in their contracts of employment that make searches a requirement that if refused could result in disciplinary action. This section will explore the legal tools of private security staff to carry out searches in these different circumstances. Unlike many of the legal tools discussed so far, search must be based upon consent, as there is no right to conduct a forcible search. Nevertheless as will be shown there are a wide range of strategies security officers can use in-order to secure consent.

1) Searches as conditions of entrance to private property

There is no legal right for a security officer to forcibly undertake a search of the person or belongings of an individual seeking entrance to private property. As the SITO basic training course states, 'Security officers must remember they are not policemen. They have no special authority to search' (from ohp). Owners of private property, however, can insist upon a search as a condition of entrance. Usually conditions of search will be notified through signs at the entrance to an area or stated on the ticket. The security officer must gain the consent of the individual to search their person and/or personal belongings. However, if they refuse permission they cannot be forced to undergo a search. Nevertheless if permission to search is refused the security officer can deny them entrance or as the SITO distance learning materials for aviation security officers and door supervisors state respectively, 'No Search. No Fly' and 'No Search. No Enter'. Clearly this is a very strong incentive for an individual to submit to a search that in many occasions amounts to a *de facto* power. For instance if an individual wanted to enter a museum they would have to submit to a search to enter. If the person entering is also an employee or under contract there are additional sanctions that can be imposed that will shortly be discussed.

Once someone has entered private property the similar sanctions can also be applied as above. If an individual is asked to submit to a search and they refuse they can be asked to leave. This sanction may not be as strong as on entrance, as the individual may have secured the pleasure, service etc they sought. Thus they are willing to leave the private property rather than consent to the search. For instance at a leisure facility if a security officer suspected someone possessed drugs and asked them to empty their pockets the individual might have enjoyed their time there already, refuse, and therefore accept removal. However, if it was on entrance they might be less likely to refuse. Thus a sanction also exists once someone is on private property but it is weaker than on entrance.

In most of the instances where the above types of search take place there is usually a clear contract between the individual and the owner for entrance to the property. Where someone is invited on to the property, such as in a retail environment this is not as clear. However, access to retail stores is invariably linked to a condition of good behaviour and that can be withdrawn. Thus in the event of an individual refusing to give permission to be searched they could be asked to leave. In a retail store, however, this kind of sanction would be much weaker compared to a nightclub, museum etc. This type of search has become increasingly likely with the advent of Electronic Article Surveillance Equipment (EAS) where goods are tagged and if not deactivated at the checkout will activate an alarm at the exit on attempting to pass through it. If a shopper leaving activates such an alarm and a security officer asked them to open their bag, if they refused they could not be forcibly searched and they would be free to leave. However, the security officer might have enough evidence for a 'citizens arrest', although if the only evidence is the activation of the alarm, this would not amount to 'reasonable grounds' because of the many other factors that might activate the alarm system.

2) Searches as conditions of employment or contracts

Many organisations have employees who have access to valuables that if they so desired could relatively easily steal. Some organisations operate in locations where there are combustible materials that could be ignited by a careless smoker. To prevent these types of risks occurring a range of strategies are pursued to address them. One of the most common is the searching of employees' personal belongings and outer clothing by security staff or management before entering or leaving the workplace. As with all search rights for private security staff consent is required to undertake a search even with express contractual provisions for such searches in an employee's contract. If security staff do not secure consent and forcibly search an employee they could be guilty of the criminal offences of assault, battery, indecent assault and false imprisonment. Additionally employees might also be able to pursue civil litigation for compensation for which the employer might also be vicariously liable (Baker 1999). Thus if searches are not carried out properly there is a substantial risk of the employer not only losing valuables through pilferage but also having to pay compensation for unlawful searches to those they suspect of it! There are, however, a range of strategies that employers use to ensure the lawfulness of their searches and make consent more likely.

For employers to insist on a search policy they need to adopt the express right to do so and link this to clear procedures which are followed (Baker 1999). The most important requirement is for an express clause in an employee's contract of employment or link to code of practice setting out the employer's right to undertake searches and the consequences for refusal. The following extract from a Sainsbury's contract of employment is typical of many.

3.14 Searches

The Company undertakes searches as a security measure, both to guard against potential danger and to ensure that unauthorised goods are not removed from the premises.

It is a condition of your employment that you agree to be searched at any time whilst you are on company premises. The search may include your person, anything you are carrying, your desk, your locker, and any vehicle in your charge. You may be stopped outside the boundary of the Company premises and may be invited to return to the building for the purposes of a search. Searches may be carried out by a member of the security staff or a member of the management. Whenever necessary, more thorough personal searches will be conducted in private by a member of your own sex in the presence of another security officer or a member of management.

If it is found that you refused to submit to a search, disciplinary action, which could lead to summary dismissal, will be taken (Search and Seizure Files Institute of Personnel and Development Library).

There is much advice for organisations to ensure their searches are lawful. The policy on searches should make clear in what circumstances a search may take place, what might be searched, who may undertake the search and the conditions of the search. In terms of the latter, general guidance to employers suggests securing the express consent from an employee such as through the signature to a search authorisation form (Croner Employment Digest 1992). To further strengthen the employer's position security staff (or other designated staff) should be properly trained and searches should be restricted (with consent) to the employee's bag, vehicle, pockets and outer clothing. Even with consent it is doubtful if any search, which was more intimate would be lawful. To ensure the policies are followed and that there are no allegations of misconduct there should also be a witness to the search (Croner Employment Digest 1992). The importance of the transparency of the search procedures was illustrated by *British Railways Board v Czarnecki*, which was cited in the Croner Employment Digest 1992. In this case the employee was found to have been unfairly dismissed after a search revealed the possession of forbidden property, because the employee's attention had not been brought to the consequences of such action.

Even with the consent of the individual employee the employer must be careful to ensure that an individual or groups of individuals are not disproportionately searched. For instance in *BL Cars Ltd v Brown* [1983] IRLR 193, the Employment Appeal Tribunal held that the employer, after asking gate staff to stop and search all black staff after the arrest of one black employee for theft of a car part, had contravened the 1976 Race Relations Act. The giving of instructions by employers to security staff to carry out such searches may also breach the legislation. In both *Showboat Entertainment Ltd v Owens* [1984] ICR 65 and *Weathersfield Ltd (t/a Van and Truck Rentals) v Sargent* [1999] IRLR 99, it has been held unlawful to penalise an employee for refusing to carry out a discriminatory search policy.

In the vast majority of cases employees will submit to a search. Even where employees do not wish to be searched in most cases they will consent because of the fear of disciplinary action and potentially losing their job. The disciplinary sanction is therefore an important 'stick' to ensure consent is gained. However, another sanction an employer could also pursue if the search is related to a potential criminal act is to threaten to call in the police to investigate. The fear of disciplinary action and the potential loss of job might not be enough of a threat for some employees, whereas a police investigation, prosecution and potential criminal record may well be. Although, generally, employers prefer not to get the police involved because of the potential bad publicity, the higher burden of proof required and the length of time it may take to get a conviction (George and Button 2000). If treated through internal disciplinary procedures the employee can be dismissed on a lesser burden of proof, it can be achieved relatively quickly and probably with limited publicity.

Thus this section has illustrated a security officer has the delegated right from an employer to conduct searches of employees with their consent which are not discriminatory in accordance to the employers search procedure. They can secure consent through a range of measures the most important of which are the threat of disciplinary action and ultimately dismissal, combined with the threat of calling the police in to investigate.

3) Search after arrest

Once an individual has been arrested there are no special rights for a citizen or security officer to search the suspect. However, they can 'seize' the 'fruits' of the offence and they can remove any weapon that is being carried. This would have to be overtly available and could not be found through a routine search.

Miscellaneous powers

Depending upon the requirements of a particular assignment, private security officers may exercise various other rights of property owners and employers. One of the most common is wheel-clamping which takes place on the private property of many organisations and is generally enforced by security officers. Where an organisation has a policy on clamping that meets all the necessary requirements set through case law and statutory regulation (under the Private Security Industry Act 2001) a security officer may clamp a car and seek a fee for the removal of it (Home Office 1993). Similarly in some organisations there might be penalties for the breach of other rules that may result in fines or other sanctions. This might be also related to the enforcement of car parking regulations (without a clamp), the speed of vehicles or other issues such as no smoking policies. In some organisations security officers may utilise the rights of property owners and employers to conduct intrusive surveillance on people entering private property and/or employees. This may involve the use of covert cameras or ordinary CCTV. Again this would be subject to the surveillance meeting the increasingly complex web of legislation regulating its use.

Models of security officer

The preceding analysis illustrated the different range of powers available to private security officers, with all possessing 'universal' tools and some 'select' tools. Security officers generally operate in three types of space: public, 'hybrid or quasi-public' and private. Each of these provide a different range of 'select' legal tools. It is possible to distinguish different models of security officer according to the type of space and node of governance they operate within.[4] Figure 3.1 below illustrates these three models of ordinary security officer. A-typical security officers with special legal powers provided by specific legislation such as court security officers are excluded from this analysis.

The models begin with the 'basic' security officer who operates on public space engaged in policing those where there is no form of contractual arrangement. This covers security officers employed by local communities and authorities to police public streets as illustrated by Noaks (2000) and Sharp and Wilson (2000). The second model of private security officer can be termed the 'semi-empowered' security officer who can additionally draw upon some of the 'select' legal tools from operating on quasi-public space. As was discussed earlier with legal challenges to the power of property owners in this type of space, these rights are increasingly likely to based upon reasonable justification (Gray and Gray 1999c). These security officers are generally found in private space environments such as leisure facilities and shopping centres as researched by Wakefield (2003). Finally there is the 'completely empowered' security officer who can potentially draw upon the full range of 'select' legal tools from operating on private space as well as legal tools deriving from contracts, particularly employment based as well as the 'universal' legal tools. The legal tools derived from operating on private space are not subject to legal challenge as those on 'quasi-public space' and can be considered more arbitrary. These officers are generally found in factories, office complexes where entrance is for the workers and by invitation for visitors. The emphasis in the models is the development of the tool box given the 'basic' officer's legal tool box is relatively bare, the 'semi-empowered' nearly full, while the 'complete empowered' officer has a full tool box. As with any tradesman having a toolbox full of tools does not necessarily mean they will all be used. There might be organisational decisions and a culture of not

---

4   Some security officers do not have a permanent site and 'float' between different sites. These may have different spatial characteristics and therefore a different set of legal tools are available to them. Indeed as was to be found at Pleasure Southquay so called 'floaters' in the space of a few days could find themselves at assignments with very different legal tools open to them. Their ability to adapt to this clearly poses challenges and is an area that requires further research.

using some of the tools an/or an individual officer might not wish or know how to use the tool (as was to be found in the two case study sites used for this book). Thus this model only offers the potential capacity of security officers in using their legal tools. The research that will be explored later in this book will examine the actual use, which will lead to a further dimension of this model that will be outlined in the concluding chapter.

Model	Powers available
Basic Security Officer	*Universal Legal Tools* To ask To arrest To use reasonable force to prevent a crime
Semi-Empowered Security Officer	*Select Legal Tools: Property Based (Reasonable)* To exclude entrance to private property To remove from private property To enforce conditions on private property To search person on condition of entrance
Complete Empowered Security Officer	*Select Legal Tools: Property Based (Arbitrary) and Employment and/or Contractually Based* To enforce conditions on private property or other area To search person on condition of entrance To search person on exit from private property

Figure 3.1   Models of security officer power

As with any model when applied to the real world there will no doubt be examples where this model does not quite work. However, most places where security officers operate fit one of the three categories so it will be useful in most cases. This model, does however, exclude the a-typical security officers with special powers. If their powers were superimposed upon the above models it would demonstrate the very impressive range of legal tools some guards operating on private space – such as aviation security officers – have access to in their 'tool box'.

Conclusion

This chapter has illustrated some of the most important legal tools available to security officers. It has shown that there are 'universal' legal tools that all private security officers possess and there are 'select' legal tools that security officers possess through operating on private space and policing those engaged in employment and/ or other forms of contracts. Additionally there are 'a-typical' security officers who possess special powers because of special legislation passed. From this analysis of these legal tools it was possible to identify three models of security officer: the 'basic security officer', the 'semi-empowered security officer' and the 'complete empowered security officer'. Research on security officers in North America has found varying levels of knowledge and commitment to the use of their legal tools (Kakalik and Wildhorn 1971d; and Rigakos 2002) and this was also found in this research and will be developed in subsequent chapters.

Chapter 4

Nodes of Governance: Pleasure Southquay and Armed Industries

Introduction

There is a growing literature that challenges state centred conceptions of the governance of security, recognising, instead, the importance of the corporate sector, non-government organisations and the voluntary and informal sectors as well, in governing security (Johnston and Shearing 2003; and Shearing and Wood 2003). Some scholars researching and theorising these changes have advocated the principles of 'nodal governance' (Shearing and Wood 2003). Shearing (2004, 6) has defined nodes as,

> ...locations of knowledge, capacity and resources that can be deployed to both authorise and provide governance. Nodes may or may not form governing assemblages, and they may or may not develop networks that traffic information and other goods to enhance their efficacy.

A node could be based upon a territorial basis such as a town, a housing estate, a gated community, a shopping centre or a factory to name some. A node may also not necessarily be based upon physical space. It could be a community founded upon membership of a specific group such as a church, professional group or sporting body that is geographically spread. The maturity and complexity of the governing structures could vary from relatively simple informal arrangements to complex state-like structures.

These nodes may fall within and/or cut across one another and a person might be permanently located in some nodes but also in the course of a normal day fall within the boundaries of others. Within this complex web of nodes, the governance of security is provided by an equally diverse range of agents. They range from state actors such as the police, to security officers, staff with security responsibilities and volunteers. Each node has differing compositions in terms of this security balance. These nodes also have varying relationships with one another that are constantly changing.

Loader and Walker (2004), however, have criticised Johnston and Shearing's use of the term 'nodal governance'. They argue that in places it is used to describe the structures of governing security, while in others it is used as 'the *principles* of nodal governance' (Loader and Walker 2004, 224). It is important to distinguish the critique of the principles of nodal governance Johnston and Shearing advocate, from the analytical framework nodal governance provides for researching security. Central to this is that nodes do represent more than yet another descriptive term such as place, site etc. Nodal governance recognises that places, sites etc are more than just physical space, but that there are also, of varying degrees of sophistication, governing structures for security linked to them. Nodes are also different in establishing that the governance of security does not necessarily have to be linked to physical space. For these reasons this chapter is called 'Nodes of Governance...', rather than 'Places of Governance..'. It is also recognised, however, that many nodes are based upon a particular location, site etc as was the case with Pleasure Southquay and Armed Industries.

Linked to their nodal analysis, Shearing and Wood also make a case for denizens rather than citizens. They argue that people increasingly operate across multiple governmental domains and the traditional conception of citizens and their rights and responsibilities, that were linked to a specific domain, has become much more tenuous. Therefore the term denizen, which has emerged from the literature on citizenship and immigration, has been advocated referring to '...an affiliation to any sphere of governance and its associated rights and responsibilities' (Shearing and Wood 2003, 408). Thus denizenship might be permanent or temporary based upon the node they are within.

Johnston and Shearing (2003) (with Stenning) have provided a useful structure to analyse the structures of governance based upon eight dimensions. These include who makes the rules, the nature of the rules, the focus of governance, who executes governance, the mode of governance, the processes of governance, the technologies of governance and the mentalities of governance. These are aimed more broadly at governance, but clearly some of these dimensions can be used to analyse the governance of security at the two nodes studied for this book.

This study relates to two nodes of governance that are based in the corporate sector. Clearly the aim of this book is to examine the contribution of private security officers to the policing of private space and not to examine the broader issues of the governance of these two nodes. It is important, however, to understand some of the foundations of the governance in these two nodes if the contribution of security officers is to be truly understood. Therefore this chapter will seek to undertake an analysis of the governance of security in these two case study sites utilising the eight dimensions identified above where they apply, before providing some more detailed information on the main agents deployed at the two locations to provide security, the security officers.

Pleasure Southquay

'Pleasure Southquay' is a retail and leisure waterfront development in the South of England. It opened in February 2001 as a £200 million development based upon 33 acres of former Ministry of Defence land. At the time of the research (there has been a substantial increase in the number of units since) there were 65 designer shopping outlets; 20 waterfront restaurants, bars and coffee shops; 2 nightclubs; an 11 screen cinema; a 26 lane bowling complex; 1450 car parking spaces; 500 metres of prime berthing space; and 100,000 sq ft of office space. Construction was also continuing of 310 homes (some of which had began to be occupied as the research continued), further retail leisure units, 2 hotels and a major millennium attraction. Pleasure Southquay at the time of the research represented 33 acres of private space with access limited to three entrances or via the berths.

This 'oasis' of shopping and leisure is also located next to one of the most deprived areas of the city where crime and insecurity were high and policing provided only by the state (there were no wardens or security firms operating to supplement the public police). CSO 11's view of the location of Pleasure Southquay illustrated this division very well,

> Nice place, wrong place definitely wrong location. Paradise one side of the railway, Beirut the other, Don't mix, told them that from the beginning but they don't listen.

Thus the division of society between what Castells (1989) calls the low waged poor, those on state benefits and/or working on the margins of society, alongside the spending elite was there in microcosm around Pleasure Southquay. There was therefore an immediate challenge faced by the management in attracting those spending consumers Pleasure Southquay required to be profitable, while excluding the 'undesirable' neighbours without creating a fortress environment that might discourage the former. A vast array of strategies have emerged in shopping malls and town centres to exclude 'undesirables' and enduce appropriate behaviour that range from the design, access to even background music (Reeve 1998; and Hopkins 1994). Reeve (1998,75) argues these are based upon, '...socially controlling strategies in management, design, promotion and policing...'. More specifically these are based upon the promotion of a certain image, the design and characteristics of the facility, the creation of rules, and systems of surveillance and security. Central to the governance of security was therefore an attempt to create an appropriate mentality amongst the denizens who visited (or did not) Pleasure Southquay.

Creating an appropriate mentality amongst denizens

Johnston and Shearing (2003, 29) argue a mentality is '...a mental framework that shapes the way we think, the way we react to the situations and circumstances we encounter in our daily lives.' If denizens can be conditioned to behave in the appropriate manner, then other capacity to provide security becomes less important. Clearly to prevent a certain type of behaviour is far more effective than having to deal with. Pleasure Southquay sought to create a mentality by utilising a range of technologies as well as agents.

Mentalities through image   A distinctive image for a city centre or shopping facility has become increasingly important (Harvey 1990). As Raco (2003, 1870) has argued, '…creating safe, aesthetically pleasing public spaces requires the removal of 'social pollutants' – those individuals and groups whose (co)presence may threaten the perceived and aesthetic quality of an urban space.' At Pleasure Southquay the management were starting from scratch and given the 'threat' from the neighbours and the need to attract a large number of consumers from beyond the city, developing a distinctive image was a very important task. Research has also noted how higher expectations of behaviour can be created through what has been called 'domestication by Cappuccino' or the creation of a more bourgeois environment where different norms of behaviour are expected and tolerated (Zukin 1995; Atkinson 2003; and Massey 2005). The marketing and image of Pleasure Southquay was therefore incredibly important, as it has become in many similar developments (Raco 2003). The promotional literature for Pleasure Southquay sought to create an image as an exclusive and unavoidable shopping location. Some of the prominent headlines on the literature at the time included, 'Destination Unmissable', 'The Ultimate Destination for a Unique Christmas Experience', 'Ultimate Shopping Destination', 'Ultimate Lifestyle Destination', and 'Ultimate Leisure Waterfront Destination'. This literature contained pictures focusing upon yachts and sailing – a very exclusive and expensive pastime. Exclusive 'designer' outlets such as 'Gap', 'Ralph Lauren', 'Tommy Hilfiger' and 'Paul Smith' were promoted. Literature also focused upon 'restaurants' and 'cafes' and dining 'al fresco' and entertainment based upon 'contemporary artists' and comedy. A style of entertainment distinctly different from the traditional working class pubs across the road. As the Marketing Director explained,

> Pleasure Southquay is all about the customers' experience. It is a leisure destination and we fit more in the tourism category, I mean all the awards we have won have been in that category. It is a unique waterfront destination and these days there is no such thing as customer loyalty. Customers will flip about to where they have had the most satisfaction, most recently. So the challenge is… ensuring those customers that do come have a great time every time they visit. It encourages new customers to come down because we haven't encouraged all the customers we have wanted to reach.

By focusing upon images of shopping based upon exclusive trade marks and 'upmarket' leisure activities the image created was one that appealed to consumers able or aspiring to lifestyles based upon the display of consumer wealth. Many of the local youths, unemployed and low paid would not consider such a place for undertaking their shopping or pursuit of leisure because of the image and the expense. Therefore the promotion of an image based upon a more exclusive type of shopping and leisure would make many unwilling to go there simply because of cost, and others would be likely to feel uncomfortable in such exclusive surroundings. Indeed Lees (1997, 339) found such an effect in the opening of Vancouver's new library,

> …homeless or street people and other so-called social deviants are not specifically excluded by library policy, the fortress style architecture, security consciousness, and middle class ambience (bourgeois playground) of the library, in general, does nothing to attract them or make them feel at home.

Such was the importance of the image of Pleasure Southquay that the Marketing Department also assumed a central role in all decision-making, including security. Indeed security officers were called Customer Service Officers (CSO) and had a uniform designed to make them look more customer friendly. Thus there were no hats and the security officers wore grey trousers, white shirts, black ties, maroon jumpers and bright yellow and maroon overcoats (known to the CSOs as 'rhubarb and custard'). The Marketing Director explained the rationale for this distinction,

> CSOs emerged because we thought security might put people off. The image of security is often very police like. We wanted the customer experience to be central so we decided upon customer service officer. If you like, we wanted a more 'fluffy' approach.

In the early days of Pleasure Southquay such was the importance of creating a certain image to the site the police were not welcomed fearing it would give them the wrong kind of image. The Security Supervisor stated that the first Operations Manager (who had resigned before I came on site) had gone out of his way to prevent the police coming on site. In one incident the Operations Manager actually stood in front of a police van attempting to stop it coming on site to respond to an incident. The police threatened to arrest him if he didn't get out of their way. The police sergeant for the area also supported this view, he stated,

> The original operations manager wished to appear as helpful as possible to the police, but when we weren't there he would tell the security staff he didn't want us there. The most senior management have always gone out of their way to encourage us on site. At an early stage we were offered a room. That is still ongoing. The conflict is Pleasure Southquay is a business and their aim is to encourage as many people as possible to come to a safe environment. The public don't want to see blue flashing lights, fights and store detectives arresting people. This does not fit with the environment they are trying to create – although it is actually a relatively safe site. On the other hand you are always going to get an element attracted to a site like this – with all the goodies there are – to steal from it. You have to choose how to deal with this. I think they could have been harder at the beginning to deal with some of these elements.

Mentalities through reputation   The above quotation also illustrates the importance of reputation in undertaking the wider policing function, something the police sergeant was clearly concerned had not been established in the appropriate way in the early days of Pleasure Southquay. During the research the 'no police on site attitude' had also clearly changed and Pleasure Southquay management were very keen to encourage a police presence, but clearly the early days had damaged the commitment of the police to provide officers, particularly late at night and at weekends when the clubs and bars were closing and there was a risk of significant disorder. The CSOs therefore found themselves dealing with a significant amount of disorder and associated problems which in many ways they were not suitably trained to deal with. This will be explored in greater depth in subsequent chapters.

Mentalities through design   The design and characteristics of Pleasure Southquay were also important in the governance of security. Designing out crime has assumed a significant place in the development of new shopping facilities (Oc and Tiesdell 1997; and Crawford 1998) and much of this knowledge was applied to Pleasure Southquay (Poyser 2003). These same strategies to address crime also create exclusivity. Indeed Reeve (1998, 74) argues malls are characterised as, '…a place of social control in which individuals are both physically constrained to behave in ways conducive to the ends of production.' Indeed Pleasure Southquay was designed with clear lines of sight and open space to maximise natural surveillance. The site was very well lit, particularly in the car park. The mixed usage of retail and leisure meant people would be attracted during the night as well, minimising the chance of an 'empty' centre and the feelings of insecurity that might create (Poyser 2003). Pleasure Southquay was also very clean, largely due to a team of cleaners of equal size to the security force. Anyone or any activity that compromised 'uncleanliness' would clearly be out of place. Consequently there were also few signs of urban decay such as graffiti, vandalism, decrepit buildings etc, which have been linked by some to increasing fear of crime and likelihood of further action to exacerbate the signs of such decay (Wilson and Kelling 1982). The access control strategies (which will be examined in depth in Chapter 7) also aided exclusion. Most consumers were encouraged to arrive by car and this entrance had no uniformed officer present. The main pedestrian entrance, however, which was also likely to be the entrance used by those from the nearby estate and those travelling on public transport was staffed by a security officer.

Rules of governance

Who sets the rules and their nature is another important aspect to the governance of security. At Pleasure Southquay there were formal rules as well as informal rules, which were based upon national law, decisions of Pleasure Southquay management (particularly marketing) as well as the operational decisions of security staff. These rules set out the appropriate forms of behaviour. These cover drinking in public, smoking in public, litter, access of dogs, use of bicycles and skateboards and even dress-codes to name some examples. As will be developed in more depth in Chapter 7, at Pleasure Southquay there was no easily accessible 'rule book' or signs generally prohibiting certain types of behaviour. This was a conscious strategy on the part of Marketing not to 'compromise' the shopping experience. Instead there was largely a series of unwritten rules enforced according to the discretion of security staff – something that will again be developed in Chapter 7.[1]

---

1   However, it is interesting to note that since the research was completed Pleasure Southquay have decided to introduce a formal set of rules with sanctions for their breach.

The agents, mode and technology of governance

When the preventative measures described above fail the security and surveillance systems become the central strategy in ensuring order prevails. There has been much research to illustrate the importance of security officers and CCTV in securing shopping malls (McCahill 2002; Wakefield 2003; and Goold 2004). At Pleasure Southquay some officers expressed the views that management had underestimated the potential problems from the adjacent estate. As the following extract illustrates,

CSO 22

> ...Initially the management were so naive about the type of customer we were going to have. They were so sure we were not going to have no socially deprived people on site. We were just going to have nice clients. We weren't going to get shoplifters, drunks etc. The management at first also didn't get on the best terms with the police, who were made to feel unwelcome. A different manager made a difference. Whenever you have a shopping centre on the edge of a socially deprived area you are going to have problems. This is not the best place for a middle-class development. The management team here are now much more responsive. Ultimately we get the same people who cause problems on the seafront.

During the research security capacity amounted to a total of 31 security officers (there was 1 vacancy at the time) (of which 29 were interviewed). All of these officers were employed by a major contractor and were divided on various shifts and locations. There were 4 main shifts composed of five CSOs led by a team leader working 2 days on, 2 nights on followed by 4 days off (12 hour shifts). 5 CSOs worked a permanent night shift of 7pm to 5am working a mixture amongst themselves of 5 nights on, 2 off, 10 nights on and 4 off. 3 CSOs also worked 2 days on, followed by 2 nights and 2 off. Finally there were 4 CSOs based in the car park who worked their own shift pattern that provided 24 hour coverage of this location. The different roles and experience of the officers led me to divide them between the 'backroom' officers which included the one officer on each shift permanently based in the control room and the car park based officers vis-à-vis the 'frontline' officers who were interacting with the public most of the time. Their involvement in 'policing' and their orientation varied significantly, as will be illustrated in subsequent chapters. Although some of the 'backroom' officers did occasionally do overtime in 'frontline' roles. The officers were paid £6.00 per hour, control room staff £6.25 and team leaders £6.50. This was a very good rate in the context of the local labour market for this type of work.

The nature of the contract meant that so called 'floaters' would also frequently be used to cover gaps in provision. These are security officers without a permanent site who fill in at a range of locations. As they were not permanently there it was decided not to interview these officers. The contract manager – who was not based at Pleasure Southquay – because of the size and prestige of the site also took an active interest and would regularly visit and even work with the CSOs at key times. The contractor was one of the major security companies, a member of the BSIA and registered with the Inspectorate of the Security Industry (ISI) which meant it complies with the industry code of practice for this sector BS 7499.

Supervising the CSOs were 3 control room supervisors who were employed in-house and only worked days (7 till 7). In charge of overall security was a Security Supervisor – again employed in-house – who reported to an Operations Manager who also had responsibility for cleaning and other related services. The Security Supervisor told me he was really a 'manager' but the company frequently used 'supervisor' across a range of functions in order to pay them less. There was no permanent police presence, but on Friday and Saturday nights usually about half-a-dozen police officers would turn up at around 11 pm and leave at around 3 am. These officers would be given a radio for the site so that security staff and police could communicate with one another. During the day the visits of the police were on a more ad hoc basis.

The organisation of the security staff did vary to an extent depending upon the Team Leader. During the night shift, however, the following was typical. First of all one of the officers would be permanently based in the control room monitoring the CCTV, alarms, telephone and radio. The CCTV system was central to the organisation and deployment of security officers on the ground. The system was fully digital with over 150 cameras. The system covered every aspect of the site where the public *should* be, although as some of the officers were to show me there were some back corridors with gaps in surveillance that enabled them to escape for breaks without the eyes of the controller upon them! The control room staff would patrol the site with the system and deploy staff according to what they viewed. Security officers would be deployed to randomly patrol the site and would take turns to have a break. One security officer – sometimes accompanied – would also have responsibility for checking all the offices and back entrances to ensure all doors were locked. At certain times such as pub and club closing times the officers would observe those leaving these locations and would also stand by the taxi rank. From 3am onwards security officers would patrol the site. Throughout the whole shift security officers would be deployed to deal with incidents ranging from fire alarms to observing suspicious activity. The organisation of the duties did vary from team to team as someone would clearly identify meal break times and responsibilities, whereas others would be more vague.

During the day shift there were some special positions. At the main pedestrian entrance, or 'Punchthrough' as it was called by the officers, a dedicated security officer would stand with the purpose of deterring known troublemakers. A security officer was also dedicated to the main entrance for the delivery vehicles. Otherwise the security officers would patrol and stand at strategic points providing a presence dealing with incidents as they were directed to respond to them. In the car park at both day and night the officers would monitor the access control barriers and deal with any requests from drivers. They would also patrol the car park to provide a preventative presence. In addition to these staff many units also had their own security infra-structure. Most of the pubs and night-clubs employed door supervisors, some of the retail units employed their own security and many had CCTV and tagging systems. These 'unit' staff would work in partnership with the CSOs through both formal and informal structures.

The processes of governance

Another aspect of governance is the means by which governance is achieved. Is it based upon coercion or the threat of it, or is it based upon negotiation? As has been inferred in the analysis above the fundamental basis of governance at Pleasure Southquay was that of consent and negotiation. However, coercion and the threat of it was also used, particularly in dealing with incidents in the night-time economy (NTE). This will be explored further in Chapter 6.

The success of security

The Police Sergeant was able to make available the recorded crime statistics for Pleasure Southquay and compare them to the main shopping area of the city. It would be unfair to treat it as a comparison of like with like as the main shopping area is much larger and includes a much more diverse range of retail outlets. At Pleasure Southquay it was also the first year of operation and many of the outlets did not open until April in that year. Although a later report using a slightly different analysis of codes for crimes in this area for the police found 171 in total for 2001 and 190 in 2002. As with any recorded crime statistics there are also many that go unrecorded. Nevertheless what the figures reveal is a relatively low volume of crime recorded at Pleasure Southquay.

Table 4.1 **Recorded crime in Pleasure Southquay compared to the city's main shopping area 1 January 2001–31 December 2001**

Crime	Pleasure Southquay	Main shopping area
Theft	41	709
Assault	31	295
Crime and disorder	22	160
Public order	10	150
Robbery	0	23
Deception	12	144

Further evidence of the safe environment at Pleasure Southquay is illustrated by the police response required. Between the 1 April 2001 and 30 November 2002 there were only 232 control room responses to Pleasure Southquay. Of these 8 per cent required an immediate response, 46 per cent a response within 30 minutes, 32 per cent within 2 hours, 3 per cent to arrange a visit and 11 per cent not requiring a response. This means that over these 20 months there were only 125 incidents that required an immediate response or one within 30 minutes, an average of 6 per month. This indicates that given the size and nature of the development it was not a high crime spot.

Armed Industries

'Armed Industries' is a 'list x'[2] major manufacturer of defence equipment based in the West Country. The site studied was one of many based around the UK. Divided into two parts by a public road the site is a mixture of manufacturing and office complexes. Armed Industries is secured by a perimeter fence and entrance is only open to pass-holders and escorted visitors through 7 gates. The site had a total of 4,500 staff employed but there were over 8000 passes issued, many of these included contractors.

Rules and process of governance

One of the security officers described the site as a small village and compared their role to the police in a village. Given the numbers involved perhaps a better analogy would have been a small town. The emergence of corporations pursuing their own governmental agenda with their own 'police' departments to enforce it has been well documented (Spitzer and Scull 1977; Shearing and Stenning 1982; and Macauley 1986). There is evidence of corporations defining their own rules, systems to enforce and identify breaches of them (as well as the law), combined with private systems of justice that define guilt and apply sanctions. Moreover some of these systems actually deal with serious offences such as theft and fraud which could be dealt with by the state criminal justice system (Shearing and Stenning 1982). Ultimately they may have as much if not more influence over an individual as the state.

As stated above in relation to Pleasure Southquay the aim of this book was not to get embroiled in the system of governance operating at the 'village' of Armed Industries. The private justice system will also be explored in more depth in Chapter 7. However, it would be useful at this point to examine the general principles of governance at Armed Industries combined with a more detailed analysis of the security department. The site investigated was one of several operated by the company. All employees, contractors and visitors were bound by rules and procedures set out in the employee handbook. The extent to which this could be applied to visitors and some contractors was not clear, however. The handbook was issued by the Director of Human Resources for the company, but was written in consultation with the trade unions. The rules and procedures in the handbook covered an extensive range of issues from discrimination, expense claims, security issues, safety issues to the use

---

2   List x manufacturers have to comply with requirements on security set by the Ministry of Defence as a condition of their contracts. For further information on this see George and Button (2000).

of company telephones, in total 12 pages of the A5 sized handbook. Deviance was clearly defined, but not the sanction as the following extract illustrates.

16.10 Letters

The use of the Company's address for personal letters is not allowed.

Breaches would be dealt with by the company's 'Code of Industrial Discipline', which was designed to ensure evidence is gathered, substantiated and properly weighed and that the employee has an opportunity to defend him/herself or be represented by an appropriate person. The document did not set out the role of security in enforcing these rules and it was clear that some would be beyond their remit – such as abuse of telephones. There was, however, a wide range of security and safety rules which clearly fell to security. How some of these were dealt with will be the focus of Chapter 7, so will not be considered here. Nevertheless whilst coercion was a basis of the process of governance at Pleasure Southquay, this was negligible at Armed Industries, where it was based on consent and negotiation.

The agents, mode and technology of governance

Protecting the site from intruders as well as other security risks, enforcing Armed Industries rules, and contributing towards creating a safe environment were the central tasks for Armed Industry security staff. At the time of the research there were a total of 22 security officer posts and a Security Manager permanently based on site. The security officers worked a mix of 12 hour shifts. 12 security officers were on a pattern of shifts that involved days and nights known as the '168' over 7 days per week. The other 10 security officers covered a mixture of permanent days Monday to Friday and flexible positions to cover gaps in provision. There was a rank structure that was similar to the police with three sergeants and one staff sergeant (included in the 22 posts). On the night shift there would be 4 officers on site including 1 sergeant and during a weekday there would be 11 officers on site. All 22 officers and the manager were employed by a contract security company, which held a national contract with Armed Industries for all their facilities management services. The company is not a large or a well known security company, although it is a member of the BSIA and registered with an appropriate inspectorate meeting BS 7499. The Security Manager reported to the Facilities Manager on site and the Security Controller depending upon the issue.

The security department at Armed Industries up until 1994 had been known as Armed Industries Constabulary. They had worn uniforms that were very similar to the local public constabulary. Indeed many documents I was shown during the course of the research had stamped on them 'works police' and there was still some active documents that stated these words, such as one version of a visitors pass which stated, 'Return this pass to the police post on departing'. Indeed the old 'works police' culture permeated many aspects of the modern department. The Security Manager, Staff Sergeant and one of the officers had all once been 'works police officers'. Not all the officers were impressed by the 'old' Armed Industry Constabulary culture, however, as one officer told me.

SO 8

> ...The managers are from Armed Industry Police and still try to run it like a police force. Security is different, we've moved on. That's my view, lots of room for improvement.

With the 'old' Armed Industries Constabulary staff there were frequent references to the 'good old days' when there were three times as many officers, they worked 8 hour shifts and were paid very well. Indeed the Security Manager had only two years ago reached the salary he had been earning as a works police officer 10 years previously! When the in-house works police were first contracted out the security budget for Armed Industries for this site went from £1½ million to £500,000. This was largely achieved through fewer staff and cuts in wages (hourly rates went from £5.20 to £3.20 per hour). The current security officers earned £5.80 per hour, (40p more for a sergeant) and were entitled to only 20 days holiday per year. In many ways the composition of the staff had gone full circle. At one point the works police was a place for the old and injured from the shop-floor to serve out their days. It had then moved towards a younger more dynamic organisation and with the contracting out in 1994 had returned to an older profile of worker (see below). The Security Manager told me,

> In the (works police) days there was a bigger mix of staff. I came here when I was 32 and they were just starting to change the base of the works police. 25 years ago it was mainly older people who were too old to carry out their functions on the shop floor so they were put on the works police, if they had a disability they were put on the works police. But the guy in charge of the works police in those days was an ex-police inspector and he made the job more attractive to a younger person and recruited younger people. So that's what happened they had a mix and gradually the older person retired.

Indeed such was the attractiveness of a job in the works police the only opportunity to secure a position was for someone to die – so called 'deadman's shoes'. In many ways the old culture of the works police left a gap in the nature of security provision. The department still had many procedures and expectations of the old works police where staff were much more committed and professional. Yet many of the officers actually employed just did not have the same level of commitment. This left gaps and caused some problems, which will be outlined later in this book.

The security officers on the day shift were organised according to the gates or 'boxes' as they called them. The sergeant and/or staff sergeant on the shift would be based in the control room, monitoring the CCTV, alarms, radios and answering telephone calls. Each of the 7 gates would have a security officer deployed to monitor access, check passes and randomly search vehicles entering and exiting the site. There were also two positions on desks that were more receptionist orientated in function. If there was the full deployment of staff one security officer would be roaming the site giving breaks to those on gates and desks. Similarly depending upon the number of staff available security officers would go on patrol. During those patrols they would undertake parking enforcement duties. On certain occasions the Security Manager and officers would take a speed radar gun out and check the speeds of vehicles on site to enforce the 10 mph limit. On the night shift the 4 officers on duty would have one in the control room and 3 patrolling the site. The patrols would include locking and unlocking rooms, depending upon the location.

Mentalities of governance

Unlike Pleasure Southquay there was no need to consider measures to maximise the attendance of certain groups of consumers. As a manufacturer of defence equipment only those who worked, were contracted or legitimate visitors were entitled to enter Armed Indutries property. Indeed given the design of the site with perimeter fencing and barriers it would be very difficult for a member of the public to accidentally wander on site. Thus the design of the site with perimeter fences and security staff and barriers guarding entrances was part of a strategy to create a mentality amongst non-denizens of not entering the site. This self-policing of following signs, avoiding barriers and the importance of borders has also been illustrated by South (1993), Shearing and Stenning (1987) and Franzen (2001). Denizens who did need to enter either as employees, contractors or visitors were subjected to other strategies to create a mentality of compliance with Armed Industries rules. These strategies will be explored in more depth in Chapter 7.

Personal characteristics of security officers

In introducing Pleasure Southquay and Armed Industries earlier in this chapter it was stated that they were typical of many locations where private security are found. It is much more difficult to assess how typical the officers are, however. This is largely because of the absence of national research identifying the typical profile of security officers. Thus basic data such as the age, sex, race, educational achievement, level of training etc does not exist in the UK. In the USA the study by Kakalik and Wildhorn (1971a-e) based upon a significant survey of security officers provided a profile of an American security officer as an ageing white male who is poorly educated and paid, with only a few years experience of private security. Unfortunately because of the lack of a valid national survey in the UK it is not possible to come to conclusions about the typical officer in the UK. There are, however, some studies that can be drawn upon to provide some background information to compare with Pleasure Southquay and Armed Industries officers.

The main British trade association for the security industry, the BSIA, has commissioned two major studies of the manned guarding market over the last decade. The first, published in 1994, found the total market was worth £1.53 billion divided between 67 per cent contract and 33 per cent in-house. The contract sector was made up of 51 per cent BSIA members, 24 per cent International Professional

Security Association (IPSA) members and 24 per cent non-affiliated. At least three quarters of the industry were therefore claiming to be operating to the minimum industry standard of BS 7499, as these are conditions of membership of the BSIA and IPSA. The non-affiliated would be likely to contain a mix of companies some operating to high standards, some to none at all. The research estimated there were around 130,000 security officers, although unfortunately no profile of these officers was provided (BSIA 1994). Further research commissioned by the BSIA in 1998 estimated the number of officers had fallen to 125,000 of which only 13.7 per cent were now employed in-house (BSIA 1999). Jones and Newburn (1998) in their research found there could be as many as 333,631 employed in the broader private security industry. They also found evidence of many security firms employing ex-police officers and armed services personnel. Possibly one of the only consistent features of national research in the past has been by the trade unions representing security officers identifying generally low pay and conditions (see Button and George 1994; and Home Affairs Committee 1995). Indeed it would be fair to say that most security officers are now paid at or near the minimum wage.

There may have been no national research on the profile of security officers, but there have been other case studies of private security officers. Michael (2002) interviewed 50 security officers from one of the leading security companies (a member of the BSIA). Of the 50 security officers interviewed only 6 were female and she found an age profile of 30 per cent 18–24, 34 per cent 25–39, 30 per cent 40–59 and 5 per cent 60 or over. In terms of race she found over three quarters were from white British origin, with only three guards from Asian and two from Afro-Caribbean origins. Four guards in her study came from America, Australia, New Zealand and South Africa. She also sought information on their marital status and found 48 per cent married, 30 per cent single, 12 per cent engaged, 6 per cent divorced and 4 per cent cohabiting. Michael's study also found low levels of educational achievement with 40 per cent having no qualifications, 24 per cent 5 CSEs/O Levels or less, 10 per cent 5 CSEs/O Levels or more and the rest either had either A Levels, Diploma, HND, degree or were taking a break from their degree. It must be remembered that Michael's study was of a BSIA security company and as such it was likely to be better than the average security company.

The largest study of security officers conducted in the UK was a PhD study by Flynn (1997), although this was primarily based upon the larger companies who are members of the BSIA (which at the time accounted for about 40 per cent of the market (BSIA 1994). In this study based upon questionnaires completed by 259 security officers drawn from the contract and in-house sectors Flynn (1997) found three quarters were in the age range of 18–42. He also found 55 per cent had no qualifications such as O Levels, A Levels, diplomas, degrees etc and that around a third had left school at 15 with no qualifications. The median officer based upon his research had received two days training, was male and aged 31 to 35 years old, worked 56–60 hours per week, was paid £3 to £3.49 per hour, had no educational qualifications, and had been working in the private security industry and for the same employer for 5 to 10 years.

Wakefield (2003) in a study of security at three shopping/leisure facilities found that of the 56 security officers interviewed 48 per cent were 18–29 years old, 36 per cent were 30–49 and the other 14 per cent were 50 and over (figures do not add to 100 per cent). She also found a majority of officers were British and white in origin. However, at one of her three case studies 35.7 per cent of the officers were female, a much higher proportion than any other study so far. Wakefield also profiled the officers' length of service, and in all three case studies found 30.6 per cent with under 1 year of service, 22.2 per cent with 1 to 2 years, 19.4 per cent with 3 to 6 years and 27.8 per cent with 7 years service or more.

It is difficult to assess (in the absence of a representative national study of private security officers) to what extent the officers interviewed in this study represent the general picture. As will be illustrated shortly, however, the profile of security officers at Pleasure Southquay was similar to Michael's and Wakefield's. Here officers were largely male, white and under the age of 50. At Armed Industries, however, the profile was very different in terms of age, with 70 per cent over 50. It may also be the case that Pleasure Southquay officers were slightly better qualified than the normal security officer. Indeed the Contract Manager told me during his interview,

> This site should be only for a certain type of security officer it is a special type of work. There is for example one security officer I know who should never be down here doing this type of work. The other week the co-ordinator put him on down here and he shouldn't. I was on duty that night and I had to stand next to him all night. It is a different beast here, you get the drunks out of the clubs and all they want to do is punch the police or a security officer. The next day they are a different person. I am a football referee and see it all the time: people being different the minute they get on the football pitch. Most of it is drink related and you have to know how to handle it. The other week there were 25 guys fighting outside *club j* and 2 of our guys in the middle of it. You have to think of health and safety and so I called them out.

Therefore these caveats must be borne in mind when considering the following analysis of the personal characteristics of the security officers interviewed for this study.

Table 4.2   **Personal characteristics of security officers interviewed at Pleasure Southquay and Armed Industries (%)**

	Pleasure Southquay	Armed Industries	All
Male	86	90	88
Female	14	10	12
White	93	95	94
African	7	5	6
Age 18–30	45	10	31
Age 31–50	45	20	35
Age 51+	10	70	35
N = 49			

The security officers employed at both sites were overwhelmingly male, white and educated only to the age of 16 years old. Both sites had around 90 per cent male and over 90 per cent describing themselves as white in ethnic origin. Pleasure Southquay had a slightly better profile in terms of education with just over 70 per cent educated to the age of 16, compared to 90 per cent at Armed Industries. The age structure did vary between the two research sites with Armed Industries having a much older profile with 90 per cent over 30 years old and 70 per cent 51 years or over, compared to Pleasure Southquay having only 55 per cent 31 years or over.

Table 4.3   Educational achievement of security officers interviewed (%)

Educational achievement	Pleasure Southquay	Armed Industries	All
Left school with limited or no qualifications	35	75	51
Left school at 16 with 5 GCSEs or equivalent	38	15	29
Educated to 18 with A levels or equivalent	21	10	16
Educated to degree level	7	0	4
Educated to postgraduate level	0	0	0
N = 49			

The level of training that security officers undergo has frequently been criticised (Home Affairs Committee 1995). In Chapter 3 some of the main training qualifications were examined and it was illustrated that the industry standard BS 7499 specifies two days off the job and one day on the job as minimum (as set by SITO). As both of the contract companies operating at the two case study sites were BSIA members they should have been meeting at least this level of training. More importantly one might expect security officers being trained further in specialist in-house courses and pursuing further industry training qualifications. The general picture at these sites did not reflect this, however. Before some of the findings on training are examined it is important to set out what training actually took place.

Table 4.4   Training received by officers interviewed (%)

	No training	SITO Induction only	Old AI Induction only	PS Induction	Professional Guard One
Pleasure Southquay	0	38	n/a	62	0
Armed Industries	25	55	5	n/a	15
All	10	45	2	37	6
N = 49					

As Pleasure Southquay was a new development, before it opened the original team of security officers had undergone six weeks of induction before the site opened to the public, in addition to their BS 7499 minimum. This had covered further security training, site familiarisation, health and safety, radio etiquette and customer service. Only 62 per cent (18) of the original security officers remained and all new officers since the opening had had to learn this additional information on the job. All the officers at Pleasure Southquay had also undergone the SITO basic training.

In the case of Armed Industries the level of prior training was not as good. The official procedure should have encompassed security officers undergoing the SITO basic training followed by a programme of on the job training at Armed Industries. Indeed one of the responsibilities of the Staff Sergeant was to train new recruits. However, the recruitment crisis facing the department at the time of the study meant new recruits were not receiving the latter and were being placed straight on active duties, but more worrying were some who had not even undergone their SITO basic training. In total 25 per cent (5) officers had not undergone this basic training. The older profile of staff also meant that there were some who had been there in the old constabulary days and had therefore also not undergone the SITO basic training. There were also three officers who had secured the Professional Guard Part 1 training course.

The research also revealed a wide range of additional specialist courses being undertaken by the security officers at both site. Some of these included: first aid, health and safety, fire, risk management courses. However, there did seem to be a desire amongst some of the officers for more training and a feeling that not all the opportunities they could pursue were offered to them. The security officers were also asked to rate the quality and suitability of the training they had received. Because of the very different training regimes at the two case study sites, this will be considered separately.

Table 4.5   Attitude towards the suitability and quality of training for current job at Pleasure Southquay (%)

	Very good	Good	Average	Poor	Very poor
Initial classroom training	21	43	29	4	4
On-the-job training	19	42	23	15	0
N = 28 for initial classroom training and N = 26 for on-the-job training					

Given the more extensive training undertaken by most of the officers at Pleasure Southquay it is not surprising to find that just under two thirds rated it good or very good. This compares to under half at Armed Industries where some had had no training and most had received only the industry standard of two days training. Only 8 per cent at Pleasure Southquay rated the training poor or very poor, compared to 25 per cent at Armed Industries. The on-the-job training was similarly rated at Pleasure Southquay to the classroom training, but at Armed Industries the on-the-job training was rated average to very poor by nearly two thirds of officers. This probably reflected many officers having been thrown straight into 'frontline' duties because of the recruitment crisis, without undergoing a period of on-the-job training.

Table 4.6   Attitude towards the suitability and quality of training for current job at Armed Industries (%)

	Very good	Good	Average	Poor	Very poor
Initial classroom training	13	31	31	0	25
On-the-job training	20	15	40	10	15
N = 20					

The more extensive training at Pleasure Southquay led to some quite positive comments from officers about their training.

CSO 1

All been very clear, no problems. Good quality training.

CSO 21

The PS training is fine, but there are quite a few faces who have not received it who should.

CSO 26

Over the six weeks of training there was plenty of things for them to absorb. Time to think about training and by the time it opened I was raring to go.

There were, however, negative views expressed about their training from both case study sites, as the following extracts from the interviews illustrate.

CSO 4

Very basic. Turned up on site, given a clip board and told to get on with it. On the night shift you pick up as you go along.

CSO 19

People who were giving us training didn't know what they were on about. Some of the instructors looked like why should I be taking this.

SO 2

I went straight to work, for me it was a case of learn for yourself.

SO 4

The courses don't tell you anything.

SO 5

I was taken round in the van and shown the gates. Then I walked around. There was very little training.

SO 7

The opportunities for training on this site are poor. You never get the chance to go on a course, there are never enough to cover. When I came on site you had to be first aid trained. This has now expired and I could have gone on a two day top up, but didn't get the chance, so now need 4 days. There is no money put into training.

SO 11

I had the induction training 6 months after I started the job, you are suppose to have it before you start!

SO 17

I was left to get on with it and develop how I wanted. I wasn't given any proper training as such, I was just left to work it out for myself.

Even the contract manager for Pleasure Southquay – a senior manager with a BSIA member company – revealed to me his views on the basic SITO training,

The nature of the industry makes it very difficult to improve the standard of training. I would agree 100 per cent that the two days is not enough. We have some go through Professional Guard 1 and 2 and not even that is enough. The SITO induction is even easier, all you have to do is get over 68 per cent and if you cant get that you should be walking the streets as a tramp. The SITO training is a joke, its not hard enough. I want to do more, but there is not a lot you can do.

Indeed during the observation at Pleasure Southquay I began talking with two officers about their training. They told me that the contract company provide a passport of training and at the initial training are told that if there is any training they think they need to approach 'Adam' who will arrange it. In reality when anyone approached him he would say 'what do you need that for?' One of the officers told me that he had just left the Royal Navy and required customer service training because he was not used to the public and it had never been given to him. This officer also told me the initial (two days) training was 'complete bollocks' and a 'waste of time'!

Conclusion

This chapter has examined the two nodes of governance that are the main subject of this book. The chapter began by examining Pleasure Southquay describing its characteristics, image and organisational structure of security. The chapter also examined some of the other strategies used to secure social control there. In doing so particular focus was drawn to the challenges posed by the location of this 'oasis' of shopping next to one of the most deprived areas in the city. The chapter then went on to examine the other site, Armed Industries, illustrating the 'village' structure of this case study. The unique 'police' orientated history of the security department was also examined. Finally the chapter assessed some of the personal characteristics of the security officers studied, drawing upon other studies to illustrate their representativeness. This section examined the sex, age, race, educational and training profile of the officers studied. In doing so it also illustrated the views of staff on the quality and quantity of training they had received. This book will now assess the security officers' knowledge and understanding of their knowledge of the legal tools available to them.

Chapter 5

'Knowledge is Power?': Security Officers' Understanding of their Legal Tools

Introduction

There has been very little research conducted internationally on security officers' knowledge of their legal tools and none on British security officers. As Francis Bacon once said, 'knowledge is power', and a sound understanding of what can and cannot be done by a security officer vis-à-vis their legal tools should give them an advantage in achieving their goals. Similarly as many security officers regularly make use of these tools it is important to find out whether security officers know what they are doing is lawful. Therefore it was decided as part of this study to test security officers' knowledge. The security officers were asked 13 questions to test their understanding of their legal tools to arrest,[1] use force and search in varying circumstances. Individual analysis of each of these questions is provided as well as an overall picture of the security officers' performance. Additionally security officers were asked to rate their degree of confidence in their knowledge of their legal tools as well as the quality and quantity of the training they received in this area. Before these results are considered, however, it would be useful to briefly recount the findings of the only other research that has been conducted of security officers' knowledge of their legal tools.

The only other research on the knowledge of security officer's powers was the Rand study published in 1971 (Kakalik and Wildhorn 1971b). American security officers were presented in this survey with a series of scenarios and asked what they would do. They found that the average respondent was wrong 25 per cent of the time and that the average number of errors per respondent was 11 (of a possible 44). In relation to gross errors (that could lead to a law suit or serious criminal charge) there were on average 3.6 of these per respondent. They also found that 97 per cent of respondents made at least one gross error. In terms of their confidence they also found that 18 per cent stated they did not know their legal powers and that 23 per cent were unsure of them. Further, less than 50 per cent knew their arrest powers were the same as a citizen.

---

1   As noted in Chapter 3 the any person powers of arrest have been amended by the Serious Organised Crime and Police Act 2005. The findings relating to the knowledge of legal powers of arrest in this chapter therefore relate to the old powers.

Clearly as this research was based upon the USA its relevance to England and Wales is limited. However, given the low level of training and education amongst some of the security officers surveyed, which also seems to apply to the wider British private security industry, one could suspect that a similar level of knowledge and confidence might apply in the UK. These issues will now be explored.

Security officers' confidence in their knowledge of their legal tools

Before security officers were tested on their knowledge of their legal tools they were asked to rate their level of confidence in their legal tools to arrest, search and use force. This would enable a view as to generally how confident security officers were with using their legal tools. Table 5.1 below illustrates the results for this question for all security officers combined and for Pleasure Southquay and Armed Industries separately.

Table 5.1   How well security officers think they know their legal tools

Case study	Level of confidence	Powers of arrest	Powers of search	Powers to use force
Pleasure Southquay	Very well	28	45	55
	Fairly well	52	35	28
	Somewhat unsure	17	17	17
	Don't know	3	3	0
Armed Industries	Very well	25	40	35
	Fairly well	55	50	35
	Somewhat unsure	15	10	25
	Don't know	5	0	5
All	Very well	27	43	47
	Fairly well	53	41	31
	Somewhat unsure	16	14	20
	Don't know	4	2	2
N = 49				

The table illustrates that security officers were most confident in their legal tools to use force at Pleasure Southquay and search at Armed Industries. This partly reflects the extent to which security officers were using these tools, as will be demonstrated in subsequent chapters these two tools were the most commonly used at the two case study sites. This would seem to suggest that the more commonly used a tool the more confident the security officers are in using them or vice versa. In the case of search at Pleasure Southquay, however, officers rarely used the tool to search, yet their confidence in this tool was also very high. This confidence, however, probably reflected they would not need to use it.

Nevertheless on the negative side at both case study sites there was a significant minority who expressed a view that they didn't know or were somewhat unsure of their legal tools. At Pleasure Southquay around 20 per cent were somewhat unsure or didn't know their legal tools relating to arrest, search and the use of force. At Armed Industries around 20 per cent fell into this category for arrest, but on search it was much lower with 10 per cent somewhat unsure and none who didn't know. Where as with force nearly a third expressed a view that they were somewhat unsure or didn't know. Overall the results reveal that the majority of security officers interviewed were not very confident about their understanding of their legal tools.

Quality of training in legal tools to arrest, search and use force

In Chapter 4 the level and type of training for security officers generally was considered. Given the importance of training in providing the knowledge to undertake the use of legal tools, this is also an important issue. Security officers were also asked to comment on the training that they had received vis-à-vis their legal tools to arrest, search and use force. Table 5.2 below illustrates their rating of the training for these tools.

The above table illustrates differences between Armed Industries and Pleasure Southquay where in the former there were a larger number of security officers who rated the training either poor or very poor. This is not surprising given that 25 per cent of (or 5 officers) security officers had received no training at all! At this site around one third rated the training either poor or very poor for arrest, search and force. Apart from search, the rating was either very good or good for only about a third of officers. At Pleasure Southquay the views on the training they had received in these issues was much more positive. Only 13 per cent rated the quality and quantity of the training on arrest and search either poor or very poor and for force this figure was only 17 per cent. Also on the positive side around half the officers rated the training on all three issues either good or very good. This is not really surprising, given the extensive training these officers were given in comparison to most industry standards.

Table 5.2   How well security officers rated the quality and quantity of their training in their legal tools (%)

Case study	Level of confidence	Powers of arrest	Powers of search	Powers to use force
Pleasure Southquay	Very good	24	24	24
	Good	34	28	34
	Average	28	34	24
	Poor	3	3	7
	Very poor	10	10	10
Armed Industries	Very good	15	15	15
	Good	15	35	20
	Average	30	20	25
	Poor	25	20	25
	Very poor	15	10	15
All	Very good	20	20	20
	Good	27	31	29
	Average	29	29	24
	Poor	12	10	14
	Very poor	12	10	12
N = 49				

Security officers' knowledge of their legal tools

The security officers interviewed for this study were subjected to 13 questions testing their knowledge of their legal tools. The answers to the questions fitted a number of categories. The worst performance would be an answer that was a **major** error (answers that fall into this category are distinguished in **bold**). This would be a course of action that could lead to the officer (or organisation they work for) being prosecuted and/or subjected to civil litigation. A *minor* error would be a course of action that would not necessarily lead to the courts, but would not be appropriate behaviour for a security officer (answers that fall into this category are distinguished by *italics*). Finally there were answers classed as satisfactory where the appropriate action has been identified. In some of the scenarios below there were often more than one of the categories above. Clearly questions that ask a person to predict future behaviour are problematic, as people often say they will do things that in reality they would not (Moser and Kalton, 1971). Indeed on some of the questions below security officers answered that they would arrest a person when they had no experience of undertaking such action, and I was doubtful they would have the courage to do so. Nevertheless the questions do provide original information on the quality of their knowledge and some indication of their orientation towards the job.

Comparison of legal power to arrest to other occupations

In this question security officers were asked to compare their legal powers of arrest to other well known occupations and an ordinary citizen. A police officer has greater powers of arrest relating to issues such as suspicion and non-arrestable offences. A special constable has the same powers as a police officer, although restricted to their force area. Traffic wardens and ordinary citizens have no special powers of arrest that differ from what those a security officer has. Therefore in this question if a security officer answered they had greater or equal powers of arrest vis-à-vis a police officer or special constable this was considered to be a **major** error as thinking one has greater powers than one actually has may lead to situations of abuse of those legal tools. Similarly with traffic wardens and ordinary staff if the security officer answered 'greater than', this was also considered to be a **major** error. On these two occupations if they answered 'less than', this was considered to be a *minor* error as this was incorrect but unlikely to lead to any risks of litigation. An answer of 'don't know' was also considered a *minor* error because a security officer should have an awareness of what their legal tools are vis-à-vis these occupations.

Table 5.3   All security officers knowledge of their legal power to arrest compared to other occupations (%)

How do you think your legal powers as a security officer to arrest a person compare to the following occupations?				
	Greater than	Same as	Less than	Don't know
Police officer	**0**	**10**	90	*0*
Special constable	**2**	**29**	55	*14*
Traffic warden	**8**	78	*10*	*4*
Ordinary citizen	**6**	92	*2*	*0*
N = 49				

The table illustrates that generally security officers had a good knowledge of their legal tools to arrest vis-à-vis other occupations. There was, however, a very small minority that caused concern about their level of knowledge. 10 per cent of security officers thought they had the same powers as a police officer to arrest an individual. This degree of knowledge worsened when special constables were considered with 31 per cent considering they had the same or greater powers than a special constable to undertake an arrest. However, as many of these probably did not know what powers a special constable hold this error was not as bad. These same comments apply to traffic wardens. When ordinary citizens are considered, however, these comments do not apply. Here 8 per cent got this answer incorrect with 6 per cent considering they had greater powers to arrest than an ordinary citizen (2 per cent thought they had less). Given the comments about special constables and traffic wardens above, a fair overview of the performance of security officers on this question (all 4 answers) would be very good.

Table 5.4   Pleasure Southquay officers' knowledge of their legal power to arrest compared to other occupations (%)

How do you think your legal powers as a security officer to arrest a person compare to the following occupations?				
	Greater than	Same as	Less than	Don't know
Police officer	0	7	93	0
Special constable	0	31	58	10
Traffic warden	10	76	10	3
Ordinary citizen	7	93	0	0
N = 29				

Table 5.5   Armed Industries officers' knowledge of their legal power to arrest compared to other occupations (%)

How do you think your legal powers as a security officer to arrest a person compare to the following occupations?				
	Greater than	Same as	Less than	Don't know
Police officer	0	15	85	0
Special constable	5	25	50	20
Traffic warden	5	80	10	5
Ordinary citizen	5	90	5	0
N = 20				

When the analysis is split between the two case study sites similar profiles of answers also emerged (Tables 5.4 and 5.5). Although on the more important question relating to comparison with a police officer, double the percentage of officers at Armed Industries felt they had the same powers as a police officer to arrest compared to Pleasure Southquay. On a positive basis, however, at both Pleasure Southquay and Armed Industries 90 per cent or more knew they only had the same powers as an ordinary citizen to arrest. This confident performance in general amongst security officers was also to be found in subsequent questions, as will now be considered.

Question 22

In this question the aim was to test the security officer's knowledge of their citizen's right of arrest. The question provides the scenario of clearly witnessing what reasonably seems to be an arrestable offence under section 24 (4) and (5) of the Police and Criminal Evidence Act (PACE) 1984, which therefore entitles a person to undertake a citizen's arrest. Some security officers raised the scenario that it might be someone locked out of their own car smashing the window to secure access. However, if the person runs away that would be reasonable grounds for suspecting they were committing an arrestable offence of theft from a motor vehicle, rather than breaking into their own car. Therefore this answer would be the most satisfactory answer for a security officer.

Table 5.6   Security officers' answers to Question 22 (%)

22. You are patrolling the car park of the building you guard when you see a man smash the window of a car and pull a bag from it. When he sees you he begins to run away but is in an enclosed area and you soon catch up with him. What do you do then? (Please indicate one answer which relates to what you think a security officer should do and is legally correct)			
	Pleasure Southquay	Armed Industries	All
1. Ask him to leave and escort him to the exit	3	5	4
2. Ask him for identification and his name and address and then escort him to the exit	0	5	2
3. Arrest him using your citizen's right of arrest and call the police	83	45	67
4. Call the police	14	45	27
5. *Do nothing*	0	0	0
N = 49			

Nevertheless undertaking an arrest is a risky practice that may result in the security officer being injured or worse. Therefore an answer of call the police (or some said their controller) would also be a satisfactory answer. Answers 1 and 2 would be unlikely to lead to serious litigation, however, this would illustrate incompetence on the part of the security officer. Therefore answers 1 and 2 were classed as *minor* errors. To witness such an incident and 'do nothing' would also smack of incompetence but would be unlikely to result in serious litigation, therefore this was also classed as a *minor* error.

Two thirds of security officers said they would arrest the man using their citizen's right of arrest, with a further 27 per cent stating they would call the police. During the interviews a number of officers expressed the view that rather than call the police they would call their controller or a superior to ask them to call the police. These responses were also allocated to answer 3. In the explanations of their answers a number of security officers were concerned about their safety and would prefer to call the police or a superior rather than tackle the person themselves. As the following extracts from the interviews reveal,

CSO 2

If violent would call the police. If I thought I would be under any threat I wouldn't arrest.

SO 4

I would inform the controller to catch on camera and then monitor the situation. They don't pay me enough to get hurt. I certainly wouldn't arrest him.

SO 5

Call the control room to call the police. I couldn't confront them because I have a bad leg.

The explanations of some officers also revealed a very good knowledge of their citizen's right of arrest, as the answer from SO7 reveals.

SO 7

Because the police have the power of arrest and search and we don't we have to be careful in detaining someone. You have to have strong grounds for undertaking a citizen's arrest. I would endeavour to call the police to undertake that part. To arrest someone they need to have done a crime that carries a 5 years jail sentence and there aren't many of them.

Some officers considered it could be a man breaking into their own car after having lost their own keys and stated they would approach the person first before deciding what to do. What was most striking about this answer, however, was the much greater willingness amongst staff at Pleasure Southquay to arrest the man. At Pleasure Southquay 83 per cent stated they would, compared to only 45 per cent at Armed

Industries, whereas 45 per cent would call the police at Armed Industries compared to only 14 per cent at Pleasure Southquay. Bearing in mind the problems with questions that seek to predict future behaviour, this large difference does perhaps illustrate the more active law enforcement oriented culture of the Pleasure Southquay officers, something that will be considered further in Chapter 9.

Question 23

The aim of question 23 was to test security officer's knowledge of their ability to undertake a search of a member of staff. This question, given the retail context, was familiar to the Pleasure Southquay staff. However, given the rarity of conducting searches it was more appropriate for the Armed Industries staff where they regularly performed this function. Despite this familiarity, however, one Armed Industries security officer refused to answer the question.

Table 5.7   Security officers' answers to Question 23 (%)

23. You are a security guard in a retail store. A shop assistant (employee a) on the perfume counter tells you that she thinks she has seen one of her colleagues (employee b) put some perfume in her bag and that she hasn't paid for it. You ask if she is certain that she saw it and she says she only thinks she has. What do you do? (Please indicate one answer which relates to what you think a security officer should do and is legally correct)			
	Pleasure Southquay	Armed Industries	All
1. Ask employee b if you can search her bag with her consent	69	88	77
2. Call the police to arrest employee b on suspicion of theft	7	0	4
3. Arrest employee b on suspicion of theft and call the police	**0**	**0**	**0**
4. Search employee b's bag without her permission on grounds of suspicion of theft	**24**	**0**	**14**
5. Do nothing	0	10	4
N = 48			

Answer 1 was the most appropriate answer as the security officer could ask to look in her bag if consent was given to investigate this allegation before further action was considered. However, there is no right to search and if she refused the security officer would not be able to force a search. Therefore answers 3 and 4 would be

major errors. The officer has not witnessed an arrestable offence and would not have reasonable grounds for believing an arrestable offence has occurred. Also there is no right to search without consent. Either of these answers could lead to litigation for false arrest, assault etc. Answer 2 would not be a **major** error but to call the police on the basis of such an allegation would be an over-reaction and it would be much better to call management or pursue some other action first. Calling the police to ask to arrest would also be inappropriate behaviour as you would in reality be calling the police to ask them to come and investigate further. To do nothing would also be inappropriate behaviour for a security officer.

The table above reveals that for this question the overall performance of security officers was not as good as the previous question. Just over two thirds of security officers answered the correct answer at Pleasure Southquay, compared to 88 per cent at Armed Industries. It is also a concern that nearly a quarter of security officers at Pleasure Southquay would search the employee's bag without her consent. This would constitute a **major** error. In defence of the Pleasure Southquay officers they rarely were required to search and given they were not based in stores this would also be an unlikely scenario for them. It still, however, raises questions about the level of knowledge of security officers vis-à-vis their legal tools to search. Indeed a number of security officers stated they would search or arrest according to the local store's policy. Some of the explanations for *minor* and **major** errors are listed below.

CSO 12

As only thought she saw I would do nothing.

CSO 15

I don't have the powers so I would get the police in to arrest her and search the bag.

CSO 27

If allowed to search at random I would request an ordinary search.

One security officer, however, was clearly aware of the risk of undertaking a forcible search, as the extract below illustrates,

CSO 1

I've always been taught to do nothing unless actually seen. If you've seen it I will back you up. I will do nothing, because not seen it. If she's got nothing she could sue me for thousands.

Other officers were keen to pass responsibility for the appropriate action to either a manager or the police. As the extracts below illustrate,

CSO 11

If there was a manager around I would try and get them involved. Management should deal with this type of incident.

CSO 26

I would get the person away from the public and ask the member of staff to repeat what she has said to me in front of her. If she still repeated it I would then ask if I could look in her bag. If the items were there I would then ask if she could produce a receipt. If she couldn't I would then refer it to management. If she could I would offer my apologies. If she refused to co-operate I would threaten to call the police.

This question perhaps shows that security officers may have less knowledge in relation to areas of activity they rarely get involved with. It does illustrate the need to raise the standards of knowledge of security officers at Pleasure Southquay in search. Although they were rarely confronted with such situations, it could occur and there would be a significant risk of a major error if some of the officers actually did what they said they would.

Question 24

This question also tested the security officers' knowledge of their legal tools to undertake searches. Given the activities of security officers at Armed Industries this question was highly suited to them, compared to Pleasure Southquay where it was much less appropriate. The satisfactory answer was the first, as the officers have no right to undertake a forcible search and should allow the official to leave writing down the details of the incident to inform management for further action. Answer 2 would by a *minor* mistake because although you could call the police, what they decide to do would be based upon the circumstances and they might decide to take no action. Also in most organisations (as was the case at both Pleasure Southquay and Armed Industries) the first stage would be to inform management rather than involve the police. Answers 3 and 4 would be **major** errors as there is no right to arrest as there has been no observation of an arrestable offence or is there reasonable grounds of suspecting one has taken place. There is also no right to search him without his consent. To do nothing would also not be appropriate behaviour for a security officer in these circumstances.

Table 5.8   Security officers' answers to Question 24 (%)

24. You are a security officer in a motor vehicle factory. You are at the entrance of the factory conducting random searches of employees leaving the workplace. You stop a senior trade union official and ask him to search his bags. He claims you are discriminating against him because he is a trade unionist and refuses to be searched, even though there is a clause in his employment contract referring to a company policy on searching and the consequences of refusing to be searched. What should you do? (Please indicate one answer which relates to what you think a security officer should do and is legally correct)			
	Pleasure Southquay	Armed Industries	All
1. Write down details of the incident to inform management and allow him to leave without being searched	86	95	90
2. Call the police to arrest and search him on reasonable suspicion of theft	*3*	*0*	2
3. Arrest him using your citizen's right of arrest and then search him with his consent	3	0	2
4. Search him without his consent	7	5	6
5. *Do nothing*	0	0	0
N = 49			

Given that the security officers at Armed Industries regularly undertake this type of search one would expect a large number indicating option 1, which 95 per cent did. Even at Pleasure Southquay where the officers did not face this kind of role, 86 per cent still answered correctly. There were only a handful of officers who felt they had the right to undertake a forcible search. The officer who answered search without consent at Armed Industries had not received any training, but the answer illuminated other issues as well, as the extract below reveals,

SO 2

> I would search without his consent. I had a similar situation with a black man I kept stopping to search. It was only on the third day when he said to me why do you keep stopping me that I realised. I was shocked. I didn't realise what I was doing. I was searching him every day. I was picking on him because he was black. He was a very nice man though about it.

One of the officers at Pleasure Southquay who answered forcibly search did so because of the clause in the contract.

CSO 21

I would search him because of the clause in his contract.

Perhaps more revealing in the answers to this question were the strategies that security officers mentioned they would use to try and secure consent. Some described how they would use a form of language so that it would be difficult for the person to say no,

CSO 3

If there is a notice that it is company policy to carry out a search I would carry out the search. I would say 'Do you mind being searched?' I would try and use phrases so they can't say no.

This type of approach is regularly used by police officers to secure compliance without recourse to using actual legal tools (Dixon 1997). Another approach identified by Dixon vis-à-vis police officers is to threaten to actually invoke the legal sanction available to them, such as to arrest. In the case of security officers this was not always available. They could, however, threaten them with other sanctions, such as calling the police or a manager and there was evidence officers would do this to try and secure consent as the following extracts illustrate.

CSO 9

I would call the police because it is in the contract, referring to be searched. It makes life easier. If you mention the police they are more likely to say yes.

CSO 23

You can't stop them in this position. I would try and call my superiors over without him leaving. I certainly wouldn't forcibly search him or restrain him. He may have a good reason for refusing the search. You could threaten to call the police, but it would depend upon what the superiors said.

CSO 26

If a superior not around I would threaten to call the police. If he still refused I would actually call the police.

Finally the other strategy identified would be to stress the potential consequences for the person's employment if they refuse to submit to a search.

CSO 10

I have actually experienced this and I would hold the person there. I wouldn't let him leave and would stress to him it could be instant dismissal if he continues to refuse to be searched.

Overall the security officers interviewed at both case study sites showed very good knowledge of the rights to undertake searches. There were a handful of officers who were confused on this issue. The question also revealed a wide range of strategies officers would use to try and secure consent and this has been well documented in relation to police officers who use similar strategies to secure consent (Dixon 1997).

Question 25

The aim of question 25 was to test the security officer's knowledge of trespass and search. Given the nature of both case study sites all security officers should have had a good knowledge in this area. Answer 1 was the correct answer because it is private property and as it is a condition of entrance to submit to a search they have the right to refuse entrance unless a person agrees to a search. Answer 2 would be inappropriate behaviour because this might be someone impersonating the police officer with deviant motives in mind. It would also defeat the objects of the search policy on the entrance. It was classed as a *minor* mistake, although if this was a person with a criminal motive the negligence of the officer could conceivably lead to litigation. To do nothing is also not an appropriate course of action for a security officer in these circumstances. Answer 3 would be a **major** error as refusing to be searched is not a criminal offence and therefore would be no grounds for a citizen's arrest. There is also no right to undertake a forcible search so answer 4 would also be a **major** error.

Table 5.9   Security officers' answers to Question 25 (%)

25. You are guarding the entrance in a hotel to a conference on international terrorism. As part of the requirements for entrance to the conference all delegates and staff must be searched before entering the conference. A delegate turns up late claiming to be a police officer who is due to speak and refuses to be searched because he is due to speak. What do you do? (Please indicate one answer which relates to what you think a security officer should do and is legally correct)			
	Pleasure Southquay	Armed Industries	All
1. Refuse entrance unless he agrees to be searched	93	100	96
2. Take his name and address and allow him entrance on the grounds that he comes back to be searched after speaking	*3*	*0*	*2*
3. Arrest him for refusing to be searched	**0**	**0**	**0**
4. Forcibly search him	**3**	**0**	**2**
5. Do nothing	*0*	*0*	*0*
N = 49			

The security officers generally showed excellent knowledge in this area. 100 per cent of Armed Industries security officers answered correctly. At Pleasure Southquay 93 per cent answered correctly. One officer did, however, state they would forcibly search the person and this was because it was a 'terrorism' conference. The officer stated,

CSO 13

I would forcibly search because it is a 'terrorism' conference and there are police there.

It seems in this case the issue of terrorism influenced the security officer's answer and if it had been any other kind of conference this would not have occurred.

Question 26

The aim of this question was to test security officers' knowledge of their ability to use reasonable force. The options available also enabled an assessment to be made on how prepared they would be to undertake the use of force.

Table 5.10   Security officers' answers to Question 26 (%)

26. You are walking on a public highway between two buildings you have responsibility for guarding. You see a man with a brick who looks like he is about to smash the side window of a car. What should you do? (Please indicate one answer which relates to what you think a security officer should do and is legally correct)			
	Pleasure Southquay	Armed Industries	All
1. Use your citizen's right of arrest on the grounds that he is about to commit an arrestable offence	**3**	**0**	**2**
2. Call the police and monitor him	41	60	49
3. *Wait until he has smashed the window and then use your citizen's right of arrest to arrest him*	*34*	*20*	*29*
4. Use reasonable force to prevent him committing a crime and then call the police	17	15	16
5. *Do nothing*	*3*	*5*	*4*
N = 49			

Answer 1 is a **major** error as a security officer has no right to arrest on the grounds a person might commit an arrestable offence. Answer 2 would be a satisfactory answer and would demonstrate a reluctance to get involved in confrontational situations. If the security officer waited until they smashed the window to arrest the individual this would also be a legitimate course of action. However, it would be better to prevent a crime from occurring, so this answer was classed as a *minor* error. Under the Criminal Law Act 1967 section 3 (1),

> *Any person* may use such force as is reasonable in the circumstances, in the prevention of crime, or in assisting or affecting in the lawful arrest of offenders, suspected offenders or of persons at large.

Therefore answer 4 would also be a satisfactory answer and would also show a willingness to engage in confrontational situations. Answer 5, again, would not be an appropriate course of action for a security officer.

The question did provide the greatest degree of diversity in answers. Again all officers bar one avoided a **major** error. There was a significant minority at both Pleasure Southquay and Armed Industries, 34 and 20 per cent respectively, who would wait for the crime to be committed and then use their citizens right of arrest. Again this showed a greater willingness amongst the Pleasure Southquay staff to engage in confrontational situations. The answers revealed a knowledge of citizens right of arrest, but also a lack of knowledge of the Criminal Law Act 1967, as the following answers reveal.

CSO 14

He might not do it if he sees you. If he does smash the window you can arrest him.

CSO 26

This is difficult because he could have locked his own keys in. If it was his I would ask him to prove it. Where was it taxed? What is the registration? If I was satisfied it was his I would leave it at that. If I wasn't satisfied I would ask him not to proceed with his intentions. I would then call the police and stay and observe. If he then smashed the window I have the power of arrest.

There was a similar number at both case study sites who would use reasonable force to prevent the crime occurring with 17 and 15 per cent at Pleasure Southquay and Armed Industries respectively. These answers were based more upon a notion of preventing damage, rather than the exact legal basis as the extract from the interview with SO 14 reveals.

SO 14

He is going to cause damage if you don't do anything and you're here to protect property. So I would try and stop him.

Probably the biggest indicator of the lower willingness to engage in confrontational behaviour was the large proportion of officers who would call the police at Armed Industries with 60 per cent compared to 41 per cent at Pleasure Southquay. As one security officer answered,

SO 2

Its too dangerous these days. You don't know what they've got, they could be carrying anything. So I would call the police.

SO 16

As a security officer I would be inclined to call the police and monitor him. You don't get paid enough as a security officer to get bashed over the head with a brick.

A number of officers also stated they would approach the person first to try and find out what they were up to before deciding what to do.

CSO 10

I would wait and see what happened. If it was on private land you have more authority to approach them and ask them what they are doing. If I wasn't happy with their explanation I would call the police.

SO 8

I would ask him what he is doing as you can't pre-empt what he's going to do. I would take it from there.

Question 26 provided the most diverse range of answers and particularly illustrated the different orientation towards conflict between officers at the two sites. Overall, however, the performance in terms of satisfactory answers was good to this question.

Question 27

In question 27 the security officers were presented with a series of statements to further test their knowledge of the limits to their legal tools. The first essentially sets out what a citizen's arrest is and therefore legally correct. If the security officer answered no this was regarded as a *minor* error because although they do not know what an arrestable offence is it was impossible to determine from this answer if they thought they had greater rights, which clearly would be a major error.

The second scenario proved to be less transparent in retrospect for many of the interviewees were confused as to whether this meant a consensual or forcible search. In such occasions this question was clarified as a forcible search. Although it would be contentious if a person was 'arrested' whether consent would be valid. There is, however, scope to 'seize' the 'fruits' of the offence and remove any weapon that is being carried. However, these would need to be overtly available and could not be found through a routine search. Given the advice security officers are given to not search, it was considered that if the security officer answered yes they were committing a **major** error. The third and fourth scenarios were much clearer and in both cases answering yes was classed as a **major** mistake.

Table 5.11   Security officers' answers to Question 27 (%)

27. Which of the following is legally correct?						
	Pleasure Southquay		Armed Industries		All	
	Yes	No	Yes	No	Yes	No
A security officer can arrest a person who he has reasonable grounds of suspecting has committed an arrestable offence	72	28	75	25	73	27
A security officer can search a person who has been arrested for committing an arrestable offence	**45**	55	**30**	70	**39**	61
If an employee's contract states refusal to submit to a search by security staff is a disciplinary offence, the security officer can forcibly search them	**3**	96	**10**	90	**6**	94
A security officer is entitled to use greater force when arresting a person than an ordinary citizen	**0**	100	**10**	90	**4**	96
N = 49						

The table above illustrates there was a degree of confusion on what constitutes an arrestable offence, with around only three quarters in both research sites recognising what it is. On the issue of search after conducting an arrestable offence there was a great deal of confusion. As stated above on this question with many officers it was clarified as a forcible search. Nearly half of the officers at Pleasure Southquay thought they could search a person once they were arrested and at Armed Industries it was nearly a third. This shows a degree of confusion over what the rights to search are once a person is arrested. There were a handful of officers who in the last two scenarios thought they have the right to forcibly search a person if their contract states it is a disciplinary offence and who also felt they had greater rights to use force than an ordinary citizen.

Overall performance

Overall analysis of the answers of security officers to these questions reveals that of the 13 questions security officers would on average make 1 **major** error, 1 *minor* error and answer 11 satisfactorily (for median as well, but for mode 0, 0 and 11 respectively). The preceding analysis revealed the types of questions security officers generally got wrong. Some of them were more related to their knowledge of what their powers were vis-à-vis other occupations and could be considered as less serious **major** and *minor* errors. Such analysis is also prone to be skewed by a small number who get a large number of answers wrong. Indeed overall on **major** errors 3 of the 49 officers accounted for nearly a quarter (13) of the 55 **major** errors and for *minor* errors 6 of the 49 officers accounted for a third (18) of the 54 *minor* errors. This illustrates that there was a small minority who had a much worse knowledge than the average. Overall, therefore, these figures illustrate a good knowledge amongst these security officers of their legal tools.

Table 5.12   Mean number of answers per security officer which were satisfactory *minor* and major errors

	Pleasure Southquay	Armed Industries	All
Mean number of satisfactory answers	10.6	10.9	10.7
Mean number of *minor* errors	1.2	1	1
Mean number of **major** errors	1.1	1	1.2
N = 49			

The small numbers of officers (and even smaller sub-groups in terms of sex, age, race and small variations) made detailed statistical analysis of performance against these criteria pointless. It was decided, however, to undertake further analysis of the mean numbers of correct and incorrect answers relating specific sub-groups of security officers to training. The greater amount and quality of training would be expected to produce better results. Given that some of the Pleasure Southquay officers had undergone several weeks' training in their induction covering these issues one might expect the best results amongst them. As Table 5.13 illustrates this was not the case. Bearing in mind the very small samples of some groups the best all-round performance was amongst those who had undertaken only the SITO Basic training. However, perhaps the other striking finding – and probably the most important – was the much higher number of **major** errors amongst those officers who had received no training, with a rate of 2.4, exactly double the all round average.

Table 5.13   Mean number of answers per security officer according to level of training which were satisfactory, minor or major errors

	No training	SITO Basic (n = 22)	Professional Guard One (n = 3)	Pleasure Southquay Induction (n = 18)	Old AI Induction (n = 1)
Mean number of satisfactory answers	9.8	11	10.7	10.7	10
Mean number of minor errors	0.8	1.1	1.3	1.1	3
Mean number of major errors	2.4	0.9	1	1.2	0
N = 49					

Another distinction was between the 'frontline' and 'backroom' officers at Pleasure Southquay. Given the greater use of legal tools amongst the 'frontline' officers one would expect and hope a better performance than the 'backroom'. This was not the case, although the differences were minor. 'Frontline' security officers secured a mean of 10.5 correct answers, 1.3 minor errors and 1.1 major errors. This compared to the 'backroom' staff of 10.9, 0.9 and 1.3 respectively.

Conclusion

This chapter has illustrated that in terms of confidence security officers are more positive about the legal tools they use regularly or never have to use. There is also a significant minority who are unsure or don't know certain legal rights. Generally the officers interviewed were positive about the training they received in their use of their legal tools. When knowledge was assessed, the overall results were much more positive than some of the inadequacies found by Kakalik and Wildhorn (1971b) amongst American security officers in the early 1970s. It is difficult, however, to determine from such a small sample whether this would reflect the wider private security industry in England and Wales.

Overall this analysis generally reveals a good knowledge amongst security officers of their citizens right of arrest. Security officers presented with scenarios asking them to consider whether they should undertake an arrest or not generally had the right idea of what to do. The results also illustrated some gaps in knowledge. There is a small minority of staff who do not know the legal limits to conducting searches. Given that some regularly undertake such functions this is an area that illustrates the need for measures to improve knowledge amongst officers. Similarly very few officers were aware of their right to use reasonable force to prevent a crime and this is also an area that should be given greater priority in education and training. The answers to many of these questions also revealed similar strategies being used by security officers to secure consent to those undertaken by police officers. Evidence of avoiding demands and requests based upon the law or contracts by security officers and instead using appropriate language based upon questions and by invoking the threat of sanctions was also found. Bearing in mind the small sample there was also evidence of the higher likelihood amongst staff who have received no training to make **major** errors. Finally the answers – accepting the caveat that what is said is not what is always practiced – illustrated differences in orientation vis-à-vis the willingness of security officers to put themselves in positions of greater risk. This is an issue that will be developed further in subsequent chapters.

Chapter 6

Universal Legal Tools: Consent, Coercion and Commonsense

Introduction

Earlier in Chapter 3 the legal tools of private security officers were divided between 'universal', those that all possess such as the right to arrest and use force in specific circumstances; and 'select', those such as exclusion and search privileges, which are based upon the nodal context. In this and the next chapter these two types of legal tools and their use in practice at the two case study sites will be examined. The focus of this chapter will be the legal rights to arrest and to use force. It will also provide data to illustrate the different commitment of security staff to make use of their 'universal' legal tools. The chapter will also examine the attitudes of security officers towards the grant of additional special powers and the right to carry non-lethal weapons. In Chapter 1 the emergence of police powers was also briefly examined and it was illustrated this has been characterised by gradual extension of legal powers and a focus upon consent in officers securing compliance (Dixon 1997). A theme this chapter will develop is that many of the practices used by police officers are also used by security officers. In policing their workplaces security officers rely on a variety of strategies to secure consent. This approach, does fail sometimes, and as a consequence they often have to resort to coercion if they are going to achieve their outcome. Another theme that will emerge is that strategies to secure consent and the use of coercion are usually rooted in notions of 'commonsense' rather than detailed knowledge of what their legal rights are to actually pursue a course of action.

The right to arrest

The security officers interviewed were asked to estimate the number of times they had undertaken 'arrests' and to describe an example of one they had undertaken. During observation of the security officers further evidence also emerged on the issue of arrest. It was clear, however, that when they were asked to describe their experience they were answering in relation to the number of detentions that they have made, rather than formal arrests. In the absence of a definition of an arrest in the Police and Criminal Evidence Act 1984, what constitutes one has largely been determined by common law. It is usually considered to involve some form of touch (or reasonable force) or the arrestee acquiescing when told they are under arrest

(Stone 1997). In the incidents described to me the security officers were generally persuading the alleged shoplifters to go to a private location in the store to wait for the police to arrive, where they would be presented with evidence, and if satisfactory when the police arrived, they would formally arrest them. It was rare for a person to resist, requiring the security officer to use coercion. Clearly in these situations even if the security officer does not state the person is under arrest the use of force to restrain them would constitute an arrest (Stone 1997). Indeed Adu-Boakye's (2002) covert study as a security officer in a large inner-city supermarket revealed the ambiguous treatment of 'arrests' for shop-theft by management, with only 1 of the 29 'arrests' conducted during his research being handed over to the police. Such was the disinterest in arrests from management Adu-Boakye resorted to exercising his own discretion when catching shoplifters and frequently asking the offenders to replace the goods and leave the shop without recourse to management.

When considering the statistics below on arrest the vast majority were really apprehensions or an act that fell short of a formal arrest because of the tactics used by the security officer. Indeed security officers are encouraged to use a lexicon that avoids describing what may have occurred as a crime or the action as an arrest. The handbook for staff at Armed Industries stated,

> If you see a theft and stop a suspect say only this:
> 'Sir/Madam, I have reason to believe you have goods in your possession that have not been paid for, would you please accompany me to the Manager/Security Office.'
> At no stage should you mention **stealing – shoplifting**, or theft (Contract Company at Armed Industries Staff Handbook, their emphasis).

The other striking finding was the variation amongst security officers in the extent to which they had undertaken an 'arrest'. There was a large cohort of security officers who had never undertaken an arrest. Given that to 'arrest' someone risks verbal abuse, assault and perhaps worse; as well as the potential legal consequences if the action is legally flawed, it is probably more surprising given the training and pay security officers receive that they actually do 'arrest'.

Table 6.1 reveals that at Armed Industries conducting arrests or apprehensions were very rare with only two officers or 10 per cent indicating rarely. And for both of these officers it related to the same incident where they had chased a suspected burglar at night and caught him in partnership with local police who had also joined the pursuit. At Pleasure Southquay well over half, 59 per cent, had not undertaken an arrest. There were about a third of security officers, 10, who were regularly conducting apprehensions on a weekly or monthly basis. Indeed when the Pleasure Southquay statistics were subjected to further analysis distinguishing 'frontline' staff from 'backroom' (those who worked in the control room or in the car park) it revealed around half the frontline staff were actively pursuing apprehensions on a weekly or monthly basis. There was an active group of security officers prepared to use their legal tools to undertake arrests, but undertaking the same 'frontline' functions were also a group who were not using their legal tools.

Table 6.1 **Number of 'arrests' security officers have claimed to have made (%)**

	Once or twice a week	Once or twice a month	Once or twice a year	Rarely	Never
Pleasure Southquay All	10	24	7	0	59
Pleasure Southquay 'Frontline'	14	32	9	0	46
Pleasure Southquay 'Backroom'	0	0	0	0	100
Armed Industries	0	0	0	10	90
All	6	14	4	4	71
N = 49					

Securing consent

The structured interviews revealed that the security officers that had undertaken apprehensions were clearly aware of the appropriate lexicon to use to secure consent and in undertaking their functions most suspects complied as some of the extracts from interviews reveal (The most relevant parts relating to arrest are illustrated in bold).

CSO 3

Let me get it right first. We went to *shop r* about 1.30 today called by their staff. They have a radio that connects with us. There was a fraudulent card been passed over. They asked us what to do so I told them it was up to them whether they wanted to make it a police matter. We backed them up. I said, **'Would you mind coming with me?'** and I took him to a backroom until the police arrived. He was very good, very calm, they can be a handful, physical, verbal and violent. He just accepted it.

Have you ever had someone you have had to detain get violent?

They are more shocked than anything at getting caught. They just want to get away – although luckily at the moment.

CSO 9

Just 'Joe Public' shoplifters. Made the selection, the concealment I observed him, he made no attempt to pay, left the store at which point he has committed theft. **You stop him and**

explain who you are. At no time do you say 'you are under arrest' as you get into the 'every thing you say will be....' Nine times out of ten once they're stopped they generally come back anyway.

CSO 23

It is much easier here than being in a shop the whole day. **Here we basically detain, unless it is serious. 9 times out of 10 there is no problem. We get 'nicks' here but not arrests.** Some team leaders have a different attitude to what to get involved in. Some have different outlooks and experience and their actions reflect that.

It was also clear from their statements that there was generally compliance from the suspects once they had been approached by a security officer, as the following statements reveal.

CSO 1

We got called to *store r* a 14 year old who had decided to take a £14 hat off the shelf and put it down his trousers. He had £20 in his pocket. We took him to the back of the shop took his name, age, address and the police turned up, his rights were read, it was fairly straightforward from there and they took him away.

Were you called there?

The shop actually called us in there and it was myself and a colleague who went in there. **The child gave in as soon as we arrived, he could not deny it**.

CSO 12

The first that springs to mind is someone that ran out of *store t* with a couple of sweaters he had stolen. Two staff followed him to the car park towards the North gate. He was quite heavily drugged and exhausted through running with so many sweaters on. So there was no real struggle he knew the game was up. He just walked back to the management block where we waited for the police.

What did you say to him?

I can't remember the exact words, but it was something like, **'you are going to have to come back to the management block with me'**.

This was confirmed when asking one CSO about having to use force.

CSO 21

Generally apart from when the clubs chuck out is the arresting of shoplifters and so far **we have had all the quiet ones that once they have been nicked they come quietly we take their names wait for the police** do the statements…

When all else fails commonsense requires coercion!

Arrests involving coercion did occur at Pleasure Southquay, but were relatively rare (although not in relation to disorder as will be discussed later in this chapter). During observation at Pleasure Southquay only one apprehension by security staff was witnessed and that did not relate to shop-theft. This occurred at 02.45 hours on a Sunday morning after the clubs had shut. Two men who were drunk walked by and we overheard one say something like 'I'm gonna spike him'. As they headed towards one of the nightclubs the door staff were warned that two men were heading towards them. We followed the two men and they turned the corner out of sight and within seconds we heard on the radio that they were attacking the doors of the nightclub. The CSOs ran to the club and I followed and 2 of the door supervisors were wrestling one of the men to the ground and the other was held by 2 CSOs. In securing them to the ground punches were exchanged and the man held on the ground by the door supervisors was bleeding from the nose. The man held by the CSOs was lying face down with a CSO each holding one arm and he was not struggling. While holding the man to the ground one of the CSOs asked him if he would mind if he 'patted him down' to check if he had any weapons or sharps in his pockets; to which the man agreed. Nothing was found. They were held there for about 10 minutes when a police van arrived with officers who asked what had happened. As soon as it was explained that they had attempted to smash their way back into the club – from which they had been removed earlier – they were arrested and handcuffed by the police officers and driven away in the van. The security officers and door supervisors were asked to supply statements. I was told a few days after the incident that the men had been charged with affray, but like the officers never found out whether they were prosecuted, found guilty and if so what their sentence was.

At no time during this incident were the men told they were under arrest by the security officers, but they were clearly being restrained to prevent them escaping by the use of force and therefore under arrest. There were good grounds for believing that they were guilty of affray as they were threatening violence against the door supervisors. As they were also attempting to kick the windows in they could also be reasonably viewed as attempting to cause criminal damage (which is an arrestable offence). In these circumstances the security officer could draw upon a number of different justifications for the arrest. First because of the attempt to kick the door in and cause criminal damage, under section 24 (4) (a) of the Police and Criminal Evidence Act (PACE) 1984 '*Any person* may arrest without warrant – (a) anyone who is in the act of committing an arrestable offence.' If the two men had not kicked at the doors then the situation would have become more interesting, but there would have still been a justification. The officers could have drawn upon the Criminal Law Act 1967 section 3 (1),

> *Any person* may use such force as is reasonable in the circumstances, in the prevention of crime, or in assisting or affecting in the lawful arrest of offenders, suspected offenders or of persons at large.

It would have been reasonable to assume that they were about to commit a crime against the staff of the nightclub. Finally the security officers could have used the justification under common law that any person may also arrest anyone committing a Breach of the Peace while it is happening and if he has reasonable grounds for believing that it will continue. This usually means behaviour that is or is likely to cause violence, such as a fight between two people. Clearly this incident fitted this category as well. Therefore the security officers had a range of justifications to draw upon.

In reality, however, the officers never actually told the man they were restraining that they were under arrest. It was the police when they arrived and had surveyed the situation who formally arrested them and read them their rights. Talking to the security officers after the incident they did not justify their action in terms of relevant legislation or common law. They simply talked in terms of responding to an incident, preventing disorder and calling the police to deal with that side. Thus they undertook this action without reference to their legal tools preferring to deal with it in a practical way and based upon consent where possible and ultimately 'commonsense'.

'Commonsense' was also illustrated in an incident that was the closest I came to witnessing an 'arrest' for shoplifting at Pleasure Southquay. In this incident I was patrolling with two CSOs when we were asked to go to a sports clothing store. One of their staff briefed us outside that there was a 'black man' who had been seen playing with trainers and he suspected he was trying to remove the electronic tag. We waited outside and the suspect then proceeded to walk out of the store, when he reached the exit point the alarm activated and he immediately turned round and went back to where he had been playing with the trainers. A few minutes later he then returned to the exit and walked out of the store. This time the alarm did not activate. The CSOs consulted with the in-house member of staff and he brought out a box with the trainers. He showed us that one tag has been removed, but not the second. He stated the view that the suspect must have thought the trainers only had one tag. No action was taken against the suspect other than CSOs tailing him and standing outside every store he went in with a tip off to the staff inside to keep him under surveillance. After a few more hours shopping he eventually left the site with no formal contact or action taken against him. For some the actions of this suspect might have warranted at least stopping the suspect to question him, after all he had activated the alarm. Ultimately, however, for the security officers there was no clear evidence he had removed a tag, activation of the alarm does not warrant 'reasonable grounds' for a citizen's arrest and he had never left the store. If the suspect was attempting to steal the trainers then he would no doubt have been aware of their interest in his shopping habits for the rest of his trip to Pleasure Southquay. Hence the officers had prevented theft and avoided a tricky legal situation through the pursuit of 'commonsense'.

Some of the officers were also keen to tell me of arrests they had undertaken at other assignments that involved force. These illustrated, not only how force was often required and used by security officers, but also their bravery in doing so.

CSO 6

It was a Romanian claiming asylum over here living in *city y* in a bedsit. He stole a leather jacket and basically gave us the run around for an hour. He couldn't get out so he decided to give us the jacket back and then kick out. He was a short squat chap. I basically had to bring in my training and restrain him. It was pretty scary. He was muscular and panicking.

CSO 11

We had a bloke called Jerry who was basically HIV pos. He was in *shop z* in the *shopping centre b* I was in *shop k*. If you have ever been to the *shopping centre b* it is right opposite. I actually hid behind a dummy and watched him put a load of teeshirts up his jumper and then proceed to walk out the front. I kept eye contact with him from the actual taking to the arresting. As I say with Jerry pretty disgusting bloke who would spit blood at you. HIV positive and we all knew it and we could act on it. Being naive at the time about HIV you thought a mouth full of spit could do the honours on you so your first reaction was to stop him spitting. You take him down to the ground and in Shopping Centre B we use to carry handcuffs, so he was cuffed, picked up and dragged him along to a backroom out of site out of mind to await the police wagon. In the end he walked with a limp because he had a needle snap off in his ....basically in his legs and his arms had gone had collapsed his veins from drug abuse. So it snapped and went septic.

Grey policing

Research by Hoogenboom (1991) in the Netherlands has demonstrated how rank and file agents from different policing agencies often co-operate by using each others' powers and sharing intelligence in what he calls 'grey policing'. There was evidence at Pleasure Southquay of a strong partnership between the security staff and the police. This was most prominent in dealing with disorder in the NTE, but there was also evidence in arresting shoplifters. As the following extract from an interview with a female security officer illustrates, the police were even prepared to ask a security officer to undertake a search for them because of sexual balance issues.

CSO 22

We have had a report from *shop y* and a number of stores that there are two suspicious females around. One in an orange jacket one in a denim. And they have large bags on them and the stores suspect they have stolen from them but not quite sure. One of our guys goes into *shop y* puts on a plain clothes jacket and can see them actually concealing goods. There is a WPC in uniform in the complex and I am in touch with her with my radio and she then joins me outside *shop y* where the two women females exit the store. We stop them and they are obviously druggies, jumpy jittery and I don't know if they are going to run or not. We take them back into the store into a store-room in the back and they both have bags full of gear. She arrests them and we left by the back exit through the service corridor where the WPC takes hold of the one in the orange jacket and asks me to take hold of the other and starts walking them through the service corridor. The one in the orange jacket does not want to go at all and starts self harming herself, banging her head against the wall, punching herself, pulling her hair out and we just have to stop her doing that. Fortunately we have cameras. She was a definite self harmer she had bruises on her face which she attributed to her boyfriend, but you don't know do you? The other girl that I was gonna hold just stood there and shook, she was frightened to death and she had never seen her do it. The police officer called for the police van, they took her handcuffed her – really so she couldn't harm her self – and put her in the police vehicle. **At the request of a police officer as there was not a female police officer present they have asked me to go through her pockets for sharps, not stolen goods, just anything they could harm themselves on.**

The role of security officers undertaking apprehensions in relation to shoplifting was also seen as invaluable to the police. The police sergeant responsible for Pleasure Southquay argued,

> The security staff have the right to arrest someone for an arrestable offence. We don't have a problem with that. We have no problem with *shopping centre b* security staff carrying handcuffs. They clearly have a right to do this. By definition security has a role to detain shoplifters. The police (or representative of us) train the security within strict guidelines. The use is to keep people safely secured to prevent injury and prevent escape. In practical terms dealing with a disturbance is more a matter for them rather than us. If there is a group on site misbehaving the responsibility for ejecting them is theirs not ours.

Thus there was evidence of a strong partnership between security and police in dealing with shop-theft at Pleasure Southquay. This partnership was even stronger when the policing of the NTE was assessed and the need to use force to resolve issues.

The right to use of force

In addition to the number of times they have ever arrested a person the security officers were also asked how many times they have had to use force. Again these statistics illustrated a different orientation amongst officers towards using force, although many more were willing to use force than arrest someone. The statistics in table 6.2 below illustrate that at Armed Industries it was relatively rare for security officers to have to use force with 95 per cent never using it and 5 per cent (one officer) rarely. At Pleasure Southquay around half the officers were regularly using force, either once or twice a week or once or twice a month, which corresponded with the smaller group regularly apprehending suspects. When the 'frontline' officers were considered over three quarters of these had used force in the past year and nearly two thirds were using it at least once or twice a month. Given the nature of Pleasure Southquay with bars and nightclubs where disorder is common on Friday and Saturday nights this was not surprising.

Table 6.2   Number of times security officers have used force (%)

	Once or twice a week	Once or twice a month	Once or twice a year	Rarely	Never
Pleasure Southquay All	17	35	10	7	31
Pleasure Southquay 'Frontline'	23	46	9	5	18
Pleasure Southquay 'Backroom'	0	0	14	14	71
Armed Industries	0	0	0	5	95
All	10	20	6	6	57
N = 49					

The interviews with the security officers revealed a range of scenarios where force had been used. The vast majority related to the NTE dealing with drunken males after the pubs and nightclubs shut. These were invariably situations where it was not possible to use strategies to secure consent because an incident was already occurring. In using force, however, generally the officers used 'commonsense' rather than legal justifications in using it. The incidents described and observed ranged from the breaking up of simple fights between two males to dealing with a virtual riot. They also differed in terms of whether the security officers were working alone or with the police, providing further evidence of 'grey policing'. Some of the examples given in the interviews will now be examined to illustrate the scale of incidents.

Dealing with acts of disorder alone

Many of the security officers discussed scenarios where they had had to deal with simple acts of disorder frequently with no police support. These were usually related to the breaking up of fights or stopping some other form of misbehaviour that required the use of force. CSO 4 described how a fight situation and damage to property had required him to use an appropriate level of force to deal with the situation.

CSO 4

We had a fight situation and we were involved in preventing damage to property. The only way you can do that is by restraining culprits. We can only use force that is appropriate in relation to other people. It is a case of moving a person out of the way or trying to confine them in a space. That is the reasonable force used. A simple arm-lock the more they struggle the more it hurts.

Sometimes incidents required a great deal more bravery by the security officer. CSO11 described how a fight broke out next to a pub that involved quite a serious assault. It illustrated the significant amount of force the security officer had to use to stop the incident, but also how the force used may have bordered on excessive. Grabbing an individual by the throat poses particular dangers that could lead to the person being choked to death in the heat of the incident. Clearly this was a dangerous incident and is the type of incident that illustrated the need for the officers to be appropriately trained in dealing with these types of situation.

CSO 11

A few months back a fight kicked off outside *pub c*, it was a big old brawl. Basically a couple of nutters from *city y*, a couple of boys, who were shall we say fighters. I had one of them pushed him away but he started to go for it again. I started to talk to him – believe it or not about the football – because I think England had dipped Germany and that calmed it down. But in the melee one of my blokes got nutted in the lip. Burst his lip and basically I thought his nose was broke. Blood pouring out. We chased him down to the gate and I had my hands on him and I literally screwed his shirt up. About three or four of his mates tried to help him and his little stocky cousin came running in from the side and tried to be the 'he man'. You have to do what is necessary. You don't know what he has got, Friday Saturday night all sorts of bottles that anyone could pick up. And all I could see was him coming in at a rapid rate of knots from my right so my hands immediately let go and his cousin was flying through the air at me, so I batted him away and let him get on with it. He was still going for it so you take him by the throat and give him a little squeeze, God knows what they could pull on you. It's a battle of wills if some guy has got a bottle in his pocket and he is willing to use it if you just use a little bit of force on them and they might just not pull it. We have had to use force down here loads of times because people get stupid we are not talking about teenagers as such , we are talking about middle aged or God knows what else and they will fight. Nice place, wrong place definitely wrong location. Paradise one side of the railway, Beirut the other, Don't mix, told them that from the beginning but they don't listen.

The extracts from the interviews of CSO 13, 16 and 22 also illustrated how they often had to deal with aggressive women. This poses the greater challenge of men not only having to use force to deal with aggressive behaviour, but also against the opposite sex. There was a female officer on each shift, but they could not be guaranteed to be at the place where incident breaks out immediately.

CSO 13

A girl had hit one of the doorwomen and she tried to bottle me and another CSO so we had to restrain her. She was kicking like a donkey. A couple of male CSOs came over and restrained her and the police came and she was arrested.

CSO 16

If you have a fight when there is a female involved – we had one a couple of weeks ago – where a gentleman wouldn't stop abusing her and punching her in the face. Took his arm away and told him to stop.

CSO 22

On my first Sunday night working here at the *bowling club* we suddenly have a fight between three females and two of them were partners and the third was most offended by the comments they were making at her in front of children. All of a sudden all three of them were in an almighty great fight in central square. There was hair coming out there were fists flying and we had to restrain them. They were quite vicious and I would much rather arrest a man than a woman any day. Women don't have a stop button. Men will very rarely hit a woman. These three went on and on and one managed to get away, there were handfuls of hair and all we were trying to do was to stop them harming one another. So we had to physically restrain them. That was our first one. They didn't want to harm us, just each other. There was history to it that we weren't to know.

CSO 23

I have seen heated arguments between men and women and me and it has got very personal and we have had to intervene and try and separate them. We usually have to talk to them and try and calm them down. They have got personal back to us and got very out of order. They have sometimes threatened – 9 times out of 10 – well I'm gonna do so and so to you and so forth. If they persist on doing it and refuse to leave we have had to like ask them to leave or the police will be called. If they have kicked off or will not stop fighting each other or they start on us we have basically had to arms behind the back put them against the wall one on one arm the other on the other and had to detain them. I've never had to kick, punch of thump anyone – never done that. Even down here 9 times out of 10 they are very shocked – even when I have been hit – they're expecting you to turn around and hit back. When you detain them and don't hit them they are completely dumbfounded. Its like the people who do it aren't ready for that. I could go into numerous types of events like this down here but you would probably run out of tape.

The extract from the interview by CSO 23 also reveals how restrained the security officers can be and how shocked those they are dealing with can also be. However, during my observation one night a security officer confided to me that there had been an incident the previous Friday where one of the people who had been restrained had their nose broken and there was a feeling amongst some of the officers this CSO had used excessive force. No complaint was made against the officer, however, and therefore no action was taken. Indeed in relation to door supervisors, the NTE and the use of excessive force Lister et al (2000) found there was a reluctance for people assaulted to report such incidents to the police.

Some of the incidents security officers had to deal with alone involved more than two or three men or women fighting. The extract from the interview with CSO 5 illustrates how the security officers got involved with a brawl with 25 plus men in order to remove them from site with no initial police presence.

CSO 5

> There was a big fight outside *club j* on Friday night. There were about 25–30 blokes who decided to kick off after a few too many drinks. The bouncers were doing their job, but after they had dealt with them it was down to us to get them off site. They were still fighting. But we have not been trained to do anything like that so it was quite difficult. We were waiting for the police to turn up, but you try your best while your waiting. When a fight kicks off they don't care who you are. They want to take on whoever is in front of them. They are not fussy.

Dealing with disorder with the police: more 'grey policing'

The police did generally provide a presence for a period on Friday and Saturday nights, so there were often occasions where the security staff and police would work together. The following extracts illustrate how security officers work with police in dealing with incidents. CSO 1 describes an incident where under police supervision he had had to use full force to detain a man involved in a fight with a bottle.

CSO 1

> I have to go to court this Friday due to a bloke putting a bottle over another's head. I wont mention names. I stood back and observed the fight, there was, one came up, he was a boxer – but I have had all sorts of martial arts training – I knew exactly what he was going to do. Under police supervision – I ran across put him to the ground, put him in all the proper locks and then the police came over, handcuffed him and put him in the back of the police wagon. This was gonna get violent, so full force was required.

Some of the incidents security officers have found themselves embroiled in have been much larger. One incident described to me by several security officers bordered on a riot and involved a local group of football hooligans orchestrating a major brawl that lasted for an hour and twenty minutes. Initially the security officers dealt with it alone, but when the police arrived they found themselves supporting the police in trying to restore order. The incident also revealed how determined the management of Pleasure Southquay were to ensure this incident was not described as a riot by security staff.

CSO 22

> The second was a riot. Although I am not allowed to call it a riot only a violent disorder. It was the day of a football match, in May, there are a gang of hooligans called the 657 crew. This crew are about two decades old, they were originally called this because they use to catch the 6.57 train to football matches. Some are now middle aged. A fight started – I was stood outside the *bar h* – and we don't get a lot of trouble from *bar h*. You could sense a degree of animosity. I was stood outside with my team leader and all of sudden I saw this

stool fly through the air and hit somebody over the head. It was crowded and all I could see was the crowd disperse and a man covered in blood. Called on the radio for the police and a ambulance. This crowd was outside *bar h* and there were only 5 or 6 of us on duty at the time and there are about 30 men wanting to fight. We managed to keep them calm. One of the *bar h* staff who was off duty pushed one of our guys into the middle of this and said 'do your fucking job and sort it out'. Well no one person can sort out 30 drunks wanting to fight. We were pretty annoyed that this person had done this, but they didn't want to fight us – they really didn't. The police arrived and as they arrived we managed to stop the guy who had been hurt – he didn't want attending to. The ambulance wouldn't come up here. The crowd started moving and the 657 crew are quite organised it is almost like a script. Something to watch. Never experienced anything like this. A fight started at the end of the tunnel and the police were there and they would stop that, but there was one guy who would be a goader and would say, 'you picked on him, you picked on him....' And then that person would get arrested not the instigator. He was a very clever man, clever to watch, the police are well aware of who he is. He does it a lot and this incident went on for an hour and twenty minutes with sporadic fights in this end of the tunnel, in the middle of the tunnel and the far end of the tunnel. We were just totally shocked. There were police units from all over *city y* in the end and they ran out of units to send. There was one dog van, the ambulance was trying to tend to the injured man and then he spotted the man who originally hit him and went after him. It was awful. I think 11 people were arrested that night. It was horrendous it went on for a solid hour and twenty minutes. The longest fight that actually went on, went on for 11 minutes. This is a long time to be solidly struggling and fighting. It was awful. We referred to it as a riot. Police have different terms for a riot, violent disorder, affray and all that.

We are not police officers we were in it and to us it was a riot. One of the management team, one the original I spoke about earlier, 'wiped the floor' with me for referring to it as a riot. He stamped his feet standing there shouting at me. I almost walked out at that point. He hadn't been there we had and we were the ones who actually had to police it.

In another incident described by CSO 23 he described how he and his colleagues actually supported the police in dealing with an incident when they were overwhelmed.

CSO 23

When I was called to the *bowling club* once there were two youths, I think one called over two PCs who were in central square and waved them across to sort out two blokes who were arguing who had been ejected from the *bowling club*. They were involved in a heated argument and while the one PC was trying to talk to this bloke and calm him down the other PC was trying to prevent his mates coming out of the *bowling club*. I realised it was getting out of hand. There were a couple of my partners down the stairs so I go and try and help this PC out. When this PC is on the floor when somehow this bloke he is trying to detain is on the floor with him. I have jumped into help him detain this bloke. The other copper is by himself trying to keep the other six lads from trying to do what they are gonna do. So I called up for more backup, more police have come up, and even an off duty police officer who was here at the time and the other CSOs. Its just one big mass of bodies and arms flying. I had lots of abuse. And there was no respect for myself or the police. And while I'm down there bending over at the time over one bloke with the PC at the side someone thought it would be great to smack me in the side of the head with his fist and I was caught on the side of the ear and head and I turned round and all I could see was a mass of bodies and heads and the noise and you just go back to what you were doing. You can't leave this bloke because your head hurts. In the end it sorted itself out. It took four of us to get this bloke down and handcuffed and the rest were made to disperse. Never did find out who assaulted me, it was just impossible.

Indeed when the police sergeant responsible for this area was interviewed he was very positive about the role of private security staff dealing with these kind of incidents. He stated,

The CSOs should also be able to get involved with incidents at night, indeed most of them want to get involved, but are constrained by management. Their training course originally had control and restraint in it but *L* was told to take it out! There has also been a cut back in numbers from the original plans. There is a constant tension between profit and security. When they cut back the number of officers late at night I told them they didn't have enough officers for their emergency action plan. This led to a change in policy. I have also told them they need to have enough staff observing clubbers leaving who are properly trained.

The extent and nature of the use of force at Pleasure Southquay is even more interesting when the policy on this issue at Pleasure Southquay was considered. The Operations Manager told me,

The role of the CSO in an incident at night is to observe and report. It is not to get involved in a fight. They are not trained for that kind of role. I do appreciate, however, that when an incident occurs it is difficult not to get involved.

Despite this view and policy the officers were clearly willing and able to put themselves in dangerous situations and use force where necessary to restore order. This culture is probably best illustrated by the comments of the Security Supervisor,

It is the difference between two people on the shop-floor. PE has been there CD hasn't. He wanted a soft approach and was more concerned with the safety of the shoppers not involved in incidents, rather than solving the problem. I have been on the shop-floor the buzz is arresting someone or sorting a problem out. I think all the CSOs want this and if they don't they won't enjoy their job. CD had the idea that you call the police if there is a problem and let them deal with it. But you need to stop a fight escalating as once it starts it could get out of hand. If an incident starts we need to take it out of the public view as soon as possible. We want the public to leave site not having witnessed an incident.

Thus many officers at Pleasure Southquay were quite prepared to put themselves in situations of danger, but did this lead to them wanting special powers and privileges to carry non-lethal weapons? And were there significant differences with the views of Armed Industries officers? These issues will now be explored vis-à-vis officers attitudes towards being given special powers and the right to carry non-lethal weapons.

Security officers' attitudes on special legal tools and non-lethal weapons

The security officers at the two case study sites were also asked about their views on being given special legal powers and the right to carry non-lethal weapons during the course of their duties. The latter has proved a peripheral debate in the private security industry in the UK with most mainstream industry opinion opposed to such privileges being granted to private security officers. As was discussed in Chapter 1 it was quite common for some security officers to carry non lethal weapons and even firearms in the post-war period (Draper 1978; and South 1997). There are also a growing number of security officers who are carrying defensive tools, such as handcuffs, with the support of the police (Ralph 2004).

In recent years, however, there have been some vocal calls for private security officers to be armed with non-lethal weapons, most notably from Sir Stanley Kalms (Chairman of Dixons) and Gene Plews (Managing Director of Guardian Security) (Plews 2001). These calls, however, have been opposed by the most important interest groups and companies in the private security industry (Button 2004).

The grant of special powers to private security officers has solicited a different response. As was illustrated earlier in Chapters 1 and 3 there have been numerous statutes that have given special powers to private security staff undertaking specialised functions. Most notable is the Police Reform Act 2002, which enables a wide range of special powers to be given to accredited security staff operating in public space. Concerns have been raised with some of these initiatives, however, in that they may change the way such empowered personnel operate with those they police (Crawford and Lister 2004a). However, in terms of the security officers at the two case study sites, their views were relatively similar on the two issues with a clear majority opposing both additional legal powers and the right to carry non-lethal weapons. Nevertheless there were significant differences between those staff who were more frequently at risk of violence and who had to regularly use force, the 'frontline' security staff at Pleasure Southquay, vis-à-vis all other officers in the two research sites.

Table 6.3   Should security officers be granted additional special legal powers (%)

	Yes	No
All	33	67
Armed Industries	35	65
Pleasure Southquay	32	68
Pleasure Southquay 'Frontline'	43	57
Pleasure Southquay 'Backroom'	0	100
N = 49		

A clear majority of the security officers interviewed for this research did not see the need to be given special legal powers, with over two thirds against. It was also interesting that the split was almost identical at both research sites with around two thirds against. However, when the security officers at Pleasure Southquay were split between those who were 'frontline' and 'backroom' this balance changed significantly. 'Frontline' officers were divided 43 to 57 in favour of special powers, whereas 'backroom' were 100 per cent against. The security officers were also asked to explain the rationale for their decision and if they favoured special powers to outline what kind of powers they would like. Some of these answers will now be explored.

The security officers that indicated they would like greater legal powers largely outlined powers that reflected their working environment. The Pleasure Southquay officers generally wanted greater powers to arrest, detain and use force, where as the Armed Industry officers generally sought greater powers of search, although there were some that sought additional powers that did not reflect what they largely did. For instance one security officer at Pleasure Southquay wanted powers to stop and search and another at Armed Industries wanted greater powers to use force. Another officer at Armed Industries felt they should be given the same powers as a police officer! Some of the answers from Pleasure Southquay officers illustrate the answers seeking greater powers of arrest and detention.

CSO 10

We should be given powers to detain a person for lesser crimes.

CSO 11

You could get a 19 year old come in here and become a little Hitler. Yes, sometimes a greater power of arrest than just citizens would be useful. Greater ability to search would also be useful.

CSO 13

Power to arrest and use handcuffs.

CSO 14

More powers of arrest and ability to use force. Especially in this job.

The other power Pleasure Southquay officers sought related to the ability to remove people from private property and the right to use force. The answers on this also revealed that some of the officers were not entirely clear in their understanding of their rights on this issue, as they already have the right to use reasonable force to remove trespassers.

CSO 12

You should be allowed to use force to remove someone from private property.

CSO 23

With trespass if a person fails to leave it could be useful if we had more powers in those situations. There could be a lot more occasions where we could act.

At Armed Industries the answers divided between those who sought greater powers of arrest and detention and those who sought greater rights to undertake search. Given the lack of arrests/detentions being undertaken by the security officers at Armed Industries it did seem unusual that some sought this right. Given the large number of searches they undertook, however, it is not surprising that some sought greater powers of search.

SO 1

I would say that security officers should have greater powers of arrest. They should be upped so that a security officer has greater powers on the job to arrest.

SO 11

Some special powers to use force could be dodgy, but greater powers to arrest and detain would be useful because if they struggle on a citizens arrest they are not allowed to hold on.

SO 12

In a place like this you should have better powers of search. Although maybe if I knew the policy here I would have different views as I've never been told.

SO 13

Better powers of search.

SO 15

In todays society I would say yes. A guy could come on with a brief case that has a bomb. We should have the power to search anyone who comes on to this site in any circumstances.

The rationale of the security officers also revealed some interesting insights on the nature and role of security officers. Some of those who were opposed to additional legal powers were concerned about the implications such a rise in powers would have on their role. There was a general theme that private security officers were not police officers and shouldn't be given rights that elevated their status.

CSO 16

We are not trained enough to have special powers. We are there for prevention and deterrence not to be police officers.

CSO 26

Getting into dodgy areas. You're not trained as police officers.

SO 8

We're not police officers we're security officers. There are a lot of differences.

SO 16

It would put you in conflict with the police and they are the experts so leave it to them.

SO 20

It's better in the hands of the police than security. It takes special training to use powers. The legal system is complex and you don't want to get tangled up in that.

Another theme that emerged was the perceived capabilities of security officers and the potential dangers should they be given special powers. Some officers felt that some security officers would not be capable of using them, where as others felt they might abuse them.

CSO 22

Not at all they would be not capable of using them. Some security officers are right 'numbskulls'. Some also think they are policemen.

CSO 24

No because you would get certain security officers who would abuse it, particularly those who want to be police officers.

SO 10

It would be Armageddon! Unless properly trained and pay and professionalism improved in the industry.

Similar debates emerged when the issue of security officers being allowed to carry non-lethal weapons such as truncheons, CS gas and pepper sprays. Before some of these answers are explored let us first consider the quantitative data relating to this question.

On the issue of the right to carry non-lethal weapons, however, there were significant differences between some of the security officers. In terms of *all* security officers there was a split of just under a third in favour, against just over two thirds against. However, when the individual responses from the case study sites were examined at Armed Industries 90 per cent were against the right to carry non-lethal weapons compared to 57 per cent at Pleasure Southquay. When the distinction between 'frontline' and 'backroom' staff was also considered this revealed just over half 'frontline' staff in favour of the right to carry non-lethal weapons, compared to an overwhelming majority of 'backroom' against such a right. As was revealed earlier in the chapter these 'frontline' officers make greater use of their rights to detain and use force compared to other groups. It will also be shown in chapter 8 they experience higher levels of verbal abuse and assault. Therefore it is not surprising they seek such weapons for greater protection. Again the security officers were asked to elaborate upon their answers.

Table 6.4   Should private security officers be allowed to carry non-lethal weapons such as truncheons, cs gas, pepper sprays etc to to defend themselves (%)

	Yes	No
All	29	69
Armed Industries	10	90
Pleasure Southquay	43	57
Pleasure Southquay 'Frontline'	52	48
Pleasure Southquay 'Backroom'	14	86
N = 49		

Because of the dangers they faced many of the security officers at Pleasure Southquay were very attracted to non-lethal weapons to protect themselves. There was a preference for sprays and cs gas over truncheons, although there was also a concern it might be abused by some officers.

CSO 4

If my life in danger or a colleagues. Would use it to stop them. Pepper spray would be the ideal solution.

CSO 11

In situations where you are vulnerable it could be useful. Some junkies will use anything. But you might get someone who once they put on a uniform will spray someone for a laugh.

CSO 15

In a place like this with nightclubs, and drunken groups of lads it would be useful sometimes for self-defence.

CSO 23

For self-protection truncheons would be useful. Full training would be needed to be given otherwise it could be dangerous.

At Armed Industries one security officer was concerned at the risk at night should he be confronted by a burglar, while another felt it wouldn't be appropriate at Armed Industries, but could see the rationale at riskier sites.

SO 11

We're out on our own and if you come up against a burglar all we can do is phone the police, so having weapons would be useful. But we are not police officers.

SO 19

It depends upon the site where you're operating. Where there is a high risk to their life they should be allowed to carry these weapons.

Some of the security officers who answered yes ruled out truncheons as a potential weapon.

CSO 9

Pepper spray to calm the situation would be useful. Truncheons would cause more problems.

CSO 28

If they have proper training, although not truncheons.

As with the question relating to greater legal powers there was a divide amongst those opposed between those who felt it would change their role, that they were not police officers. One officer also expressed the view it would change his role and he didn't get paid enough to be put in such potential situations of danger.

CSO 7

Sometimes it would come in handy. But if we carry these other people are more likely to carry weapons. We are not the police.

SO 14

I wouldn't want this, I wouldn't want to spray someone with gas or hit them with a truncheon. That's a job for the police not a security officer's.

SO 20

They could be used against you. An SO is here to protect property. You don't get paid enough to get killed.

A large number of security officers were concerned at the suitability of many of their colleagues to use such tools. Linked to this was a fear that they then might be used against them.

CSO 22

Some would use them when they shouldn't do. If in life threatening situation you should be able to use them, but personally I would not want to carry a weapon.

CSO 26

They could be misused or actually used against us.

CSO 27

As soon as you give security officers weapons there is much room for abuse.

CSO 29

It would go to some of their heads and they would use them when it was not necessary.

SO 4

Force begets force. If they think you have a stick they will get a bigger stick.

SO 7

You will get the cowboys who will go overboard no matter where you are. You get some security officers who as soon as they put on a uniform think they are above the law.

A common argument against arming all police officers has been it would lead to an escalation in violence leading to criminals becoming routinely armed. This view was also expressed by a security officer, who argued,

CSO 10

Once you give security staff these you might as well give them a 9 mm. It would only encourage everyone to take up a weapon.

Another security officer felt that one should be capable of dealing with potentially violent situations without using non-lethal weapons,

CSO 19

If you come into the security industry and can't handle yourself, you are in the wrong occupation. If you can't handle violence you shouldn't be in the job.

It also became clear during the research that some security officers were already carrying non-lethal weapons unofficially anyway. Indeed one security officer in answering this question stated,

CSO 6

I have seen too many cowboys on the job. I have seen some security officers come to work with everything bar a sawn off shotgun!

Perhaps more revealing, however, was one security officer when asked what two things could be done to improve his job began talking about counselling for those who had experienced violence, but in doing so also revealed he carried a torch which could be used as a weapon and had been encouraged to do so by a senior police officer.

CSO 23

…I carry a torch just in case the 'lights go out'. I was told to do this by a Chief Inspector and I would use it if my life was in danger. It cost me £30 for the 6 cell torch. I've had to deal with shoplifters with needles and there is nothing in the SITO training that tells you how to deal with that. The police are paid twice as much as us and have twice as much training. Some of the shifts don't help as much as they could.

Have you ever used the torch?

CSO 23

It's come out, but never been used.

Another officer also told me most of the 'frontline' security staff carried a torch. Given such torches could be as lethal as a truncheon by sheer fear and necessity many of the staff were becoming *de facto* armed with non-lethal weapons anyway.

Conclusion

This chapter has explored the use of 'universal' legal tools used by security officers and their attitudes towards being given special legal powers and rights to carry non-lethal weapons. The chapter began by exploring arrest illustrating the differences amongst the two research sites and between types of security staff in the extent to which they have undertaken arrests. The chapter also illustrated how strategies to secure consent predominate when officers attempt to undertake arrests. When this fails security officers may resort to force and in doing so this is often based upon 'commonsense' rather than a complex understanding of their legal rights to pursue such action. There is also evidence of 'grey' policing in the arrests undertaken with security and police co-operating in such situations. The use of force is much more commonly used, particularly those from Pleasure Southquay. This relates largely to the challenges of dealing with revellers in the NTE. Again the officers' approach to using force is based largely upon commonsense rather than legal justification. Finally this chapter examined attitudes of officers towards special legal tools and non-lethal weapons. There was a majority against such measures. However this declined significantly when the officers who were most active in using the tools of arrest and force and were most at risk of abuse and violence were considered.

Chapter 7

Select Legal Tools: Compliance, Consent and Commonsense

Introduction

In the previous chapter 'universal' legal tools were examined and it was shown that they were largely used by a minority of officers at Pleasure Southquay. In using those legal tools it was also demonstrated that consent was usually gained, although force was sometimes required. In using those tools it was also established that commonsense approaches were pursued rather than justifications relating to the law. With the 'select' legal tools the situation was different. First of all there were a different range of legal tools open to the security officers at the two research sites and even those that were used by both, such as access control, were used very differently. Second, Armed Industry officers were much more active in their use of these tools. Third the underlying approach to achieve the outcomes desired were based upon a number of strategies to secure compliance – of which officers were only a part –and where officers did intervene their approach was based upon consent. Force was a peripheral issue within the context of the use of these tools because it was generally not lawful to use. Like 'universal' tools, however, the primary basis for use was through commonsense rather than legal or organisational rule justification. This chapter will begin by examining how security officers use their legal tools relating to access control, it will then move on to explore search before examining other tools they derive, such as those relating to the enforcement of traffic regulations. The chapter will conclude by revisiting Lukes's (1974) three dimensional model of power by applying the strategies of the two case study sites observed during this research to this model.

Access control

On private space one of the most important functions private security staff undertake is access control. Chapter 3 illustrated the significant rights private security can draw upon in deciding who may or may not gain access to the site. The two research sites presented the two extremes in access policies. At Pleasure Southquay as a retail and leisure facility the site was open access with the aim of encouraging as many people as possible to enter. At Armed Industries, by contrast, it was a List X manufacturer with a selected number of access points protected by a mix of barriers and security staff with a perimeter fence around the site limiting access. Despite these two different environments the rights of security staff to determine access were very similar. Not surprising given the very different nature of two sites the access control policies were different. These will now be considered separately.

Access control at Pleasure Southquay

In Chapter 4 it was shown that there were a variety of controlling strategies at work to encourage the appropriate persons to come to Pleasure Southquay, which at the same time discouraged other groups. These were based upon the design, image and rules of Pleasure Southquay. These were the primary strategies for maximising the control of access. The security staff were the last resort in achieving this outcome. If the primary measures failed security officers through presence, verbal interaction, force or the police would be used. When security officers did intervene to achieve an outcome – and not just relating to access control – it was also important that they were successful to re-enforce their reputation to further enhance the primary measures. Some of these issues will now be explored in greater depth.

When the research was taking place access to the Pleasure Southquay site could only be achieved through two pedestrian entrances, one vehicle entrance, or by boat through the harbour. During the day on the main pedestrian entrance (known to the CSOs as the 'punchthrough' because of the number of fights that occurred there) one CSO was placed permanently there. This was aimed at preventing undesirables and those 'informally' banned as well as providing a reassurance to the public of a security presence. This was also the entrance most likely to be used by those coming from the nearby estate and those who would have travelled by public transport – the riskiest groups for Pleasure Southquay. There was, however, another pedestrian entrance unguarded and if someone entered in a vehicle they could also bypass them. Although the other pedestrian entrance was most likely to be used by those coming from a direction of one of the most exclusive estates in the city and those who would have come by vehicles would clearly be from beyond the nearby area. There were also extensive CCTV cameras with a CSO constantly based in the control room to monitor them.

One of the most significant 'select' legal tools the security officers could draw upon is that of excluding a person. In England and Wales, as discussed earlier, there exists a reasonable right of excluding and removing a person from 'quasi-public space' and probably an arbitrary right. Security officers in many other shopping/ leisure type facilities regularly make use of this tool (see Adu-Boakye 2002; McCahill 2002; and Wakefield 2003). At Pleasure Southquay, however, this tool was not used in a systematic or effective way. First of all there was no written procedures relating to access control and removal of undesirable persons or statistics kept on such cases. For the most serious cases of unacceptable behaviour Pleasure Southquay did issue a letter. Originally only the security supervisor could do this, but this was not working, so the team leaders of shifts were then allowed to. The letter stated,

Dear Sir/Madam,

As a result of your conduct on ____ at Pleasure Southquay in ____, we write to inform you that your right as a member of the public to enter the Centre premises forthwith is now withdrawn, and that you are not permitted to enter the Centre in the future under any pretext whatsoever.

Should you disregard this notice you will be a trespasser, and we will not hesitate to apply to the Court for an injunction to restrain you from entering the premises.

Thereafter should you be in breach of the injunction we will make application to the court for an order committing you to prison.

You may wish to take legal advice.

Yours faithfully

On behalf of Pleasure Southquay Ltd

Security Manager

However, as the security supervisor illustrated to me when interviewed even this scheme did not really work or have the support of senior management,

> In one case a known shoplifter and drug addict was on site causing problems. She spat at me and threatened me with used syringes. So I banned her from site. She got her solicitor to write to me and in it claimed it breached the Human Rights Act. It then went up to the Director and he wrote and said she could come back on site if she behaved. He didn't want any litigation or any publicity about this to get out. It could cost up to £2,000 per case to go to court. I haven't told the CSOs about this as it would be bad for morale.

Most exclusions and removals happened on an informal basis, without recourse to any rules based upon commonsense. Usually youths or adults (usually under the influence of alcohol) at night would be approached by the CSOs and asked to leave. In one example witnessed, two youths of about 12–13 years old were being verbally abusive to the counter assistant on the 'ice' ring. It had started raining and they wanted their money back. They were swearing at the assistant shouting, 'Give us our fucking money back!' The CSO called to the incident radioed control and was told to give them their money back and take their names and addresses and escort them off site. The two youths gave their names and addresses, although no identification was sought to verify who they were. In the control room they then used the CCTV system to get pictures of them for future reference. They were escorted off site where they continued to give the CSOs verbal abuse all the way to the boundary. They did not return that shift. Most removals from site related to some form of misbehaviour and happened such as this. All that was required was officer presence and a verbal command and most would comply. The CSOs would tell them they were banned for the rest of the day, week, a month or some other period. The approach was based upon informality and commonsense rather than formality and legal rules.

The presence of a security officer on the main entrance combined with an extensive surveillance system that enabled security officers to be deployed to remove a person also created a situation where persistent offenders knew if they were removed they were unlikely to get back on site. There were a number of incidents witnessed in the control room where the controller while undertaking observation would spot a person or group and deploy security officers to investigate and remove if necessary. On many occasions the mere presence of security officers moving towards them would result in them turning around. Inherent in the success of such a strategy was the need to secure a reputation amongst security staff for successfully dealing with such situations. This would then feed into the primary measures.

Part of the reason for the lack of exclusion and removal was the dominance of the marketing department in organisational decision-making vis-à-vis security. Inherent in their strategies was a belief that the primary measures would secure the desired outcome. Both Reeve (1998) and McCahill (2002) have argued malls are 'instrumental' space where measures (including security) are used to maximise consumption. At Pleasure Southquay there was an overwhelming aim of maximising 'footfall'. As such marketing were very keen to avoid any notion of exclusion taking place or rules and regulations that might inhibit a visitor's 'pleasure' experience.

Access control at Armed Industries

Access control at Armed Industries was a very important part of the overall security strategy. The two parts to the site were surrounded by a perimeter fence with some sections alarmed to enable the control room operator to move CCTV cameras to observe that area if activated. There were seven main gates where pedestrian and/or vehicle access could be gained. There were also two further gates where automated access could be achieved with an appropriate swipe card (at the time of the research plans were being considered to further automate certain gates). Usual access, however, was through one of the seven gates staffed by security officers. For a pedestrian to secure access a valid Armed Industries photo identity swipe card had to be produced and shown to security staff. These were only issued to employees and contractors and because of the List X status of the site they needed to be vetted by the MoD before a pass could be issued. If a pass was forgotten staff were required to sign in and a supervisor or manager was required to come and sign to verify who they were. These requirements were clearly set out in the Armed Industries employee handbook.

Visitors to the site were required to sign in at the reception, carry and wear a visitor's pass and a member of staff was required to come and escort them on site at all times. For vehicles a valid pass was also required to enter the site. Visitors who wished to bring their car on site would also require a valid vehicle pass. Most of the gates had barriers, which the security officers operated and raised when vehicles arrived or sought to leave depending upon the gate. There were also signs in place stating identity passes must always be shown. For all of the entrances it was possible for pedestrians to enter or leave the site without the barrier being raised. No matter how well known the pass-holder was, it was their duty to show their pass to security staff to secure entrance. Similarly it was a duty of security officer to view the pass of every person entering site, no matter how well they knew them. If the person did not show their pass it was their duty to ask to see the pass. If a person refused to show their pass the contract manager outlined to me the procedures,

> If they don't show their pass or wilfully don't show their pass they (the security officer) should report the incident to me. What you have here is difficult because we do have single man gates and you have so many things going on with employees coming in, coming in to get keys, which the officer has got to be there to give them the keys and so its too many jobs for one person to carry out so you would see a lot of people coming in and out.

There were therefore extensive primary measures based upon the design and layout of the site backed up by clear rules. Sitting in the boxes with security officers it was clear that the vast majority of staff automatically showed their passes without having to be asked. Some did so walking by without even looking at the security staff. It almost seemed like the vast majority were 'conditioned' to show their passes on entrance. Although the ability to scrutinise those passes was questionable as rarely was there enough time to effectively scrutinise a pass and compare the photograph to the person carrying the pass. On many occasions such was the distance of the pass from the security officer the photograph could not be seen effectively. The success of this type of access control strategy relied heavily on the primary measures deterring intruders and the security officer not recognising a person and calling them over to scrutinise their pass more closely. There was also a small minority of pass-holders who did not show their passes.

On gate three, which was one of the quietest and most boring posts I spent two hours with the security officer. During that period six people did not show their pass. Some of the staff just completely ignored the security officer walking past, others said hello but failed to show their pass. The security officer didn't do anything claiming he knew that they worked in the factory and held passes. The security officer told me, 'I don't get paid enough to chase after them!' The security officer in this gate was clearly exercising a degree of discretion in not mandating that they show their passes. Such discretion was also shown with vehicles entering the site where the passes of the drivers were rarely sought, the pass on the vehicle was enough. In another example of exercising discretion and being flexible to staff one security officer showed me the automated turn-style machine adjacent to his gate. He told me that some staff forget their passes and get colleagues to swipe them in. Technically they should sign in if they do, however, the security officer told me he usually lets them go through. However, he told me of SO 20 who doesn't and makes them sign in. Consequently all staff were reputed to hate him for this. Security officers who did stop a person failing to show a pass were often subjected to verbal abuse. Chapter 8 will illustrate the extensive verbal abuse some security officers received as a consequence of this duty.

Despite the inadequacy of some security staff intruders were very rare on site. Indeed it would be almost impossible to accidentally wander on site and to purposefully gain access would require a high degree of confidence and belief that the security staff were inadequate – and this would require 'inside knowledge'. The security manager could only recall one major breach, which occurred on a Saturday at a time when there were no barriers at the entrance. He claimed some 'gypsies' managed to talk their way past a security officer and gain access to the site. They were allegedly looking for scrap metal and were identified by another member of the security staff. The police were called and the security manager. No evidence of theft was found and they were removed from site. As a consequence of this the security officer was removed from site.

Search

A significant function that security officers undertake at many locations throughout the UK is that of search. Research into the pursuit of search by security officers is virtually non-existent. At the two sites used for this study search was a major function of officers at Armed Industries, but was rare at Pleasure Southquay. As the table below illustrates 90 per cent of security officers at Armed Industries were conducting them on a daily basis. This compared to one officer at Pleasure Southquay who claimed to search on monthly basis and five others who did so rarely. The nature of these searches at the two sites will now be considered in greater depth.

Table 7.1   Number of searches security officers have made (%)

	Once or twice a day	Once or twice a week	Once or twice a month	Once or twice a year	Rarely	Never
Pleasure Southquay All	0	0	3	0	17	79
Armed Industries*	90	0	0	0	5	5
All	37	0	2	0	12	49
N = 49						

*The question in the interview schedule for Armed Industries was adapted from 'While working as a security officer have you ever had to search a person?' to 'While working as a security officer have you ever had to conduct a search?' As usual officers were asked to relate their answers to the specific case study.

Search at Armed Industries

Armed Industries was a manufacturer of defence equipment and was also a List x company. This means that Armed Industries have to comply with certain regulations relating to security, requiring specific strategies to be in place and also means they are subject to regular inspections. One of the strategies required as part of these regulations and for the company security strategy was a policy of search of vehicles and hand luggage on entering and leaving site. At Armed Industries the policy was clearly set out in the Assignment Instructions. They state:

Procedures for Random Searches

Employees' Conditions of Employment state that if an employee brings a vehicle or a container onto Company premises he may, on entering and leaving, be required to display its contents to Security. If he wishes, this may be done in the presence of a third party of his choice who is readily available.

Similar rules apply to others who enter site.

These rules do not give the Security an automatic right and the individual's consent is required in every case. However a refusal can result in disciplinary action being taken against an employee and other forms of sanctions being used in respect of other persons such as contractors etc. All refusals to permit such search must, therefore, be reported in writing to the Security Manager without delay.

When carrying out random routine searches in accordance with these rules Security should ensure that they do so quietly and efficiently and avoid causing unnecessary delay and embarrassment. Care should be taken to avoid searching the same individual too regularly and it should always be made clear that the proposed search is of a routine nature.

A record must be entered on the appropriate Search Sheet of details of all searches carried out.

The individual should always be firstly asked if he has anything in his possession which requires a company pass. If he refuses to permit the required search it should be pointed out to him that it is a Condition of his Employment (or a Condition of his Contractors Vehicle Pass) that he should permit such a search. If he continues to refuse the search he should be told that a report will be made to his line manager and that disciplinary action could result.

In these circumstances the Controller should be called to the Gate immediately and the individual asked to wait for his arrival. If he refuses and there are no other grounds for reasonably suspecting that he is committing an arrestable offence as defined by the Police and Criminal Evidence Act 1984, he must be allowed to leave.

There were three categories of vehicles/persons hand luggage that were subject to search. These included employees, contractors and visitors. The basis of search for the first two was based in the contracts of employment and the contracts. For the latter it was based upon accepting this requirement as a condition of entrance. For instance the visitor's pass states, 'Your vehicle and/or briefcase may be searched on entering or leaving the site,' and on entering the premises visitors sign to accept these conditions. However, it was not clear if on exiting the site if a visitor refused to subject to a search what the appropriate sanction and cause of action would then be. The methods used by security officers to conduct searches were observed and these raised a number of issues.

Selection procedure The policy outlined above set out a strategy of random searches where the same people are not regularly searched. During one observation session with a female security officer I asked her on what 'random' basis she selected vehicles. She replied, 'I do a search when I feel like it. I try and pick the easy ones where you can have a quick look.' Another security officer told me while observing him about a German who he was constantly searching. The German never said anything, but he could tell from his body language he was getting increasingly aggravated. The fact that all vehicles are searched on this gate after 7pm was not made clear to the German for some time, which would have set his mind at rest that he was not being discriminated against. Indeed another security officer admitted to me when answering question 24 that she was selecting a person for search based upon their racial origin, stating,

SO 2

> ...I had a similar situation with a black man I kept stopping to search. It was only on the third day when he said to me why do you keep stopping me that I realised. I was shocked. I didn't realise what I was doing. I was searching him every day. **I was picking on him because he was black.** He was a very nice man though about it.

The nature of selection of a person (vehicle or their baggage) by the security staff showed evidence of not being random. There was no clear random selection procedure and there was even evidence of officers picking a target based upon an easier search. This procedure gave security officers a significant degree of discretion, which also opened up the possibility that searches maybe pursued in a discriminatory fashion. There were no statistics kept on searches based upon the race, sex etc of the person so it was not possible to investigate if there was any systematic evidence of discrimination. Further issues emerged in the conduct of searches.

Conduct of search Once a security officer has decided who they were going to search the next stage was the conduct of the search itself. I asked one security officer during an observation session what she was looking for, to which she replied, 'I m looking for computer equipment, lap-tops that kind of thing. That's what we're told to look for. If they have one they need to have paperwork to show its theirs or they can't take it home.' I then asked her, 'What about plans or parts of engines which could be useful to a competitor? Do you look for those?' She replied, 'Well I wouldn't know about that.' I then asked her, 'Would you stop them to investigate further?' She replied, 'No.' The quality of the searches by this security officer revealed a similar lack of commitment. While sat with the officer she kept telling me, 'it's a joke here, it really is a joke.'

For the first vehicle stopped she walked out to the driver and took down the registration number asked the driver for his identification number and name. She then asked him, 'Can I have a look in the boot.' The driver got out and opened it. We looked in and there was nothing. He then drove off. She recorded the time and details on the appropriate sheet. Two other cars were stopped and searched in a similar way. Then the security officer decided to stop a van. In this case she just looked across the shoulders of the driver into the back. She didn't open the back of the van or have a close look. A lorry was then stopped. In this case she didn't look in the back of the lorry instead she checked the passenger side and asked him to move a coat to check if he was hiding anything underneath. Nothing was found underneath. Another van was then stopped. Again the security officer looked over the driver's shoulder. The van was full of plants as it is a company that supplies all the plants to offices at Armed Industries. She then discussed with the driver how lovely the plants were and if he had any spare ones for her. He said, 'no'. She then asked if there was, '…any chance of a job?', to which he also replied, 'no'. The driver then left smiling. She then told me, 'Well he could be nicking all the plants for all I know, it's a joke really, really is.'

On this same gate another security officer was observed conducting searches and did so with a similar approach for a number of vehicles. Generally the observation revealed an attitude of going through the motions in undertaking the searches. Indeed on this particular gate where the searches were observed there was a requirement to undertake 40 searches per 12 hour shift. The boredom and the rarity of any deviant action engendered a very low commitment to conducting searches. Any person determined to steal Armed Industries property, unless it was sizeable, would have little concern in getting caught removing the property. The observation also revealed the searches being achieved largely by asking questions to which the people targeted generally agreed. During the interviews I asked most of the security officers a supplementary over whether a person had ever refused a search and if so what had occurred. None of the security officers could recall an incident where a person had refused a search, although some noted staff who had been difficult about it. For example,

SO 1

You get a situation where someone doesn't want to wait to be searched. You might get into an argument with them then. You have to use your loaf and get the powers involved if they refuse. This has happened but very seldom. They're only allowed on site if they accept the regulations of Armed Industries.

SO 3

99% allow you to search their vehicles. Its in their contracts of employment to be searched. If they refuse you just record it and refer it to management. Generally most go along with it.

SO 18

Its not common but there are some people who object, but we wouldn't make a big fuss of it. But we should do. Its usually senior management who complain because they don't want to stop and go through all the procedures.

If security officers did fail to secure consent through a question they would resort to threats or invoking the disciplinary procedure by reporting to management. The research on search at Armed Industries illustrates a number of issues: first, the lack of commitment amongst some staff to undertake this function with any degree of real commitment; second, the very good level of compliance amongst staff in accepting the right of security staff to undertake searches, as these had been achieved through consent.

Search at Pleasure Southquay

Search by security officers at Pleasure Southquay was relatively rare as Table 7.1 above illustrated. In Chapter 6 the incident of the security officer detaining an individual after an attack on the staff of a nightclub was described. In this incident the security officer searched the man while being restrained to look for any sharp objects. Some of the female security officers had also conducted searches of female shoplifters under the supervision of the police because of the sex issue – illustrating the strong co-operation between them. Others admitted to asking individuals who had been 'detained' to empty their pockets. There was also one function on the goods entrance where the security officer was required to conduct occasional searches of vehicles. Given the rarity of this at Pleasure Southquay it does not warrant any further detailed consideration.

Other select legal tools assumed by security staff

Private space enables a wide range of other conditions to be attached on entrance which private security staff frequently find themselves policing (Gray and Gray 1999a, b and c). Some of the rules security staff enforce mirror those on public space undertaken by the public police and other agencies. The most common relate to parking and traffic regulations, which in the case of Armed Industries were a significant responsibility. At Pleasure Southquay traffic regulations were also a responsibility of the security staff, although their involvement in this was much smaller in comparison. There were also other regulations enforced by security staff, which will also be considered in this section not related to traffic, such as enforcing no-smoking policies, and the use of prohibited items to name some examples.

Enforcing the traffic regulations at Armed Industries

Probably one of the most impressive functions private security staff possessed was the enforcement of the speed limit for vehicles within the grounds of Armed Industries. The roads resembled public highways with similar signs relating to the speed, one-way systems, entrances etc. The site covered a large geographical area with a large number of vehicles using it ranging from cars to large articulated lorries. Throughout the site there was a speed limit of 10 mph. This limit was publicised in a number of ways. Primarily there were road signs similar to those on public roads stating the 10 mph limit. Additionally employees were made aware of this limit in their staff handbook. Contractors and visitors in the information given to them on entering site were given a map of the site detailing the one-way system and speed limit as well as a badge, which stated, 'Do ... observe the 10mph speed restriction.' Breaching the speed limit could ultimately result in the termination of the right to drive on site. Therefore for many staff, given the size, it was an important privilege to be able to make use of. The security staff enforced this regulation using a radar gun to randomly target vehicles at a specific point in the factory grounds at random times.

During my observation at Armed Industries for a brief half hour period the contract manager, staff sergeant and I monitored the speed of vehicles at a specific point on site. In doing so we hid behind a van so approaching vehicles could not readily recognise what we were doing. As the cars turned the corner into the area under surveillance the security manager would point the radar gun at them. A speed was registered and if it was above 16mph they were stopped. A number of cars passed and were within the 16 mph zone and so were not stopped. Then a car came round the corner at 22mph. The staff sergeant and I walked into the road to stop the car. The driver put his hands in the air to acknowledge he had been caught and laughed with the staff sergeant. It subsequently turned out they knew one another. The staff sergeant said to the driver, 'Excuse me sir do you realise there is a speed limit of 10 mph on this site?' The driver replied, 'yes', to which the staff sergeant stated, 'do you realise you were driving at 22mph?' The driver apologised and the staff sergeant took down his details for the form and informed him that if he carries on speeding he may have his right to drive on site removed. The driver was then allowed to drive off and we returned to checking the speed of vehicles passing.

While doing this the staff sergeant told me, 'I love this, it must be my warped sense of humour'. He then informed me that only he and the contract manager undertake this function with a security officer in support sometimes. They always hold the gun and this did cause some resentment amongst staff because other officers had moaned to me that they never got to hold the gun, they always had to approach the driver and take the flack.

Another car was stopped which was travelling at 19mph. This time the driver looked extremely angry and asked 'What's going on here then?'. The staff sergeant replied, 'Do you realise there is a speed limit of 10mph and that you were travelling at 19mph sir.' The driver said he didn't and apologised and then asked, 'So what will happen?' The staff sergeant explained it would be passed to his manager and that if he continues speeding he may lose his right to drive on site. The form was filled in and he drove off looking very angry. The weather worsened so we returned to the main gatehouse and while walking back the contract manager told me, 'You see we're just like a mini police department!' He also told me that one manager he once stopped was very angry and he had joked you will get either a £5000 fine or 6 months in jail! The manager had looked terrified. He also told me of another manager – who had been at the forefront of issuing memos to reduce speed had also been caught. He had put his hands in his head and went bright red. He was very embarrassed. He left shortly afterwards, although not because of this!

In stopping the cars the security officers rely on both primary measures relating to the rules and the presence of the officer. The first stage involved the officer standing in the road to stop the car. The image of a uniformed officer standing in the road combined with the knowledge of the rules of the site secured the consent of the driver. The rest of the lexicon relates to the exchange of information. Although this was one of the rare examples where security officers actually invoked the rules in their justification for their action.

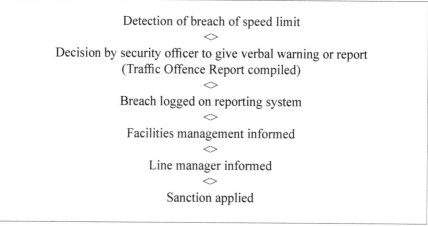

Detection of breach of speed limit

Decision by security officer to give verbal warning or report
(Traffic Offence Report compiled)

Breach logged on reporting system

Facilities management informed

Line manager informed

Sanction applied

Figure 7.1   The Armed Industries system for prosecuting breaches of the speed limit

The breach of this regulation leads to a process that mirrors the criminal justice system. The process is set out in Figure 7.1. It begins with a detection of speed above – not the actual limit of 10 mph – but the informal limit of 16 mph. At this point the security officers have a great deal of discretion as they can decide whether to initiate proceedings against the driver or not. At one extreme they could issue a verbal warning that is not recorded or they could issue a verbal warning that is recorded and reported. On most incidents the staff worked to a system whereby three verbal reports would result in a formal report to the facilities management. If they did decide to 'record' the incident the staff would fill in a Traffic Offence Report.

All these forms are then logged onto the computer management system and after the 'three strikes' are out, go to facilities management for consideration. They usually then inform the line manager who has the ultimate decision over the sanction to be applied to the offender. The ultimate sanction for speeding is the loss of the privilege to drive vehicles on site.

At every point in the system there is scope for discretion by the decision-maker. It was also interesting that the security staff rarely heard what the ultimate outcome of the breach of regulations was. The contract manager was philosophical about this. He told me, 'Its like the criminal justice system. The police catch people committing crimes and then pass on the case and they don't always find out what happened to the offender.'

During my visit to the site I was given the statistics for 2002 on traffic offences. These are presented in Table 7.2 below. In relation to speeding there were only 110 incidents recorded. These came from 23 dates, so on average there were just over 4 vehicles caught per session. The statistics reveal only a tiny proportion were reported to management, with only 10 recorded during 2002.

Table 7.2   Recorded traffic offences at Armed Industries during 2002

Traffic offence	Incidents recorded	Verbal or 'stickered' warning	Vehicle clamped	Incidents reported
Illegal Parking	232	229	3	
Speeding	110	100		10
Invalid Pass	1	1		
No vehicle tax	2	2		

The table also reveals the most common form of enforcement related to 'illegal parking'. Again like public roads Armed Industries had zones where parking was not allowed, marked by double yellow lines and those who parked in the company car parks required the appropriate pass. The latter was additionally enforced through the access control strategies of the officers. When vehicles were identified 'illegally' parking they were warned with a sticker. Similar to speeding, staff worked to the 'three strikes' rule so if they were caught a third time they would be clamped and reported to facilities management. They could also be immediately clamped if they were parked in a way that was a risk to health and safety. If they were clamped there was no fine, but the security staff 'might' make it very difficult for the offender by taking a long time to release the car. If a vehicle breached national law relating to taxation and valid MoT then the policy of Armed Industries was to involve the public police. However, as the statistics above illustrate in the two recorded cases they were actually warned.

Enforcing traffic regulations at Pleasure Southquay

At Pleasure Southquay the road network was not as extensive. There was, however, an underground car park with nearly 1500 spaces. Above ground, there was also a small network of roads leading to the delivery bays of some of the many units on site. There were no Pleasure Southquay regulations relating to speeding, one way systems etc. Therefore the only significant regulations that required enforcement related to parking.

To enter the underground car park at Pleasure Southquay in a vehicle the driver would come to a barrier where they would request a ticket from the machine linked to the barrier, which as soon as it is withdrawn, enables the barrier to rise and the vehicle to enter. The driver then finds a parking place and on leaving puts the ticket in a machine, pays the appropriate fee and then when driving out of Pleasure Southquay places the ticket in the machine which opens the barrier to leave. Because of the system in place it was virtually impossible for a vehicle to enter without a ticket. The system in place meant that security officers role in this area amounted to checking cars were parked appropriately ie not causing an obstruction to other drivers and dealing with those cars seeking to leave where the driver had not paid or not paid enough. The design and computerisation of the system meant the role of security officers was very limited in this area.

During my observations in the car park area the security officers would patrol the car park to survey for suspicious activities and to act as a deterrent for any car thieves. They had a machine that enabled them to move a car that might be causing an obstruction, but this was very rarely used. While in the control room they would have the occasional driver that had taken longer than 15 minutes from paying for their parking and leaving site, which invalidated their ticket and required the security officer to over-ride the system and raise the barrier. If they did do this they had to write a report accounting for why they had raised the barrier. They also dealt with the occasional driver who had lost their ticket and would therefore need to purchase a new one at a cost of £15.

I was told of an incident in the car park where a driver was thought to be very drunk so the car park staff kept the barrier down to stop him from leaving. He tried to then exit through the adjacent lane, which the officer then kept the barrier down again. This led to a game of 'cat and mouse' with the operator until the police arrived to investigate whether the driver was drunk. There were also some vehicles that were banned from entering Pleasure Southquay, which the security officers were required to try and prevent from entering site.

Above the ground on the roads around Pleasure Southquay the security staff did have a wheel clamp they could use to clamp vehicles parking in prohibited zones. During my time on site no security officer could recall using this device. Indeed signs warning of clamping – something that is required in case law to undertake this activity – had only just been put up. The security officers seemed to use the wheelclamp more as a threat. In one incident observed during the day by the taxi rank a vehicle parked in this area but was not a taxi. The security officer asked the driver what he was doing to which he replied waiting to pick someone up. The security officer explained to him he could not park there and might be clamped if he stayed there. This led to the driver moving to an alternative location. This also illustrated how a verbal threat by a security officer secured compliance.

Using prohibited vehicles

At Pleasure Southquay it was clear that security officers were enforcing all types of regulations, yet there seemed to be no rule book stating what these were. This was clarified to me when I asked the Security Supervisor about this. He told me,

> There is no set of rules written down anywhere. It is normal practice at any shopping centre because of health and safety regulations etc not to have people riding bikes etc. There are no signs because this could give a negative image to the public. We always try to deal with things verbally with the public. Really it is custom and practice and down to our discretion. Marketing just didn't want anything that might give a negative image about Pleasure Southquay.

The most common occurrence was visitors riding bicycles or skateboards on the pedestrian areas. Despite no public notices stating this was not allowed there also seemed to be a belief amongst those that did this that it was wrong. For instance on one occasion while walking with one of the team leaders a young man riding a bicycle headed towards us. The team leader said, 'excuse me!' and the young man immediately got off his bike. Thus without even having to tell this individual what to do he did it. This suggested a latent knowledge in the young man that what he was doing was wrong and on the other hand the authority of the security officer in achieving his goal with very limited action. In another comparable incident observed there was a youth riding his skateboard. The security officer shouted, 'no riding on skateboards!' and the youth immediately got off. Again the security officer had achieved his goal, but this time had to resort to telling the youth what to do.

These incidents revealed, first, a latent knowledge that certain behaviour was against the rules, even those rules did not exist in a written form or were publicised there. This may illustrate that rules enforced at other similar locations may condition people to expect similar rules at Pleasure Southquay. These incidents also demonstrated the importance of the presence of officers in achieving outcomes. Finally officers clearly had substantial discretion in deciding what to enforce.

Prohibited items

At Armed Industries the sensitive nature of the site meant there were some regulations based in law that they were required to enforce. The site was a prohibited place under the Official Secrets Act 1911 and 1989. One of the conditions that arose from this was that bringing any camera, radio, mobile phone, portable computer or computer media required prior approval from Armed Industries. During one observation the discretion of security officers on this issue was further illustrated. A school trip was about to leave at gate 7 and as the kids got onto the coach, the security officer saw the teacher with a camera and a member of Armed Industries staff. He told me cameras are not allowed and then pointed to a sign on the gate which said, 'No Photography'. Indeed mobile phones with cameras were banned on site. However, he didn't do anything about the camera and seemed unsure whose responsibility it was to enforce it. Instead arguing that because the teacher was with an Armed Industries employee it was down to them. I later presented this scenario to the Security Manager and asked him what the security officer should have done,

> If that has happened on site the rules clearly state that there are no photographs taken on site unless it is authorised through SC's (Security Controller) department whereby a permit will be issued and public affairs informed, they may only make use of the Armed Industries logo which is against group policy unless it has been authorised. So the officer concerned should have confronted the teacher and then sought permission. What we normally do is get the company photographer to accompany them to make sure they don't take any pictures of anything sensitive.

This policy on no cameras had been stretched to interpretation with the advent of mobile phones with cameras. The security officer cited above who had refused to confront the teacher told me of the confusion over what to do about mobile phones and the difficulty of enforcing this policy given the ubiquity of them. Indeed the Security Controller explained the nature of this policy,

> …they haven't been banned. Its an evolving world really. We have quite strict regulations on this site for the use of cameras so we say that cameras should not be brought onto site unless you've got authority. So we do have a camera permit process. With mobile phones it's a bit more difficult because we cant and you don't notice and people don't think I've got a camera. So we have put out a general policy from the centre, but we can't stop ownership we can't stop use of mobile phones and a good majority on this site are the ones issued by Armed Industries. So in some areas we've got mobile phone detectors because they are restricted use of and we've got the continual sign about use of cameras. We've created on this site because of the regulations a list of those who do own a photographic type mobile machine. The use of cameras is part of the signage at all entrances, for induction and briefing and notification and so on. A ban is a bit strong but we are strict on their use. And then you've got to be seen taking photographs and the type of background. Is it an IP issue – intellectual property or government. We have been known to borrow the camera and remove the disk, film or whatever or even develop the film and say you can have these back but you can't have this one, but that is to the extreme, because anyone coming on to site as a visitor or otherwise does and should read the health and safety thing and the rules of the site, but the host is responsible and the host should brief on what he can and can't allow and occasionally we fall foul. We've had the odd occasion where students have been allowed to take photographs outside Armed Industries saying we're visiting Armed Industry, that's quite acceptable. But when they then think we've got a licence to use the camera for the rest of the day wherever they happen to go that's taboo. So there is a little bit lack of understanding I think and clarifications on what is and isn't allowed.

These regulations were very important in maintaining the security of Armed Industries given the sensitive activities that went on there. Clearly this was an issue that was enforced differently by security officers according to their knowledge of the rules and their level of commitment. Indeed the security officer cited above told me of one colleague who did everything by the book and would enforce all regulations with equal vigour, whereas he preferred to play the situation according to circumstances showing a high degree of discretion.

At Pleasure Southquay there was also a policy that any photographs of the development would require prior permission from Pleasure Southquay management. This was not publicised anywhere, however, and required security officers to know about this regulation and then enforce it. During observations on one shift the control room notified one security officer to follow a man who was carrying a camera suspected of taking photographs. He was kept under surveillance discreetly for a period of time but found not to be taking pictures. A more common regulation in this field that was pursued was where revellers were leaving bars and clubs with bottles. On numerous occasions I observed security officers asking them to drink up or pass them the bottle. On all occasions observed the reveller gave up the bottle.

Other enforcement functions

The observation also revealed many examples of how the security officers secure good order with varying degrees of action. The mere presence of a security officer frequently secures compliance. In one example during a Saturday night after the night clubs had closed by the taxi rank, a man left the queue and proceeded to walk behind the main block. The security officer I was stood with noticed this and followed the man as he thought he was going behind the building to urinate. The security officer said nothing, but the man turned round, left site and then returned to the queue a few minutes later. It was clear the mere presence of the security officer had prevented this man from going to the toilet on Pleasure Southquay property. There were other similar examples of mere presence securing compliance.

At the time of the observation there was an 'ice' ring in the central square. This was really a large white surface that had oil placed on it during the day to replicate an ice ring. During the night it was relatively easy for people to climb onto the ring and many drunken revellers attempted to do this. On one occasion a group of men ran towards the ring and were heard to be shouting that they would go skating. As soon as the security officer moved to illustrate his presence some of the revellers stopped. Two carried on and climbed on to the ring and the security officers went over to them and asked them to leave, which they then did. Thus with the combination of presence and verbal command the security officer was able to achieve a satisfactory outcome. In another incident that illustrated compliance to verbal commands a security officer approached a group of drunken men who looked like they were trying to throw one of their friends in the water. The security officer asked them to stop and they did.

Sometimes the authority of security officers was questioned particularly when they threatened the profitability of a tenant. While attending one tenants meeting some complained that a security officer on New Years Eve had been going round the shops asking them to close on time. Some of the tenants had clearly been upset at this request, as the official time for closing had not been reached. The Operations Manager apologised to these tenants and promised to look into the matter. A few days later when attending Pleasure Southquay for further observation it transpired that the Team Leader who had undertaken this action had been removed from site, effectively sacked from Pleasure Southquay for exceeding his authority (or challenging tenants profitability!).

Three dimensions revisited

In Chapter 1 the three dimensional view of power outlined by Lukes (1974) was explored and it was demonstrated these all applied to the policing of private space. Having reviewed in this and the last chapter the more detailed use of these universal and select legal tools it would seem appropriate to revisit this three dimensional view in the light of the findings discussed. Power is ultimately about achieving 'outcome situations', getting A to do B. Lukes identified three dimensions that may achieve this. This research has found evidence of all three dimensions at work and to make an understanding of this easier figure 7.2 outlines this model, which also draws upon continuums of force that have been outlined by McKenzie and Gallagher (1989).

THIRD DIMENSION Primary Measures	Creating mentalities to achieve outcomes sub-conciously Design, Image, Rules (sanctions for breach) and Reputation
SECOND DIMENSION Secondary Measures	Officer presence
FIRST DIMENSION Tertiary Measures	Verbal questions ◇ Verbal requests (making use of universal and select legal tools) ◇ Verbal threats ◇ Coercion ◇ Call the manager and/or Police

Figure 7.2   Lukes' three dimensional model of power applied to security officers achieving outcome situations

At both Pleasure Southquay and Armed Industries the primary measures to achieve 'outcome situations' were based upon controlling measures that secure compliance without the individual necessarily realising they have complied. As Lukes (1974, 23) argues,

> ...A may exercise power over B by getting him to do what he does not want to do, but he also exercises power over him by influencing, shaping or determining his very wants. Indeed is it not the supreme exercise of power to get another or others to have the desires you want them to have – that is, to secure their compliance by controlling their thoughts and desires?

Such 'thought control' according to Lukes could be achieved through control of information, the media and through socialisation. Indeed for Foucault (1977) discipline was achieved in society through a disciplinary system that encompassed a wide range of mechanisms, other than observable orders to achieve outcomes. Such subtle controlling mechanisms have been illustrated by Shearing and Stenning (1987)'s study of Disney World in the design, signage and image that are used to secure order. Cohen (1985) has also explored the extensive range of activities that contribute to this 'social control' process in much greater depth at a state level. Many of the measures that are undertaken by the state to engender social control are pursued at places similar to Pleasure Southquay and Armed Industries, as well state social control more broadly impacting upon such locations of governance. Primarily through the design, the image cultivated, the rules that are set with sanctions for their breach and their reputation, what Johnston and Shearing (2003) would call a 'mentality' emerges amongst the 'policed', which generally secures the appropriate outcomes. They argue (2003, 29),

> Generally, we act not because we have consciously thought through and adopted a mentality that promotes a particular action, but because we constantly use methods (often embedded in habits) that imply that mentality of practical reasoning. We typically adopt these methods without thinking much about the mentality they imply.

These mentalities are created beyond the two nodes of governance studied. Other similar locations and other nodes we move within also contribute to creating such mentalities. For instance the example earlier in this chapter of the CSO at Pleasure Southquay securing the compliance from a young person to get off his bike, simply by saying 'excuse me' illustrates the rider must have had a mentality knowing that riding a bike was wrong in such places and that this was probably learnt from similar locations as well as Pleasure Southquay. The impact and success of the measures to achieve these outcomes by their very nature are hard to measure. If we go back to Pleasure Southquay the success of the strategies to discourage elements within the deprived nearby estate to come to Pleasure Southquay is difficult to assess with the methods that were used in this study. Indeed even if I had researched those groups in this nearby estate their decision to come or not to Pleasure Southquay may well have been based upon a mentality drawn from beyond the measures pursued there.

However, some of the prevailing general mentalities we can speculate existed at or around the two case study sites include:

- Armed Industries: mentality amongst general population not to enter site
- Armed Industries: mentality of some staff to automatically show identity passes without seeming to think about it
- Pleasure Southquay: mentality that certain types of behaviour are not appropriate for this site (or any shopping centre)
- Pleasure Southquay: mentality amongst some groups discouraging them from visiting

The secondary measures, relating to the second dimension, is where mere presence by security officers achieves the required outcome. This was the fundamental aim of security officers at both of the case study sites. There was a clear aim that the presence of officers at Pleasure Southquay would deter certain people from coming on site and secure appropriate behaviour when they were on site. Similarly at Armed Industries officers on gates were there to remind staff to show passes without having to ask them. On an individual level many incidents were described above where mere presence secured the appropriate outcome.

The tertiary measures relate to Lukes' first dimension, where the outcome is achieved as a result of action by the security officer. This is the last resort in the strategies used by organisation's to achieve their outcomes. The research illustrated a scale of strategies to achieve the outcome. At the base a security officer might secure consent to their request by asking a question. There was evidence of this at Pleasure Southquay when apprehending shoplifters and at Armed Industries in pursuing searches. The next level is a verbal request to do something utilising any select or universal legal tools available. Again there was evidence of this at both research sites, particularly at Pleasure Southquay in securing order in the NTE. If these fail the next stage is to resort to threats. This might be to threaten to call management or even the police. Again there was evidence of both these types of strategies being used at both sites, particularly in relation to search at Armed Industries. If all these fail and there is a legal tool available – or the situation already renders the previous strategies useless – then the next course of action is coercion. This was particularly prevalent amongst some of the security staff at Pleasure Southquay in dealing with disorder in the NTE. Force was not something that officers would universally engage in and some would move straight to the final strategy of calling a line manager and or the police to resolve the situation.

Conclusion

This chapter has examined some of the many 'select' legal tools that security officers make use of. It began by reviewing access control, then assessed search before analysing a range of other tools used by staff. In doing so major differences in the extent and type of tools used at the two sites were illustrated. Underlying these tools it was demonstrated that their use is primarily pursued as the last resort in achieving their specific outcomes. Other primary measures are the main strategy in securing compliance. However, when these tools are used they are based largely upon consent and measures to manipulate consent where that is not possible. Force is rarely used within the context of these tools at the two case study sites reviewed. It was also demonstrated, that with the exception of the enforcement of traffic regulations at Armed Industries – justification of their use was rarely based upon legal reference and more on commonsense based approaches. The chapter ended with a consideration of both 'universal' and 'select' legal tools within the context of Lukes's three dimensional view of power drawing a model of the continuum of options for outcomes to be achieved in the two sites. A consequence of using these tools is isolation, verbal abuse and violence against security staff and this will be the subject of the next chapter.

Chapter 8

Occupational Hazards: Too Many Masters, Isolation and Abuse

Introduction

The research at Pleasure Southquay and Armed Industries revealed a variety of occupational hazards confronted by security officers. At one level security officers face the challenge of having to deal with several masters who may often have conflicting agendas. Another challenge faced by security officers is isolation. This may take the form of spending large periods of time alone to feelings of alienation from fellow workers and the general public. Finally security officers face quite significant levels of abuse, this is largely verbal, but for those officers working in 'frontline' positions in the NTE, this also encompasses regular assaults. This chapter will now explore each of these hazards in turn.

Too many masters spoil the...

Security officers often lead a schizophrenic existence serving several masters with differing agendas and having to please them all. First there is a relationship with the management and staff of the client they are providing security services to. Alongside this, if they are contract security officers – which most are – there is a relationship with the management and staff of the security company they work for. This was the nature of the relationship at Armed Industries and was relatively simple compared to Pleasure Southquay. There, in addition to the client and security company management, the security officers also had to deal with tenants in the complex, which could be divided between the retailer and the NTE tenants (who also often had conflicting agendas). The security staff at certain times also found themselves working with the police, which again could be divided between the day and night relationships. Finally there was the general public, which again could be divided between the daytime shopping public and the NTE orientated revellers. The difficulties of these relationships was illustrated by Adu-Boakye (2002, 43) who found,

> To the employer all that the security guard has to do is report for work and patrol the shopfloor as a deterrent to criminal and perhaps pray not to hear of your involvement in any incidents of violence. They expect you to call the police if the need be. Management

and staff see you differently, they expect you to go beyond a deterrent security guard. Inaction physically in the event of violent attacks is definitely not an option they expect.

The relationship between the security staff and these different groups varied significantly at Armed Industries and Pleasure Southquay, even between the same group between night and day. Some of these relationships will now be examined.

Relationship with managements

At both Armed Industries and Pleasure Southquay the security officers were contracted from security companies. This created a situation where there were effectively two sets of management above the security officers. At Armed Industries the Security Manager was based permanently on site and was an employee of the contractor. There was also Armed Industries management in the form of the Facilities Manager and the Security Controller who also had responsibilities vis-à-vis contract security. The security officers did not have to deal with the general public, but instead several thousand employees and contractors to Armed Industries.

Pleasure Southquay was more complex. The key person responsible for security was the Security Supervisor who was an employee of Pleasure Southquay. Above him, however, the Operations Manager also took a very keen interest in security. The security company also supplied a Contract Manager, but he was not based upon site, having other contracts to manage, although because of the importance of the Pleasure Southquay contract was on site regularly. There were also tenants of Pleasure Southquay many of which took an active interest in security. Tenants meetings' covered retailers for one group and bars and clubs (or the NTE) for the other. On the ground, particularly at night, these tenants would also seek to influence the decisions and actions of security, particularly as many of the tenants had their own security officers or door supervisors. The difficulties of the relationships was illustrated very succinctly by CSO 11.

> We are serving two masters and get bollocked by both. The team leaders meetings are a waste of time. The same things keep coming up and nothing gets acted upon. We are on the ground 24–7 they are only here 9 till 5 Monday to Friday. They don't take enough notice of what we have to say. We are on the ground and know how it is. They don't understand. One of these days someone is going to get topped. They need to come out with us on a Saturday or Friday night to understand what we really do.

In Chapter 6 the differences over the role of security staff was illustrated vis-à-vis intervening in disorder at night. The operations manager at Pleasure Southquay set out a policy of non-intervention, compared to the security supervisor and contract manager of one of intervention. The differences in such a fundamental policy clearly created problems amongst the security staff in what to do, hence CSO11's comments above. The differences could also prove costly in terms of a security officer's career. One officer was removed from site for encouraging a tenant to close on New Year's Eve at the appropriate time, when it was part of their role to close this area from public access as quickly as possible because of the risks of disorder. Clearly by undertaking what one set of managers wanted him to do he had upset another and paid for the consequences with his job at the site. Indeed a major hazard for contract staff is removal from site at the whim of a manager, although this is not the sack as staff are almost always offered another assignment, (although the transfer to a less prestigious and possibly worse paying client could amount to a *de facto* termination of employment). The problem of too many masters was not as bad at Armed Industries, but there was still evidence of problems dealing with more than one set of management and the quality of them.

SO 14

There is no mechanism for meetings between security officers and management. This ferments unrest. I'm easy to get on with but there is a need for a forum where you can discuss things with management and we have no trade unions to do this to protect us. There is a lot of input security officers could make, they have a lot of experience.

SO 20

There is average communication here. With personnel problems you rely on management here. There needs to be greater access to personnel. We don't even know who they are with this company (the new security contractor).

Thus overall there was evidence of the hazards security officers face in serving many masters. There was also evidence to suggest security officers were not always impressed with the quality of their management more generally.

Relationship with the police

Crawford and Lister (2004a) found varying relationships between the police and other agents from the extended policing family ranging from strong partnership to outright hostility. Wakefield (2003) in her study of three shopping centres found evidence of strong working relationships between police and security, although she also found the quality of the relationship differed between the three studies. Michael (2002) also found evidence of a positive relationship between police and private security. In terms of this study the relationship with the police was only applicable to Pleasure Southquay because the police were very rarely on site at Armed Industries. Conversely at Pleasure Southquay the police played an important part in the policing of this site during both the day and night. The relationship between the police and Pleasure Southquay when the research was undertaken was still at a very early stage, but was generally very positive. It had also shifted due to changes in the management structure at Pleasure Southquay. It is worth noting some of the most important stages in the evolution in the relationship between the police and Pleasure Southquay.

When Pleasure Southquay was being planned they had originally envisaged an onsite police facility, which the local constabulary would have been able to use rent-free. Clearly the aim would have been to maximise police presence at little or no cost to Pleasure Southquay Plc. However, the police turned this down and as a consequence there were no special rooms or facilities available to the police while the research was ongoing. When the site first opened, however, cracks began to emerge in the relationship. The first operations manager decided that a police presence on site would provoke a bad image of Pleasure Southquay and therefore sought to discourage their presence on site preferring the security staff to deal with incidents as was illustrated in the extract from the interview with the police sergeant in Chapter 4.

Such was the extent of the zeal of the first operations manager that he actually stood in front of a police vehicle seeking to respond to an incident on site and only when he was threatened with arrest did he move out of the way. Not surprisingly this first operations manager did not last very long and was replaced with a new manager who had come from the bowling complex on site which had attracted some trouble in the first few months of opening, so was well experienced with dealing with 'problematic' clients. With the new manager came a much more positive relationship. Police were welcomed and encouraged on site. During the night-time on Friday and Saturday nights a group of police officers would usually descend on site during the hours of 11pm to 3.00am. During the day police officers in both uniform and undercover would be on site at various points, largely to deal with shoplifting. The police were also regularly called on site to deal with specific incidents.

Table 8.1   Pleasure Southquay security officers' perception of police attitude when they visit (%)

In your experience how do you find the police when they visit your workplace?			
	Pleasure Southquay 'Frontline'	Pleasure Southquay 'Backroom'	Pleasure Southquay All
Are helpful when you call them	48	57	50
Are helpful sometimes, sometimes not	38	29	36
Are not generally helpful	5	0	4
Are not usually around when they are needed and take their time when they are called	10	14	11
N = 29			

Before some of the many ways in which the police and private security co-operated with one another are illustrated, it would be useful to examine some of the quantitative data from the interviews on the security officers' perception of the police. The first table assesses what security officers think the attitude of the police was when they visited Pleasure Southquay. Generally there was a positive attitude towards the police. 50 per cent of officers thought they were helpful and a further 36 per cent thought they were helpful sometimes, but also sometimes not. Only one officer (4 per cent) thought they were not generally helpful and only three (11 per cent) thought they were not around when they were needed.

The security officers were also asked what they thought the police attitude towards them was. Again the results were very positive. 71 per cent of the security officers felt the police officers thought they were providing a valuable service. A further 21 per cent of the officers felt the police were indifferent towards them. Only two officers or 7 per cent felt the police looked down on them. When this question is compared to how the security officers perceive the public perceive them there was a huge difference (see later in chapter). Thus certainly from this data there would seem to be a positive relationship, particularly from the security side. The observations and other data triangulate this view and some of the positive aspects of this relationship will now be considered.

Table 8.2   Pleasure Southquay security officers' perception of police attitude towards them (%)

In your experience what is the typical police officer's attitude towards you and your colleagues?			
	Pleasure Southquay 'Frontline'	Pleasure Southquay 'Backroom'	Pleasure Southquay All
They think we are providing a valuable service that is useful to them	62	100	71
They are indifferent towards us	29	0	21
They look down on us	10	0	7
N = 29			

There was a great deal of evidence to illustrate how the police and security staff supported one another in various operations. The most prominent examples were in the NTE. Many disturbances that occurred often initially left the police or security with not enough bodies to quell the disturbance, so frequently they would support each other in the early stages of a disturbance (see Chapter 6). During the daytime when shoplifting was a concern evidence of security staff helping the police undertake searches and restrain certain detainees was also found (see Chapter 6). The security staff also secured evidence for crimes to help police secure prosecutions. When the security staff did detain individuals without police support and the police arrived on site they would generally ask security staff what had happened and treat their word – at least initially – as the facts and arrest the individual(s) concerned. Chapter 6 also illustrated examples of 'grey' policing. The police and security shared information and also helped one another in undertaking arrests. On one of the day shifts during observation the security supervisor told me he had just been tipped off by a police contact that a well known local villain was to be let out of prison that day and that there might be plans for them to come to Pleasure Southquay for a 'celebration'. Inside the control room there were also pictures of known shoplifters and lots of intelligence was shared between the police and security on this issue.

Isolation

Isolation amongst security officers was distinguished at a number of different levels. At one level the work undertaken by security staff can be a lonely task where they work alone often for long periods of time. Second there is the nature of the role of security – rather like the police – that distinguishes them from their fellow employees that culminates in a sense of isolation from them (a cultural aspect that will be developed in more depth in Chapter 9). Finally as with the relationship with fellow staff this trait also applies to the relationship with the public – if that is applicable.

A lonely job

Many of the roles security officers undertake are positions on their own. At Armed Industries this was particularly pronounced where most of the roles meant security officers were in 'boxes' on their own for often the whole 12 hour shift. Their only contact might be with a supervisor or colleague walking past or briefly relieving them or with employees, contractors and visitors to Armed Industries (but who they were policing). At night although there would be opportunities for more than one officer to meet for longer periods, they would still spend lengthy time alone patrolling the complex. Such was the loneliness and the darkness in some parts of the factory numerous accounts emerged of officers scared to venture on their own because of the dark and ghosts! At Pleasure Southquay there was far more interaction amongst the security officers and they were encouraged to engage in dialogues with the public. There were, however, lone positions where lengthy periods might be spent isolated such as the control room, car-park, 'punchthrough' and goods entrance. During the day officers were also supposed to patrol alone, although this seemed to be ignored to a large extent, except when management ventured out into the public areas. There was, however, much more opportunity to interact with the public either though responding to their requests or simply being a friendly 'customer service officer'.

Relationship with the public and fellow staff

Further evidence of isolation is illustrated by the answers of security officers at both sites on how they felt the public or fellow workers perceived them. At Pleasure Southquay because of the significant differences in the relationship between security staff during the day vis-à-vis night the question was split. As Table 8.3 illustrates during the day there was a much better perception of the relationship between themselves and the public with over three quarters thinking the public perceive them to be providing a valuable service to them. At night, however, this fell to a third and with 42 per cent thinking the public look down on them, further evidence of how the alcohol fuelled NTE changes the relationship between security and the public.

Table 8.3   Pleasure Southquay security officers' perception of public attitude towards them at night and day (%)

In your experience what is the typical attitude of the public towards you and your colleagues?		
	Day	**Night**
They think we are providing a valuable service that is useful to them	81	31
They are indifferent towards us	12	27
They look down on us	8	42
N = 26		

At Armed Industries the question related to day and night and only to their fellow employees on site. Here 30 per cent still felt their fellow staff looked down on them, with a further 30 per cent indifferent towards them.

Table 8.4   Armed Industries security officers' perception of Armed Industries staff attitude towards them (%)

In your experience what is the typical attitude of the Armed Industries employees towards you and your colleagues?	
They think we are providing a valuable service that is useful to them	40
They are indifferent towards us	30
They look down on us	30
N = 20	

The extract from the interviews with CSO 22 and 23 and SO 5, 8 and 12 also illustrate the sense of isolation and inferiority of staff typical of many security officers.

CSO 22

(Pleasure Southquay) should treat us with more respect, there are some that deserve, others who don't. Mutual respect to make you feel better. We tend to get tarnished with the same brush as 'brainless idiots'... Older people tend to think we'll help them. But we get yobs come in and say to us, 'you get paid £3.50 to walk round here at night in the freezing cold?'

CSO 23

There are a lot of people working for Pleasure Southquay who have never seen a fight let alone a dozen blokes fighting with bottles flying overhead. The office people have no idea what we go through at night. There is no real feeling of what we feel. They don't know if we actually sleep at night. They don't realise that we may have to jump into a fight of six people with bottles flying. How no one has ended in hospital is beyond me. You can't walk around with helmets on, but with 24 plus bars and 5 to 6,000 people the management don't realise what could happen. You can't walk round like Rambo it doesn't do us any favours. I carry a torch just in case the 'lights go out'. I was told to do this by a Chief Inspector and I would use it if my life was in danger. It cost me £30 for the 6 cell torch . I've had to deal with shoplifters with needles and there is nothing in the SITO training that tells you how to deal with that. The police are paid twice as much as us and have twice as much training. Some of the (police) shifts don't help as much as they could.

SO 5

You're a contractor and they don't like contractors telling them what to do. Its them against us. On gate 7 you can say hello to everyone and they wont say anything back. They cut you dead.

SO 8

Some are really good, but the majority think we are a bag of shits. Since it has gone from Reliance Security to Armed Industries Security on the jumper we get more respect. But most think we're brainless numbskulls.

SO 12

There is a them and us culture depending upon which gate you are on. In this area people have great respect for you, but on the factory side they look down on us and think we're a pain in the arse.

The sense of isolation and to a degree inferiority will be developed further in Chapter 9 where the nature of security officers' culture will be explored, as this is a significant aspect of it. The poor relationship with some fellow staff and members of the public further manifested itself in terms of the abuse officers received, both verbal and physical.

Abuse

In previous chapters the dangerous situations faced by security officers and the wide range of enforcement related tasks they often undertook were outlined. One of the negative aspects that accompanies these roles is verbal abuse, threats of violence and even assaults from the general public and fellow employees. There has been some recognition of the dangers and stresses of a security officer as well as a growing interest in workplace violence generally (Silva et al. 1993; Gill et al. 2003; Bowie et al. 2005; and Waddington et al. 2006). Despite an overall drop in the rate of victimisation, the most at risk group are still those in the 'Protective Services Occupations', which includes security officers along with police officers, prison officers etc (Gill et al. 2003; and Upson 2004). In this group 12.6 per cent had been assaulted during 2002–03 and they were 14 times more at risk of being assaulted than the average and 3 per cent of this group also reported being threatened at work. Of those who had been assaulted nearly a third claimed the offender was under the influence of alcohol and a fifth under the influence of drugs (Upson 2004).

Table 8.5   Security officers' experience of verbal abuse (%)

	Once or twice a day	Once or twice a week	Once or twice a month	Once or twice a year	Never
Pleasure Southquay All	46	32	11	4	7
Pleasure Southquay 'Frontline'	57	38	5	0	0
Pleasure Southquay 'Backroom'	14	14	29	14	29
Armed Industries	15	10	40	25	10
All	33	23	23	13	8
N = 48					

Given the growing body of research on the NTE illustrating the violence and abuse endemic there, it would not be surprising to find it in Pleasure Southquay (Lister et al. 2000; Winlow 2001; and Hobbs et al. 2003). However, although violence was rare at Armed Industries, security staff did experience a great deal of verbal abuse, which in itself could also be considered as workplace violence (Bowie 2002). This section will now examine some of the abuse faced by security officers dealing with the public and fellow employees. The analysis will begin with security officers' experience of verbal abuse. This covers any verbal comments or outbursts directed at a security officer. It does not include a threat of violence, which falls in the next category.

The extent and nature of verbal abuse was clearly revealed when undertaking the observation at Pleasure Southquay. Indeed I experienced the abuse myself when doing nothing more than standing next to a security officer observing the taxi rank when a drunken male shouted at me, 'who the fuck do you think you are, Michael Caine!'. Table 8.5 illustrates that in both research sites security officers experience of verbal abuse was very common with nearly 80 per cent of those interviewed being subjected to it on at least a monthly basis. However, at Pleasure Southquay security officers experienced verbal abuse on a much greater level. Nearly 80 per cent of the officers working there were experiencing verbal abuse on at least a weekly basis and when the 'frontline' officers were considered this rose to nearly 95 per cent. This compared to only 25 per cent of officers at Armed Industries. Indeed, 35 per cent at this organisation only experienced such abuse either on a yearly basis or never at all. Similarly at Pleasure Southquay amongst the car park and control room staff there were 28 per cent of officers who had not experienced any verbal abuse. Some of the abuse that security officers' experienced is set out below.

CSO 14

...I have also been called a 'cunt' many times.

CSO 17

I was called a 'crazy black git' after asking a person what they were doing.

CSO 29

I had a lady who hadn't paid enough and she had to pay the rest. She called me a 'silly cow'.

SO 1

You get quite a lot of abuse when you ask to see their passes. A usual comment might be, 'bloody hell mate that's the first time you've asked to see my pass!' Everyone has to offer a pass – that's the rules.

SO 2

I reported one guy. He went over the top swearing at me saying 'you don't fucking search everyone. Why have you stopped me?' That's the worst I have had.

SO 5

I was told to 'fuck off' by one guy because he was in a hurry. Some get wound up if you stop and search them.

SO 6

On certain gates you get it. You ask where's your pass and they tell you to 'fuck off'. They say 'I've been here 30 years and I've never shown you a pass'. Its not everyday, but occasionally. Nothing happens to them they're Armed Industries. I've seen a SO chase them into a factory to see their pass. Nothing ever happens to them. Its them and us.

SO 14

It was someone who wanted access to the site in a hurry. I was the only person on the gate and I was dealing with a few other people at the time. He tried to throw his weight around and when I refused him entrance he called me a 'prick'. I put a report in and he wasn't allowed on site until he apologised to me.

SO 18

Its usually mild swearing, where someone calls you a 'wanker'.

Next in the scale of verbal abuse security officers were asked to state how many times on average they received threats of violence and to give examples of this.

Table 8.6   Security officers' experience of threats of violence (%)

	Once or twice a day	Once or twice a week	Once or twice a month	Once or twice a year	Never
Pleasure Southquay All	7	32	32	7	21
Pleasure Southquay 'Frontline'	10	38	43	5	5
Pleasure Southquay 'Backroom'	0	14	0	14	71
Armed Industries	0	5	0	10	85
All	4	21	19	8	48
N = 48					

Table 8.6 above illustrates the experience of security officers interviewed. There were significant differences between the two research sites in the experience of threats of violence. At Armed Industries it was relatively rare for security officers to experience such threats with 85 per cent of the officers never experiencing a threat of violence at work. One officer claimed to experience it on a weekly basis and two had experienced it at least once or twice in the last year. The officer who claimed to experience it on a weekly basis had only been recently appointed to the site, which

would explain this unusual result in the context of an environment where threats of violence were very rare.

When the responses of the Pleasure Southquay officers are considered, however, there was a much greater experience of threats of violence particularly amongst the 'frontline' officers. Over two thirds of the officers were experiencing threats of violence on at least a monthly basis and two officers claimed to experience them daily. Amongst the 'frontline' officers just under half the officers experienced them on at least a weekly basis and 90 per cent on at least a monthly basis. Amongst the car park and control room officers, however, the vast majority (71 per cent) had never experienced threats of violence. When analysing the research afterwards I realised that it would have been useful to divide this question between the night and day shift (as with the next question) as I suspect most of these incidents occurred at night. Some of the threats officers experienced are listed below.

CSO 12

The adults are usually fine they know they have done wrong and they are not willing to argue a toss. It is the children who now want to know why and they think they know their rights and they don't seem too keen to go.

Teenagers are the worst because they know by law you can't touch them and they know we stick to those laws as well. They will threaten you and front you up and stick their face right in yours and say, 'I'm gonna break your legs' and they know you can't do anything. You just have to try and ignore them. At which point they usually spit at you or something like that.

CSO 16

Gentleman walked out from a club and called us 'fucking this and that' and 'we know where you live', and everything like that, 'you're a dead man'.

CSO 22

'I'm gonna punch your fucking lights out.' All that sought of thing really. I've got a bit of problem because I haven't actually got a fear of threats. It doesn't actually frighten me if someone says 'I'm gonna punch your fucking lights out.' Very rarely will they do it. Especially if you say 'go on then ok.' They walk away. I actually haven't got a fear of such a thing. It's a bit strange really. They've never threatened me with a bottle, a gun or a knife. If they did that might be perhaps a bit different. These threats of violence we get off the local lads and females and they are usually 16, 17, 18 years old. And each time they come out of the place they're coming from – usually the *Bowling Club* – they know me from when I was a store detective in the town.

CSO 27

In the car park you often get verbal abuse. There was one occasion when a guy had to pay the £20 and he said he was going to come back and 'give me a good kicking'.

SO 11

I have asked for passes from some of the guys and been told to fuck off. On 4 gate I once asked to see a pass and I was told to 'fuck off or I'll kick your head in', and he then ran off. I just let it go because it was my second day here and didn't know what I was doing.

Finally security officers were asked to identify the number of times they have been assaulted and to describe some of these incidents. Two questions were asked. The first related to a minor assault covering slight bruising or bleeding. The second related to a more serious assault, which covered broken bones and/or severe bleeding. In terms of the latter only one security officer from Pleasure Southquay illustrated that they had experienced this, when they had tried to stop a suspected shoplifter in a car attempting to escape Pleasure Southquay and had been thrown over the bonnet. They had had to go to hospital with a suspected broken arm (although the x-ray revealed it wasn't). As such this incident really fell in the first category, although clearly to the security officer interviewed this fell into the higher category of assault.[1] All the other assaults identified by security officers they placed in the first category. Table 8.7 below illustrates the results.

Table 8.7   Security officers' experience of assault (slight bruising/bleeding) (%)

	Once or twice a month	Once or twice a year	Never
Pleasure Southquay All	11	29	61
Pleasure Southquay 'Frontline'	14	38	48
Pleasure Southquay 'Control room and car park'	0	0	100
Armed Industries	0	0	100
All	6	17	77
N = 48			

As with threats of violence there were significant differences between the two research sites. At Armed Industries not a single security officer had experienced assault during the course of their duties. Conversely at Pleasure Southquay assault was relatively common,

---

1   18 months after the completion of the research I heard that the contract security manager had had his finger virtually bitten off breaking a fight up, illustrating the dangers faced by security staff at Pleasure Southquay.

particularly for 'frontline' security officers. Just over a third of all Pleasure Southquay officers had experienced assault in the last year and with 'frontline' officers this rose to over 50 per cent. Indeed three officers (11 per cent) claimed to be assaulted on a monthly basis. Conversely none of the security officers in the car park and control room had been assaulted. The types of assault ranged from slight kicks and grabs to full-blown punches. Some of the 'lesser' assaults described by security officers included:

CSO 4

Whilst restraining someone. His mate took a dislike to the way I was doing it and **he repeatedly punched me in the shoulder**.

CSO 18

We had an ambulance for a casualty who had been injured on the site further up and at the time it was half 11 on a Friday night and we needed to clear the road from the taxi rank but all the people were standing in the road rather than on the pavement. So me and another sierra unit were sent to clear the road, at which point I asked the crowd to stand back from the pavement and **one guy got verbal abuse towards me and grabbed me by the throat and threatened to throw me in front of the ambulance.** At which point the police turned up and claimed the situation and asked him to sit in the corner out of the way and they dealt with the incident.

CSO 25

I was escorting a gang of kids off site. One got stroppy and **decided to kick me in the ankles** and run off.

However, some of the incidents described included much more serious assaults, usually when the security officers were trying to break up fights but also when pursuing shoplifters as the first extract illustrates.

CSO 1

I was assaulted by a car by a shoplifter. Me and my colleague followed him down to the car park. He was getting very nervous and couldn't start his car. I tried to put my hand through the window to pull the keys, **but he started the car and pulled off fast. My hand was still attached to the door, he took another CSO over the bonnet and took the barrier out. I bruised all my hand and my knuckles. No serious blood or anything**.

More typical of the types of assaults experienced were these officers who had been assaulted during scuffles where they were trying to break them up.

CSO 11

It depends upon how you treat them. Some lads down here are all right. They're little rogues, little scullies. If you treat them half right, get on a name basis with them. That's half the battle go up to them and say hello Mr so and so and they think hold up I don't know this bloke's name he's got one up on me already. So you go hello mate. Sometimes you literally pat them out. 8 times out of ten it is just a mouthful and then they go. Some play it up and show off but they go in the end. It is a matter of just getting them out the way.

One of my mate's sons who didn't recognise me they did a load of jeans or trousers from *shop t* Basically we got in front of them by *shop s* down here and one our lads gave chase, I gave chase, grabbed hold of them and ripped the trousers off them, **and from nowhere my mate's son come flying out of the air and actually twatted me one, with a right hook to the jaw, with a nice gold sovereign on. This opened my jaw a bit,** but he just carried on running but we still had the lad. But that's about the only time. You do get in little scuffles, you get punched when it is all kicking off, but you don't exactly worry about it at the time. Later on you do. That's the only time I have been twatted by someone.

CSO 21

It was outside *bar h* and again it was a Saturday night. They had already evicted 5 people out the back way. They came back round the front and *H* was around the front asking why they had let them out the back and I turned round and there were 5 or 6 fighting. So I was trying to pull one off but you still have the others fighting and at the time there was just me and *F* there, she came and joined in and one of the door supervisors from *club t* pulled a guy off me, **which I didn't realise at the time and he still had hold of him and he punched me**.

CSO 23

When I was called to the square once there were two youths, I think one called over two PCs who were in central square and waved them across to sought out two blokes who were arguing who had been ejected from the *bowling club*. They were involved in a heated argument and while the one PC was trying to talk to this bloke and calm him down the other PC was trying to prevent his mates coming out of *bar t*. I realised it was getting out of hand. There were a couple of my partners down the stairs so I go and try and help this PC out. When this PC is on the floor when somehow this bloke he is trying to detain is on the floor with him. I have jumped into help him detain this bloke. The other copper is by himself trying to keep the other six lads from trying to do what they are gonna do. So I called up for more backup, more police have come up, and even an off duty police officer who was here at the time and the other CSOs. Its just one big mass of bodies and arms flying. **I had lots of abuse**. And there was no respect for myself or the police. And while I'm down there bending over at the time over one bloke with the PC at the side **someone thought it would be great to smack me in the side of the head with his fist and I was caught on the side of the ear and head** and I turned round and all I could see was a mass of bodies and heads and the noise and you just go back to what you were doing. **You can't leave this bloke because your head hurts**. In the end it sorted itself out. It took four of us to get this bloke down and handcuffed and the rest were made to disperse. Never did find out who assaulted me, it was just impossible.

Clearly the level of abuse, threats of violence and even assault opens debates over the extent to which it can be considered workplace violence (see Waddington et al. 2006).

A grab by a person or a slight kick to some officers might not warrant recording, where as simply being sworn at by others might. Setting these subjective interpretations aside – which are a challenge for any research in this field – the extracts from the interviews illustrate quite serious levels of violence being experienced by the 'frontline' Pleasure Southquay security officers. Unfortunately there is a limited amount of research to compare the extent of verbal and physical abuse faced by the security officers studied. Given the retail environment there are some studies relating to retail staff in general. The trade union representing shopworkers, USDAW, has published research suggesting 70 per cent of respondents had experienced violence or abuse at work (USDAW 2004).[2] More methodologically sound research on shop-workers found 7 employees in every 1000 had been the victim of a violent crime, 5 per 1000 had been subjected to threats of violence and there were 10 reported cases per 1000 of verbal abuse (British Retail Consortium 2002). Another comparison would be police officers, but again there is only limited research. The Police Federation has published research based upon over 12,000 responses from police officers. This found 7.4 per cent had been threatened with a firearm, 30 per cent had been threatened with a knife and 39.7 per cent threatened with another weapon in the last two years. Further 40.2 per cent had sustained an injury as a result of an assault by a member of the public while undertaking an arrest (ERS Market Research 2003). The threats police officers were receiving were far more serious than Pleasure Southquay officers. However, in terms of assault with over 50 per cent of the 'frontline' officers experiencing an assault in at least the last year this is a comparable level to the experience of the police in pursuing arrests. Another point of comparison is the British Crime Survey and the 'Protective Services Occupation' category, which was discussed earlier in this section (Upson 2004). This research from Pleasure Southquay shows that the officers there were experiencing threats of violence and assault well above the levels found in the BCS and the 'Protective Services Occupation' levels were well above the average for all workers.

At Armed Industries there was no NTE and there was also the additional 'controlling' mechanism of employment contracts. Threatening a security officer at Pleasure Southquay was at worst likely to lead to the sanction of removal from site and probably not even this. It is unlikely the officers will know who the culprit is and they may not visit the site again for several weeks. At Armed Industries, by contrast, the security officers were likely to know who they were or could soon find out. They were likely to see offenders every day and the offence could be punished with a wide range of sanctions that could even include termination of employment. As SO 14 told me during the interview,

SO 14

They know they're an employee and if you report them they know they could lose their job.

---

2   The methodology for this research was based upon visitors to the USDAW website completing a questionnaire online and as such this research may not be representative of all shop-workers.

Thus the 'controlling' mechanisms were much less at Pleasure Southquay, and, combined with the excesses of the NTE and their front-line role, led them into situations that put them at much greater risk of verbal abuse, threats of violence and assault.

Conclusion

This chapter has examined some of the many occupational hazards security officers face based upon the two research sites. The security officers at both sites had to confront the problem of serving at least two masters and the differing agendas they had and at Pleasure Southquay this was further expanded by the relationship with tenants, the police and the public. The chapter then went on to illustrate the isolation security officers faced both in terms of their actual job and in terms of their relationship with other staff and the public. It was also illustrated, however, that there was evidence at Pleasure Southquay of a positive relationship with the police in many aspects of their work. Finally the chapter considered the abuse experienced by security officers in terms of general verbal abuse, threats of violence and experience of assault. The findings from the research revealed that amongst all officers verbal abuse is a regular occupational hazard. When confronted with members of the general public fuelled by alcohol, threats of violence and assault are hazards too.

Chapter 9

'I'm a Security Guard Get Me Out of Here!' The Cultural Characteristics of Private Security Officers

Introduction

Police culture has been the subject of much research and debate because it has affected how police officers do police work. As a consequence problems have emerged in how and to whom they exercise discretion and the rights of citizens have been undermined (Reiner 2000a). Similarly it will be shown that the culture of security officers also affects the way they undertake their work. However, in the case of the two research sites the implications of their culture focused upon undermining what the security officers were supposed to do and ultimately their effectiveness. Before we embark upon examining the characteristics of security officer culture in greater depth, it would be useful to first briefly examine what is meant by culture.

Cultures exist at national, regional, organisational and occupational levels in varying degrees of intensity (Buchanan and Huczynski 2001; and Schein 1992). A security officer may exhibit characteristics of cultures from all these levels. They might be English, from Newcastle working as a security officer for B and Q, all of which have their own cultural traits. It is, however, the occupational culture that is of interest for this chapter and this must be distinguished from organisational culture, as the latter may encompass many different occupations with their own distinct cultures. Indeed security officers are usually contracted staff to organisations that may have their own cultures such as some companies like Coca Cola, Disney and McDonalds to name some (Buchanan and Huczynski 2001). Schein (1992, 12) has defined culture as,

> A pattern of shared basic assumptions that the group learned as it solved its problems of external adaptation and internal integration, that has worked well enough to be considered valid and, therefore, to be taught to new members as the correct way to perceive, think, and feel in relation to those problems.

It manifests itself in a wide variety of ways that include artefacts, ceremonials, courses, gestures, heroes, jokes, language, legends, mottoes, myths, norms, physical layout, rites, rituals, sagas, slogans, stories and symbols (Buchanan and Huczynski 2001). Schein (1992) argues culture can be distinguished at three levels. First there are artefacts, which are the visible organisational structures and processes when encountering a group such as the physical environment, language, technology, clothing, style, emotional display, rituals, ceremonies etc. Second there are espoused values, which are the strategies, goals and philosophies of a group, which includes such attitudes as what is right and wrong in certain situations. Finally there are basic underlying assumptions, which covers the unconscious beliefs, perceptions, thoughts and feelings of a group. It is also important to note in exploring occupational culture the factors that lead to the manifestations of culture, otherwise what has been identified might be nothing more than what individuals have brought to the occupation as a result of other structural processes. For instance a machismo attitude amongst a group of workers might be a general attitude those workers possess from their broader socialisation, rather than something the structural processes in an occupation has created. It would be therefore difficult to then argue that such a facet was distinguished as part of a specific occupational culture.

A number of writers have sought to explain the processes that influence culture. Skolnick emphasised the structural factors of danger and authority influencing culture and McBarnet in research published during the late 1970s and early 1980s also noted the link between structure and action (cited in Reiner 2000a, 85–88). More recently Chan (1997) has developed a model of how cultural values emerge in the police as a result of the relationship between the field and the habitus, which can also be applied to other occupations. Drawing on the work of Bourdieu she argues a significant influence on culture is the 'field', which is '…a social space of conflict and competition, where participants struggle to establish control over specific power and authority, and, in the course of the struggle, modify the structure of the field itself' (Chan 1996, 115). The field is influenced by factors such as the political context, social and economic status of the policed, government policies as well as legal structures. The field is negotiated by agents according to a 'habitus' or cultural knowledge, which is '…a system of "dispositions", which integrate past experience and enable individuals to cope with a diversity of unforeseen situations (Chan 1996, 115).' The habitus, Chan argues, is influenced by different types of cultural knowledge. These include *dictionary knowledge*, which is the categorisation of people and events by police; *directory knowledge*, which is the way police work is carried out; *axiomatic knowledge*, the mandate to undertake a particular form of policing; and *recipe knowledge*, the way things should or should not be done. Chan argues that the field is more important in changing, and therefore influencing, police culture than the habitus and should be the focus of reforms.

There has been very little research exploring the occupational culture of the broader security community (Wood 2004), but there has been significant research in the UK and in many other countries on police culture (Foster 2003). Common traits have been identified and generally it has provided a critical perspective on policing in practice. An understanding of police culture is important because it provides an essential basis for appreciating what police do in practice. As Reiner (2000a, 85) has argued, 'An understanding of how police officers see the social world and their role in it – 'cop culture' – is crucial to an analysis of what they do, and their broad political function.' Similarly this same premise applies to private security officers and their contribution to policing. Indeed a wide variety of questions arise such as to what extent security officer culture is similar to cop culture? If it's different, in what ways? How does that culture impact upon what they are formally suppose to do? This chapter will therefore seek to identify some of the characteristics of the culture of security officers based upon the empirical research conducted for this book, as well as other relevant research. In doing so it will seek to address some of these questions. Therefore before we embark upon an analysis of the occupational culture of security officers some of the key characteristics of police culture will be examined.

Police culture

Much of the research on police culture has identified common traits as well as sub-cultures. Foster (2003) argues it is important to consider *cultures* rather than *culture*. There are sub-cultures and differences between distinct types of police officers. For instance there are variations between 'street cops and management cops', between detectives and uniformed officers and even between different police forces to name a few. It is therefore important to remember that police culture is not monolithic, there are differences and sub-cultures that exist too. Bearing these caveats in mind, however, Reiner (2000a) has sought to identify the core characteristics of police culture.

First Reiner identifies Mission – Action – Cynicism – Pessimism. This is one of the core characteristics of police culture, a belief that policing is a way of life with a worthwhile end. Policing is also seen as entertaining, challenging and a skilful occupation and these action oriented and hedonistic aspects mask the frequently mundane, unsophisticated and boring nature of the reality of policing. Linked to this is a pessimism that they are the 'thin blue line' preventing society from descending into barbarism. The extent to which this sense of mission is engrained in police officers varies and Reiner distinguishes 'uniform carriers' from 'new centurions', where the latter shirk as much work as possible (Reiner 1978). Reiner (2000a, 90) writes,

The core of the police outlook is this subtle and complex intermingling of the themes of mission, hedonistic love of action and pessimistic cynicism. Each feeds off and reinforces the others, even though they may appear superficially contradictory.

The second characteristic identified is *Suspicion*. The nature of the work of police officers breeds an attitude of suspicion based upon the need to look for potential dangers and solutions to crimes and problems. There have been some concerns that this leads to police stereotyping of potential offenders with a potential risk of overrepresentation of certain groups in the criminal justice system and consequent deviancy amplification. *Isolation/Solidarity* is the third trait where Reiner draws upon a wide range of research to illustrate the strong internal solidarity of police officers combined with the often social isolation. Some police officers find it difficult mixing with civilians in ordinary social life because of factors such as the shift work and the hostility to the police exhibited by some citizens.

The fourth trait is Police Conservatism, where evidence suggests that police officers tend to be both politically and morally conservative. Fifth Reiner identifies Machismo. Police culture is distinguished, he argues, by an old fashioned machismo based upon a degree of sexism, contempt of sexual 'deviance' combined with frequent exaggeration and preoccupation with sexual prowess. Racial Prejudice is the sixth trait identified where there is a great deal of evidence, particularly from America, of the racial prejudice of some police officers. Finally Reiner identifies Pragmatism illustrating the pragmatist aspect to policing where they are focused upon achieving their goals with as little fuss and paperwork as possible. As a consequence there is reluctance to accept innovation, experimentation or research.

It is important to state again that police culture is not monolithic and there are differences. However, police officers all face the same structural processes and are therefore likely to exhibit similar cultural traits. Now that the core characteristics of police culture have been considered the culture of private security staff will be considered.

Security officers' culture

Chapter 1 illustrated the limited number of empirical studies of private security officers using interviews and observational techniques. As such it is not surprising to also find there have been even fewer attempts to explore the culture of security officers. Recently door supervisors have been the subject of much more attention and much has been revealed about their occupational culture (Hobbs et al. 2000; 2003; and Winlow 2001). The central occupational characteristics include a pre-occupation with the body (bodybuilding), the techniques of using the body (fighting techniques) and discourses concerning violence (Monaghan 2002). However, door supervisors because of the significant structural differences in terms of their role, where they operate and the challenges they face cannot be regarded as simply security officers who work in pubs or nightclubs. Thus this research is limited in seeking to understand security officer culture.

One study that has sought to understand security officer culture was that of Rigakos (2002) and his study of an a-typical security company operating in Toronto, Canada. Rigakos identified parallels with police culture but with some significant differences. Some of the characteristics he found included a culture of 'resistance from within: the art of ghosting', where security officers seek out methods to subvert the controlling culture and systems of the organisation. Second he identified a 'crime fighting and wannabe' culture where most officers wanted to become public police and revelled in their discussions of 'pinches' or involvement in crime fighting. Third there was a culture of 'safety in numbers', which was dealing with incidents with as many officers as possible to maintain safety. Finally he identified a culture of 'fear' where officers were seriously concerned about the next threat to themselves. Given the unique characteristics of the security company studied by Rigakos it would be difficult to seek out a generalisation of this culture in Canadian security officers, let alone across the Atlantic for UK officers. This illustrates one of many caveats that need to be identified when considering the culture of private security officers.

First it is important to remember that the British private security industry is highly fragmented (George and Button 2000). There are a large number of private security companies operating in different environments to different standards. Security officers are found in armoured cars protecting cash, in shopping centres and shops where they apprehend shop-lifters, at airports searching passengers and their baggage, to officers often working alone guarding factories at night. There is a significant range in the types of duties undertaken by security officers, the types of personnel operating in these environments and the challenges they face. As such the cultures are likely to vary. Thus just as with the police where there are many more common standards it is difficult to generalise, it is even more so with private security.

Secondly this chapter will draw upon the two research sites: a retail/ leisure facility and a manufacturer of defence equipment. These may not be representative of these sub-sectors and secondly there are many other types of environment security operate within which may have different cultures. Despite the differences between the two case study sites, however, there were common traits and the limited empirical research on security officers does suggest a degree of commonality in some of these traits elsewhere. Therefore this chapter will proceed by first examining some of the core characteristics and then move on to examine some of the traits that distinguish different orientations.

'I'm a security guard get me out of here!'

Rigakos (2002) identified a 'wannabe' culture at Inteligarde based upon security staff wanting to become police officers. There was no evidence of this as a major trait at the two case study sites, but there was evidence of a 'wannabe' culture based upon 'wannabe somewhere else or doing anything else'. The research found evidence of a low commitment and orientation to the job, particularly at Armed Industries with evidence of officers falling into this type of work rather than seeking it out as a profession. Second there was also evidence of security officers actively seeking alternative employment. Indeed research by Wakefield (2003) illustrated a high labour turnover amongst security officers and in one of her research sites a reliance upon travellers from South Africa, seeking relatively easy employment, enabling long hours to earn money for further travelling. As one officer told Wakefield (2003, 145), 'Most of them look at it short-term. They're here for the money.' Michael (2002) found evidence of security staff with employment histories based upon a succession of low paid, low skilled jobs. She also found that after one year, of all the guards she interviewed, only 32 per cent remained employed with the company.[1]

---

1   Such is the rate of labour turnover with some security firms their eagerness to recruit new officers extends to conducting interviews in unusual locations. Adu-Boakye, for his

There was evidence of high labour turnover at both of the research sites. As security officers can frequently be moved between different assignments while working for the same employer, it was important to ask them more than how long they had worked as a security officer. Therefore three questions were asked. How long had they worked as a security officer, for the current employer, and for the site? Pleasure Southquay had only been open just under a year and therefore for this question the maximum would be 10 months.

The length of employment as a security officer at both case study sites ranged from a week to 39 years. At Pleasure Southquay the mean length of service was 5 years, although this was distorted by a small number of officers with long careers in the industry and the median brought this figure down to 2 years. There was a similar distortion at Armed Industries because of a few with very long service with a mean of 6 years 9 months and a median of 4 years. At both research sites, however, there was a similar profile of a small group of officers with long experience in the industry and a large group with less than a year's experience as security officers.

The length of time with current employer provided only limited data because at Pleasure Southquay the contract was a new site that had only been operating for the last 10 months and the vast majority of staff had been recruited for that contract. Here the average length of employment was 10 months (mean and median) with a range from 1 week to 3 years. At Armed Industries, where the contractor had recently changed, but most of the security staff had transferred from the previous contractor the mean and median was 3 months with a range from 2 weeks to 3 months.

At Pleasure Southquay because of the length of time the site had been open it was not surprising to find the mean length of employment was 8 months and the median 10 months. At Armed Industries where the site could trace a security team back several decades the range was from 2 weeks to 25 years. The mean length of service was 4 years 6 months and the median 2 years. As with length of service as a security officer there was a small cohort with lengthy service at the site and a larger cohort with less than a year's service.

These figures illustrate the lack of loyalty amongst security officers towards their company and a greater loyalty to their site. Indeed the contract manager at Armed Industries told me that many officers would change jobs for 10p an hour more. At Armed Industries amongst the security officers there was also generally a low commitment to the job, company and or site they worked on. Many of the officers told me this was the only job they could get. Others saw security as a relatively easy way to secure an income without much effort. It was seen as a job where you could come in and sit in a box listening to the radio and reading the paper and as such a relatively easy way to make money. Indeed when you consider the history of security at Armed Industries it originally was a place of sanctuary for those who could no longer work on the shop-floor of the factory. As Michael (2002, 131) noted in her study of private security officers, 'Security work did not appear to be a form of employment that the majority of guards had intended to go into, nor did they appear

---

covert study, was interviewed in a noisy railway station café! (Adu-Boakye 2002).

to be very attractive recruits for other employers.' Some of the comments by security officers at Armed Industries support Michael's findings and illustrate their rationale for entering employment at Armed Industries.

SO 2

It was near where I live and I wanted to work close to home. I didn't realise how long the hours would be. I also like meeting people and in this job you can meet a lot.

SO 5

I was made redundant and this was the only job I could get.

SO 7

I am semi-retired and wanted a stress free environment so I can enjoy the pace of life. I was a production manager before.

SO 8

I was made redundant from AI with a £100 per week pension. With the money from this it makes me better off.

SO 9

I've got a pension, but I work to help pay for my daughter to go through university.

SO 14

Originally I owned three petrol garages but went bust. Lost everything including my wife. Got a job for an electricity company selling door to door. Hated this job. One day after a heated discussion with one customer decided I had had enough. Walked off the job and told my partner I was quitting. Sat in the car looking at the jobs pages and saw Reliance advertising and the advert said call now for an interview. I called and demanded an interview that day. Went down there and got the job. I like security because they are good for people of my age and because I lost my pension in the bankruptcy I can still work after 65 to supplement my income.

SO 18

I was area manager at 45 and no longer required and got into this by default as a second career. For a lot of the older security officers this is a second career and it is one of the only jobs they can get. I didn't have any examinations behind me so it was all I could get.

SO 20

At 57 I couldn't get a job anywhere else so this is the best job I could get.

The lower level of commitment to their job was also revealed in the structured interviews by comparing the profile of reasons for entering current employment. At Pleasure Southquay there was a much more positive profile with 'enjoyment of work', 'job security', 'good working opportunities', 'work is stimulating' all securing over 50 per cent and 'job pays well' and 'promotion opportunities' nearly 50 per cent. This would seem to contradict their larger desire to leave, which will shortly be illustrated.

Table 9.1   Reasons for entering current employment (%)

	Armed Industries	Pleasure Southquay
Job pays well	0	48
Promotion opportunities	10	48
I was unemployed and it was the best job I could find	40	7
I could not get employment as a police officer	0	0
This is a second job to secure extra money	10	0
Good working opportunities	10	58
Work is stimulating	0	52
For the prestige of the job	5	38
I enjoy doing this type of work	30	76
Job security	25	62
Other include: chance to meet and help public, less stressful work, wanted to get into security work, security provides different challenges everyday, close to home, need flexible job to fit in with studies, and easy job to supplement pension	35	34
N = 49		

Looking at the above profile one would expect a much higher number of officers actively seeking employment elsewhere at Armed Industries. As the figures in table 9.2 illustrate, however, it was the reverse. Of those that were seeking alternative employment most were not generally looking for security work with 93 per cent and 100 per cent stating they weren't at Pleasure Southquay and Armed Industries respectively. When any other occupation was considered the figures fell to 55 per cent and 80 per cent respectively. At Armed Industries this was slightly different as there were nearly three quarters of the staff over 51 and many saw it as their job through to retirement. They had 'fallen' into this work as it was one of the few jobs a person in their age group with no or limited skills could get. In short there was no way out for many of them. Indeed of those 51 years of age or over at Armed

Industries none were actively seeking alternative employment. Of the two officers in the 21–30 category both were seeking alternative employment, of the three in the 31–40 category two were seeking employment and the one officer in the 41–50 category also answered yes to this question. Those officers at Armed Industries who were below the age of 50 were very keen to move on to alternative employment. As SO 8 told me,

SO 8

Young people on this site last less than 5 minutes. Would you want to be stuck in a box on a Saturday night when your friends are down the pub?

The trait of a 'wannabe' culture would seem to weaken the overall culture of security officers. As Schein (1992, 15) argues '…a group having either a great deal of turnover of members and leaders or a history without challenging events may well lack any shared assumptions.' However, as we will see in the following section there were a variety of other traits manifesting themselves as the security officer culture, resulting from dominant groups at the two research sites as well as other structural factors influencing these traits.

Table 9.2   The number of security officers actively seeking alternative employment (%)

	Pleasure Southquay		Armed Industries	
	Yes	No	Yes	No
Are you actively seeking employment as a security officer in another organisation?	7	93	0	100
Are you actively seeking employment in another type of occupation?	45	55	25	75
N = 49				

Challenging working conditions

The main reason for the 'wannabe somewhere else or doing anything else culture' was the next trait of challenging working conditions. Common to both research sites for the security officers were consistent discussion of their working conditions. This manifested itself largely in terms of moans about the negative aspects of their conditions, but also a degree of bravado in being able to deal with them. These included expressions of dissatisfaction and bravado concerning the long working hours, lack of breaks, poor facilities, the extremes of weather as well as their pay. Such bravado has been found in other occupations such as meat cutters in relation to the cold they have to endure (Meara 1974), slaughtermen vis-à-vis the dirt they suffer (Acroyd and Crowdy 1990) and high steel ironworkers in relation to heights (Haas 1977).

The general poor working conditions of security officers have been well documented in the past (Alfredsson et al. 1991; Cumming and Winyard 1984; Williams, George and MacLenan 1984; Button and George 1994; 1998; and Home Affairs Committee 1995). The most significant issue relates to the long working hours of security officers. It is a frequent criticism of the private security industry in the UK of 12 hour shifts and frequently 60 hour weeks. Indeed the Chief Executive of the BSIA in a recent article stated, 'Average hours worked in the manned guarding industry are still stubbornly 60 hours per week' (Dickinson 2003, 3).

In both research sites the average number of hours did not exceed this, but there was a significant difference between the two sites. At Pleasure Southquay the mean number of hours worked per week was 45 hours (as was the median) with a range from 40 to 52 hours. By contrast at Armed Industries the mean number of hours worked per week was 55 hours (the median was 56) and the range was from 36 to 84 hours per week. This compares to an average working week for males in England and Wales of 42.2 hours (Equal Opportunities Commission 2003).

These average hours, however, mask even harsher examples of the long hours worked by some security officers. While undertaking observation at Pleasure Southquay one Friday night I was introduced to the 'Chuckle Brothers'. They were 'floaters' (they did not have a permanent site or desire for one) who were notorious for working 100 hour weeks. One of the brothers told me that Friday night he was working at Pleasure Southquay from 19.00 until 05.00, then being taken to another site to work 07.00 to 19.00 and would then be back at Pleasure Southquay for another night shift. He told me it was not uncommon for him to start work on a Friday night at 19.00 and complete at 07.00 Monday morning. The officer was very keen to tell me as well as the other officers he was doing this and clearly there was a degree of bravado in his tone stating such long hours were not a problem for him.

At Armed Industries while undertaking observation there was a crisis in recruitment and as a consequence staff were put under great pressure to cover any gaps due to sickness, holidays etc. As a consequence some security officers were working almost constant 12 hour shifts. One officer with a degree of bravado and disgust told me he was in the middle of doing 17, 12 hour shifts in a row. Another illustration of the culture of long hours was the Security Manager at Armed Industries describing one security officer who worked only three 12 hour shifts per week as 'part-time'.

The impact of long hours leads to a culture of tiredness and fear of falling asleep on duty. Research by Cumming and Winyard (1984, 8) found one officer typical of many who stated 'I'm like a zombie most of the time.' Indeed while undertaking observation at Armed Industries SO 2 related to me how tired she felt and could fall asleep. She would get up at 4.30am to be on duty for 6am and by lunchtime would be frequently fighting not to fall asleep (and to do so risks automatic removal from site and possible loss of employment). The Security Manager related to me one example on Gate 7 on a Saturday afternoon. The officer had already worked 84 hours that week and fell asleep. The facilities manager happened to be walking by and caught him. The officer was removed from site as a consequence.

Linked to the long hours are frequently poor conditions. At Armed Industries because of the recruitment crisis while on site it was difficult for some security officers to get breaks. Indeed one female security officer complained to me she would sometimes have to beg to get a relief so she could go to the toilet. Some of the boxes the officers worked in had variable facilities. Some had microwaves, small cookers where as others had just a kettle and a radio. One officer illustrated the challenges very well,

SO 5

It's not hard work its just long hours. You can be on a gate for 12 hours without a tea break. You can't go to the toilet and if you really have to you have to lock the gate and then when you get back you have Armed Industries staff moaning at you.

At Pleasure Southquay the officers had access to a canteen open to all staff, but their bone of contention related to the quality of their uniforms. As they had been specially made for Pleasure Southquay, with their logo on, the officers had to wear them. Unfortunately in the extreme weather conditions of winter when there was rain, snow and extremely cold conditions they were not effective enough. The overcoats were prone to leak when it rained and were not adequate in the sub-zero temperatures of winter. Indeed I found myself absolutely freezing at night in the wind with substantial layers of clothing, when the officers had only shirt, jumper and overcoat. Not surprisingly the officers had sought to get round this by adding their own additions to the uniform to keep warm.[2]

There were also significant moans about the pay (although this is common to probably every job!). When asked to name two things that their employers could do to improve their level of satisfaction at Armed Industries every officer included an issue relating to pay as one of the answers. This was also a major issue amongst Pleasure Southquay officers, although not every officer had this in their two issues. In Wakefield's (2003) study she also found evidence of dissatisfaction amongst the officers of their working conditions with frequent moans about their pay.

The main trade union representing security officers, the GMB, has for many years campaigned for better pay and conditions for security officers. However, the strength of the trade union in this sector has been weak, with less than 30,000 members of what could be a sector employing 130,000 plus, and it has had limited impact on conditions in the industry. This low membership is the result of hostility to trade unions from some companies combined with generally high labour turnover that makes recruitment difficult (Button 1993). Recently, however, a new trade union called the Federation of Employed Door Supervisors and Security (FEDS) has been

---

2   On a lighter note, however, on one of the nights the extreme cold outside did encourage some of CSOs to be very open in their interviews to extend their time inside in the warm.

formed. Although this is primarily focused on door supervisors they are recruiting security guards. Their main rationale is the introduction of regulation and the need to create a protective body for security staff who could lose their licence (FEDS 2005). With regulation and their more conservative orientation (non-TUC affiliated) there could be more opportunities for growth than the GMB and this could represent the beginning of an organisation capable of providing a significant voice and influence for rank and file security staff.

Solidarity, isolation and inferiority

One of the defining characteristics of police and many other uniformed services that confront danger and unpredictability in their work is a degree of isolation and solidarity. The uniform itself engenders a degree of isolation and solidarity as South (1985, 53) found when conducting covert research as a uniformed security officer during duties and travelling to work, arguing, 'I began to feel how the very nature of the uniform can be incredibly powerful mechanism for inducing solidarity.' Officers operating in such dangerous and unpredictable environments soon realise that to deal with such incidents effectively they need to be part of a team rather than individuals. As Foster (2003, 203) has argued, '…police recruits soon learn that being accepted by the group has primacy over their individual needs.' As was illustrated in Chapters 6, 7 and 8 the frontline security officers at Pleasure Southquay regularly confronted dangerous incidents. As a consequence their solidarity was much stronger than Armed Industries' officers. Such solidarity did exist there, although this was more defined in terms of the alienation from the other workers on site. Similarly this also applied to officers at Pleasure Southquay vis-à-vis fellow workers and the public, particularly at night. Indeed there is much research illustrating how alienation from the public or fellow workers, such as amongst slaughtermen (Ackroyd and Crowdy 1990) and meat cutters (Meara 1974), and because of the danger amongst dockers (Turnbull 1992), firemen (Smith 1972 and 1992), miners (Fitzpatrick 1980) steel workers (Blyton and Bacon 1997), and high steel ironworkers (Haas 1977); and both danger and isolation amongst police officers (Reiner 2000a); leads to a strong sense of solidarity amongst these groups.

The degree of solidarity exhibited was different at the two research sites. At Pleasure Southquay there was a much greater risk of danger, but also officers could much easily congregate together and discuss matters during working hours. There was also a strong degree of camaraderie as well as a culture of socialising and drinking together. Indeed I was invited on a number of occasions to go out with the officers for a drink and did so on one occasion. Further, on a Friday or Saturday night if officers arrived at Pleasure Southquay off duty to go drinking there was always a degree of jealously exhibited and excessive interest in what they got up to, especially vis-à-vis the opposite sex. This solidarity also led to a strong culture of looking after one another particularly in the face of danger at night. There were frequent expressions of the goal to look after one another first, if events 'kicked off'. CSO 11, who was also a team leader, consistently told me while showing me round his main concern was his team and ensuring they were not hurt. This was a feeling echoed by many of the other 'frontline' officers.

At Armed Industries the solidarity was not as strong and there was little social interaction after hours. This probably reflected the higher age profile and the organisation of the site. The officers had few opportunities to congregate together and discuss matters and would normally start the shift in the post rather than congregating in the main gatehouse. Therefore it was difficult for them to meet as a group, although they did make regular use of the internal telephone systems to talk to one another. Added to this officers worked much longer hours and were often too tired to go out socialising with colleagues after work. There were also less dangerous incidents faced by the officers, although there were probably greater feelings of isolation that increased their sense of solidarity in the face of this.

Chapter 8 illustrated in depth the isolation of security staff at both sites. In the case of Pleasure Southquay the sense of isolation related to fellow workers at the complex and the public they were involved in policing, particularly at night. At Armed Industries as the public were rarely there, it related to fellow employees at the site. The observation also brought further evidence of the concern with their relationship with those they policed and more importantly their status. Some of the security officers were keen to illustrate the dangerous and complex work they did and to point to any evidence demonstrating their status in the local hierarchy. One team leader explained to me how they were paid more than the cleaners and that at night, when there were only security and cleaning staff on site the cleaners generally looked to security for leadership. This hierarchy was further re-enforced by the security officers taking great pleasure in referring to cleaners consistently to their radio call sign of 'Charlies'. Indeed many were pre-occupied with their uniforms, which they felt did not reflect their status. One security officer told me when asked what could be done to improve his job,

CSO 12

Give us a proper uniform. More official looking as we resemble 'bus drivers'. (Company x) uniforms are blue and white and look much more professional.

At Armed Industries a number of security officers also related to me in disgust during my observations that they were being paid less than the cleaners. One security officer told me when we were discussing his pay,

SO 6

Give all security officers a pay rise. We get £5.80 per hour, the cleaners get at least £6 per hour and we're doing a much more valuable job.

Clearly the suggestion was that the cleaners were lower in the hierarchy in the factory and that security officers should be paid more. Thus the status and degree of danger faced by security officers are significant structural influences upon their occupational culture.

Machismo

Masculinity is another important aspect of the culture. As was illustrated in Chapter 4 in both sites men were dominant. This also reflects the wider private security industry where they predominate (Flynn 1997). It is not surprising to therefore find in a male dominated, uniform orientated culture the importance of masculinity. This was distinguished on the one hand by views that female security officers were not as effective and secondly a pre-occupation with sexual prowess. Indeed South's (1985, 69) PhD concluded, '…the prejudices of white dominated security mentality with its insularity and xenophobic conservatism, conspire to condition working life in security.' Such prejudice was also found during the research for this book.

It's a man's world

At Armed Industries the contract manager had serious doubts whether women should be on the night shift. In an interview he explained to me,

> I was always of the opinion there was a divide and it was the policy of Armed Industries police. We've only had women working on this site for the last 18 months and it was recruitment driven. **I have been surprised by the female officers and how capable they are. As regards ladies being on night shift I had concerns – I've still got those concerns.** I recently had a female officer who asked to go on nights and I pointed out all the pitfalls to her like being in dark places on her own at 2 o'clock in the morning. I gave her scenarios like that. After a fortnight she was asking me to take her back on days. So I think for safety reasons for ladies on their own in a factory environment – where it is predominantly male – I think that patrolling at night should not be a ladies function. Personally I don't think they should be doing that.

These views were reflected to me by a number of other officers at Armed Industries that patrolling a dark factory at night was not a job for a woman. When I presented this evidence to the Security Controller, who was a woman, she had a very different response.

> MB
>
> Is there a chauvinistic culture here, some security officers have said this is not job for a woman?
>
> Security Controller Armed Industries
>
> Rubbish! I am quite pleased to be unique because I am in the industry and there aren't that many women security managers out there, particularly in big companies like this. M will be able to tell you about this because until yesterday he had a lady on shift. We

was always wary about a woman working a night shift. These days they can. Horses for courses, women won't want it, the problems of the dark and being chatted up on the posts. Ask this question to M as well, because if you are the right person male or female – because there are some guys who are just as daft, when I was in the airforce there were those who were scared of the dark – so horses for courses. With the company it's the same, out there on the shop-floor there are quite a few girl engineers and there are one or two senior managers, but its what came up on the AGM again, when are we getting a lady on the board? And that's across the industry, not just aero whatever, but across the world for lady representatives. So yes there's a few old fashioned thoughts out there.

'Moving to watch girls go by

At Pleasure Southquay I detected no evidence over concerns over the ability of women to work in the often quite dangerous environment. Here masculinity was defined by the way women were perceived who came to visit Pleasure Southquay, particularly the bars and clubs at night. There were frequent discourses amongst the men about the attractiveness of women, what they would like to do with them and what they had done with the opposite sex (which were also sometimes replicated by some of the female officers towards men). This is not untypical in young male working class culture (Willis 1977) and empirical research on door supervisors has also illustrated the sexist attitudes of some door supervisors in the NTE (Monaghan 2002; and Winlow 2001). Indeed there is evidence from other male dominated occupations of boasting about sexual prowess amongst car workers (Gottfried and Graham 1993), of quasi-sexual and explicitly sexual assaults amongst slaughtermen (Ackroyd and Crowdy 1990), of general sexual horseplay amongst men (Hearn 1985), and of sexual misbehaviour at work (Ackroyd and Thompson 1999).

On the night shift at Pleasure Southquay with many bars and nightclubs there were usually large numbers of women (and men) wandering towards them dressed in outfits that tend to arouse the interest of the opposite sex. Many of the security officers would move to strategic points at particular times where viewing of this could be maximised. While standing at these points both male and female officers would join in the discussions of the 'talent', 'eye candy' or 'totty' that walked by. One security officer told me the job gave him 'ball ache', while another told me 'you should see the talent here in the Summer'. He then went on to tell me with delight how some women when drunk will expose themselves to the security staff. The discussions of the talent would usually take place in the presence of female officers and they would also frequently join in. In one exchange, a male CSOs in presence of female CSO said 'nice arse', while watching two women and a man walk by, to which the female CSO retorted to me, 'he's talking about the bloke'. On another occasion a CSO (one of the 'Chuckle brothers' discussed earlier) told me while discussing some attractive women walking by that he liked 'big women', he went on, 'I like something to grab hold off'. This led to jibes for the rest of the night every time a 'large' woman walked by, as to whether she was big enough.

Given the bars and nightclubs at Pleasure Southquay this trait might be considered to be unique to this site. However, with even less opportunities for such sexual surveillance and discourse at Armed Industries this was also a trait. For instance while in the gatehouse with one officer he became excited as an afternoon shift was about to begin, which meant a group of women would be walking by his post. This almost seemed to be the main excitement for the shift for him. In the gatehouses there was also evidence of some of the reading habits of security officers with lots of past copies of the 'The Sport', 'Sunday Sport' and various 'girlie' magazines. Indeed the Security Manager told me of an old slaughter-house that was used as a store room (no longer in operation). The security officers were convinced it was haunted and would use dodges to avoid patrolling, apart from the third floor, where they were quite happy to patrol because they could watch the prostitutes at work from the windows. Thus perhaps a male dominated culture, drawing largely from the working class with a function to undertake surveillance as part of the normal job provide the structural factors to create this cultural trait.

Suspicious and risk focused minds

One of the defining differences of corporate actors is their focus on risk and minimalisation of potential loss. The police tend to be 'suspicious' but their focus is suspects who have or may commit an offence, for security officers this suspicion is much wider (Johnston and Shearing 2003). The very nature of security work requires officers to be suspicious and to look out for risks. They need to look for potential risks such as unusual occurrences, objects and persons and address them where necessary. As a consequence it is not surprising to find a similar trait to police officers of a culture of suspicion, but which encompasses a focus on a wider range of risks (Wood 2004). Indeed security officers are encouraged to look for risks and to be suspicious in their training and in their handbooks. At Armed Industries the employee's handbook contained various examples of advice that encouraged this,

> During the patrol stop, look and listen for any unusual sights, sounds or smells.
> …you must be alert for any risks.
> If you know or suspect there are intruders on the premises you must…
> (it) is important to recognise the kind of suspicious object, which might be a bomb.
> If you have any suspicion that a package may contain an explosive device, you should…

During observations at Pleasure Southquay officers would frequently stop people leaving clubs and pubs with bottles and ask them to drink up and/or handover the bottle. They were clearly profiling the potential risk of drunken revellers carrying potentially dangerous objects/weapons. Similarly groups engaged in mischievous behaviour would be observed with a view to intervening to prevent dangerous incidents. Perhaps the greatest illustration of the focus upon risk and reducing loss were the patrols undertaken by officers at both sites. These would include not only looking for any suspicious activities, but also ensuring doors were locked and lights and other electrical equipment were switched off. Indeed Shearing and Stenning (1982b) have noted the focus of security on potential risks where in a factory officers placed 'snowflakes' (or pieces of paper) on equipment/space where potential losses/ risks existed.

Wakefield (2003) has also identified the profiling techniques used by officers and how they would take interest in those who were considered 'dodgy'. Similarly McCahill (2002) found evidence of profiling and a greater likelihood of certain groups to be kept under surveillance and banned from the shopping centres. During the observations further evidence was noted of this trait. I noticed very early on in my research at Pleasure Southquay the trait of suspicion amongst many of the security officers. My presence on the first few night shifts did arouse the suspicions of some security officers (as was mentioned in Chapter 2).

At Pleasure Southquay because of the location of the site next to a deprived area in the city there were problems with certain groups of youths coming on site and causing trouble. As a consequence the CCTV operator and security officers would regularly observe youths who were known to them and follow them around removing them as soon as they caused any problems. On another occasion a vagrant wandered on to site and the security officer spent the next 30 minutes following him. He eventually left site, but the security officer was concerned he may be looking for a warm place to sleep. Many of the security officers would also regularly follow groups of young men – who were usually drunk – to ensure they did not cause any problems and intervene if possible if any trouble occurred.

At Armed Industries where random searches took place the security officers were naturally suspicious as they could pick whom they wanted to search. Naturally the security officers were aroused to search those vehicles they felt suspicious about. Some officers did not take this task seriously – as was illustrated in Chapter 7. Nevertheless many of the officers were drawn to stop certain vehicles that fitted their criteria of potentially a risk of theft. Indeed there seemed to be a pre-occupation with searching other contractors on site and those not fitting the normal profile such as a foreigner. Indeed one security officer told me he regularly stopped a German leaving site. On another occasion while sat with a security officer in his gatehouse he started actively watching a teacher and his school children who were on site because he thought he was likely to use a camera, which was prohibited unless prior permission had been given. Thus the role of security officers in their place of operation combined with the organisational requirements influence culture of security officers.

Cultures distinguished

Research from the 1960s onwards has recognised in relation to police culture that different sub-cultures exist and as a consequence different styles and cultures can be distinguished within the police (Reiner 2000a). Reiner (1978) identified the 'bobby', 'uniform carrier', 'new centurion', and 'professional' models. Other academics have sought to create different models based upon cultural orientations (see Broderick 1973; Brown 1981; Foster 2003; Shearing 1981; and Walsh 1977). As stated earlier the differences that exist between security staff mean that there are likely to be even more models that apply to security staff.

There is much less research to draw upon identifying models of private security officers, but there have been some attempts. Michael (2002) identified four types of security officer largely based upon their employment orientation. First she distinguished 'the casual', usually a younger security officer undertaking security on a temporary basis. Second there was the 'time server' generally an older employee using security work because it tends to be non-ageist in recruitment. 'The uniformed pensioner' was the third category she defined, who is also an older security officer from the armed forces using security work to supplement a pension. Finally there was the 'police wannabe' who was generally a young security officer orientated towards crime control who intended to join the police. These models were all recognisable in the two research sites. The first three types are differentiated by their employment status/orientation and it could be argued share some of the characteristics of 'watchmen' orientated end of the continuum, which will shortly be explained, whereas the latter fits the 'parapolicing' orientation.

Another attempt at distinguishing security officers does provide an interesting basis to explore some of the differences between security staff. McLeod (2002) distinguished three types of security officer. The first model he called 'nightwatchman' or 'warm bodies'. These were low skilled, low status security officers – who can't get some of the better paid jobs in society – undertaking basic security functions. They were 'young men on their way up, old men on the way down.' The second model he called 'low profile' or 'guards with blazers'. These officers were found in more prominent locations where interaction with the public was required. The officers are more presentable, have more extensive security functions but still they see the job as transitory. They are also more oriented towards observing and reporting incidents. The third model he defines as 'parapolicing' or 'private law enforcement'. These were characterised by high profile, well trained professional security staff prepared to engage in dangerous incidents and they were closer in orientation towards the police.

Even though these models were based upon Canadian security officers they do provide the basis for a continuum to distinguish British security officer cultures. There are also parallels in this continuum between Reiner's (1978) 'new centurions' and 'uniform carriers'. At one extreme of the continuum is the 'old watchmen' orientation. These officers have little commitment to their role, see their role to observe and report, seek to avoid confrontations and also have little confidence in the quality or importance of their work. At the other extreme is the 'parapolice' orientation where there is greater commitment, a preoccupation with 'real work', and a willingness to engage in dangerous situations. These are two extremes of orientation and although Armed Industries could be seen as representing the 'watchmen' and Pleasure Southquay the 'parapolice' orientations, there were exceptions within these groups of officers. The aim is to draw out the extremes of the continuum to distinguish the different models. Clearly there are also many that are likely to fall in-between.

The 'watchman' orientation

A significant trait of the 'watchman' orientation is a desire to avoid conflict and activities that might put them in situations of danger. This trait was very strong amongst most of the security officers at Armed Industries, although there were some officers at Pleasure Southquay who could also be placed more towards this end of the continuum. There was a strong sense amongst these security officers of 'I don't get paid enough to deal with that' or 'we're not policemen'. Some of the extracts from interviews at both case study sites illustrate this trait.

CSO 16

We are not trained enough to have special powers. We are there for prevention and deterrence not to be police officers.

CSO 29

I see myself as more a CSO than security. I am not really cut out for the security role upstairs. They all seem to be carrying 6 cell batteries and want to get stuck in. I would hate that.

SO 8

We're not police officers we're security officers. There are a lot of differences.

SO 11

We're out on our own and if you come up against a burglar all we can do is phone the police, so having weapons would be useful. But we are not police officers.

SO 20

Its better in the hands of the police than security. It takes special training to use powers. The legal system is complex and you don't want to get tangled up in that.

In Chapter 6 the extent of use of the legal tools relating to arrest and use of force were examined in great depth. These illustrated the much lower use of these tools at Armed Industries vis-à-vis Pleasure Southquay. Clearly the very different demands of the two case study sites explained this. However, despite an organisational policy to avoid security officers becoming embroiled in confrontations this was still happening at Pleasure Southquay.

Linked to their desire to avoid situations of conflict was also a belief amongst some of their ineffectiveness and that they make little difference. This is the antithesis of the 'mission' aspect of police culture where officers are the 'thin blue line' between chaos and order where instead they see themselves as useless pawns having little impact upon the overall order. The following exchange with one security officer while walking past her gate illustrated this well,

SO 2

'So what do you think of it? (the security at Armed Industries)'

MB

'It's ok.'

SO 2

'You know it's a sham, yes you do, I can tell you're going red, an expert like you must know it's a sham.'

Others were embarrassed by their standards and very willing to denigrate any aspect of their abilities.

The 'parapolice' orientation

At the other end of the continuum is the 'parapolice' orientation. This has strong similarities to the trait in police culture Reiner (2000a) identified as a sense of mission, action, cynicism and pessimism. The security officers see themselves in this model as the 'thin blue line' between chaos and order. The officers are pre-occupied with the 'real work' that is often more dangerous and involves the use of legal tools, even if in reality it represents a small part of their overall activities. They are also more orientated towards developing their professionalism. As one security officer told me about this 'new breed' of officer emerging.

CSO 11

...Everyone's view of security is an old bloke. There is a new breed out there and some give them a uniform and they become power crazed. If you are gonna do it you have got to do it well. Some time your arse is in the grass and you need training to do it. If you train them time after time they eventually take it in.

During my observation some of the officers at Pleasure Southquay were eager to recount to me accounts of arrests they had undertaken and drunken fights they had broken up. Indeed talking to some of the security officers one was left with the impression that they were constantly engaged in such activities, when in reality there were usually a handful of incidents on a Friday or Saturday night. Banton (1964) was one of the first to illustrate that despite the glamorous image and the discourse of police officers they generally undertook mundane and boring tasks. At Pleasure Southquay when the extent of incidents actually occurring were illustrated this also demonstrated this trait. As Chapter 6 elucidated over half Pleasure Southquay officers had never arrested a person and even 45 per cent of the 'front-line' officers had not. Indeed I secured three reports to the Board for October, November and December 2001 and these reported 12, 10 and 13 incidents of theft, 35 for one quarter of the year.[3] Thus a fair figure would seem to be that there were around 3 to 4 incidents of theft per week at Pleasure Southquay identified. Therefore given there were four shifts a 'rough' figure would be that each shift had one arrest incident relating to theft per week.

This was not as pronounced when it came to the use of force with over half Pleasure Southquay officers claiming to have to use force at least on a monthly basis. However, the impression one was left with when talking with the officers was that they were using it almost every night. In reality a 'normal' day or 'night' shift would involve most of the time patrolling the complex or standing in strategic locations dealing with the public's and superior's requests – the latter of which was usually to be told to go to specific areas to provide a presence or keep a specific person or group under surveillance. The reality of the work was boring mundane patrolling of a shopping centre. An arrest or outbreak of disorder was usually an extraordinary event for most staff on a shift.

The other aspect to this trait is the desire of security officers to deal with 'real work'. These are activities more associated with police work such as using legal tools to arrest shoplifters, removing unwanted persons from site and dealing with outbreaks of disorder. This trait has also been evidenced by McCahill's (2002) study of shopping centres in Northern England. He found security officers distinguishing between 'real' work, arguing, 'A shop theft incident constituted "real work" in the eyes of guards and close and prolonged attention was usually given to incidents involving "known shoplifters" (2002, 125).' The pursuit of 'real work' was illustrated by the security supervisor when he told me,

> I have been on the shop-floor the buzz is arresting someone or sorting a problem out. I think all the CSOs want this and if they don't they won't enjoy their job.

Foster (2003) has illustrated how the strength of police culture can override the training and formal policies of police organisations. A good illustration of this aspect of security officers' culture, as well as its strength, was the desire of security officers at Pleasure Southquay to deal with disorder at night. It was illustrated earlier in Chapter 6 that the clear direction from management was that they should not become involved in fights and that this was a responsibility for the police. In reality, however, there were a significant number of security officers dealing with such incidents at night. This was encouraged by the Security Supervisor, the contract manager, the team leaders and by the police.

The security officers also exhibited the pessimistic and cynical aspect of this culture. Many of the security officers would tell me that there were not enough staff to deal with incidents on Friday and Saturday nights and they were consistently overstretched at these periods.

CSO 19

---

3   These reports were likely to be more accurate than the police statistics because not all incidents of theft result in the police been called.

On the night-shift there is not always enough cover on certain nights and certain days. Police do respond quickly, but if you get City FC playing at home and you get a group kicking off there are only 4 to 6 of us.

CSO 21

Day shift not a problem with the odd fire alarm and shoplifter. At weekends, however, with 5 to 6000 people 5 to 6 people is not enough.

There was evidence therefore that a number of officers at Pleasure Southquay were more orientated towards the 'parapolice' end of the continuum.

Assessing the continuum

The dichotomy proposed does not mean that all security officers can be distinguished as one type or the other. As a continuum it is intended to illustrate that some officers are more inclined to one end of the continuum than the other. For instance an officer could be orientated such that under no circumstances would they get involved in a confrontation that required the use of force, one officer might happily get involved in most circumstances, while another may in certain cases get involved. Indeed Michael's (2002) typology is useful in that her 'police wannabe' could be applied to the 'parapolice' end of the spectrum. Her 'time-server' towards the 'watchman' end of the continuum, and the 'uniformed pensioner' and 'casual' may fit somewhere in the middle.

Clearly this section has illustrated a general orientation of the 'front-line' staff at Pleasure Southquay towards a 'parapolice' orientation compared to Armed Industries at the 'watchman' end. However, there were differences within the two organisations that illustrated varying commitment to these orientations. For instance two officers at Armed Industries had actually been involved in pursuing and apprehending an offender, something more associated with the other end of the spectrum. At Pleasure Southquay there were clear differences between 'front-line' and the 'backroom' staff. These differences also existed amongst the 'front-line' staff as was illustrated to me during one incident observed on a night-shift.

While patrolling the site at night with two security officers we witnessed outside one of the bars a man who had been thrown out giving verbal abuse to one of the door supervisors. He then left with another man and woman. We watched them leave and the door supervisors told us he had been thrown out for stealing a bottle of spirits from behind the bar. We then observed him as he started abusing two men who happened to be walking past him, who returned the 'compliments'. The ejected man then went over and started slapping the smaller guy on the back of the head. The taller friend then stepped in to protect the smaller man and a fight broke out. As we ran towards the fight I realised that I was in the lead and slowed down so as not to be first there. As I did this I noticed one of the security officers slowing down so as to remain behind me! The first security officer arrived on the scene and tried to break the fight up, others arrived followed by the police, but for the first 20 to 30 seconds the security officers were dealing with it. The security officer who slowed down became involved in the incident when the fight was clearly over. He was keen to be part of the active culture, but in reality wanted to step back from becoming too embroiled in the action. He exhibited a 'parapolice' orientation image, but in reality had a 'watchman' orientation. The figure below seeks to draw out the main characteristics of this continuum.

	'Watchman' ←	→ Parapolice
Dealing with disorder and conflict	Passive	Active
Use of legal tools	Passive	Active
Perception of role	Mundane and ineffective	'Thin blue line'

Figure 9.1   Watchmen – Parapolice Continuum

These different orientations are influenced by the structural factors such as the nature and demands of the workplace, the status of the security officers and the degree of boredom. For instance at Pleasure Southquay because of the violence in the NTE and shoplifting taking place there was an opportunity for security officers to get involved with these incidents, which was not the case at Armed Industries. Thus the nodal context is very important. The status of officers also influences this, because some desire to improve their standing and getting involved in this type of work provides a currency to improve it. For others resigned to low status, it also provides a justification not to get involved. The degree of boredom also contributes for some officers, as the opportunity to become involved in activities that are exciting, breaks the monotony.

Conclusion

This chapter has examined the occupational cultural characteristics of security officers and has identified a number of core traits and orientations. In doing so it has also recognised some of the major influences on these traits. The model outlined in Figure 9.2 draws together these characteristics and also identifies in italics below some of the structural factors contributing to that cultural trait. Thus the primary trait of the security officers' culture is to 'wannabe something else or somewhere else' and the structural factors influencing this trait are the generally poor conditions of employment and status of security officers. The second core characteristic was the moans and bravado relating to working conditions and this is also influenced by the general industry norm of poor working conditions. Third there was the trait of solidarity, isolation and inferiority which was also largely influenced by the dangerous situations faced by some officers, their perceived status, particularly the isolation from the public and other workers they police. Fourth there was the trait of machismo, which can largely be explained by male, working class culture combined with an occupational need to conduct surveillance. Fifth there was a trait of suspicion and risk based minds, which was also derived from their occupational role. Finally security officers can largely be attributed with an orientation either towards one end of a continuum starting with 'watchman' to the other end of 'parapolice'. This was largely driven by the workplace they operated in. The organisational needs, nature of the assignment as well as the aspirations of the officers all influence this orientation. At Pleasure Southquay the 'parapolice' orientation was driven by the opportunity and organisational need to deal with disorder, combined with aspirations amongst some of the security officers to deal with the 'real work' to raise their status in their workplace.

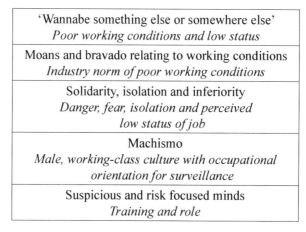

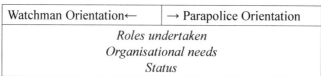

Figure 9.2   The cultural characteristics of security officers

Clearly this is one of the first attempts to map security officer culture and it is largely based upon two case study sites. It is therefore debatable – remembering the caveats identified at the beginning of this chapter about the security industry – how representative this is of the wider private security industry. Nevertheless given the structural explanations that influence the cultural traits of security officers, it is likely to be similar amongst many other officers. It is important to understand this security officer culture because it impacts on the way they undertake their job. As this book has illustrated the culture found in the two case study sites was important in undermining the effectiveness of the security officers (For example the effectiveness of search and access control at Armed Industries) and in developing their own ways of doing things, which in some cases conflicted with managerial agendas (For example at Pleasure Southquay officers dealing with disorder in the NTE). Therefore for policy-makers and managers seeking to raise standards it is important they understand the structural factors identified in this chapter that shape security officer culture.

Chapter 10

'Big Fish in Little Ponds', Security Officers and the Policing of Private and Hybrid Space

Introduction

This book has examined the contribution of security officers to the policing of two nodes of governance. There is an increasing realisation of the impact of the governing structures of different nodes on our lives and how a wide range of strategies are used to secure compliance and control within them (Johnston and Shearing 2003). Security staff are assuming increasing prominence in the policing of such space as well as society more broadly. This book has illustrated how they could access an impressive range of legal tools within their workplace. They generally have a good knowledge of the limits of their legal tools and how to make use of them lawfully. The research has also elucidated how security officers do make significant use of some of their tools, although the extent to which they are used varies amongst officers. In using these tools officers are frequently confronted with difficult and sometimes dangerous situations that lead to verbal abuse, threats of violence as well as assault. The research has also drawn out some of the characteristics of the culture of security officers and the different orientations that exist. The theme that has emerged throughout is that within the relatively small 'ponds' where security staff work they are 'big fish'. This chapter will draw out some of these key findings and from this develop some of the implications for future research and policing more generally. Before we embark upon this, however, the broader perception of security in policing more generally will be considered.

'Little fish in a big lake'

It would be fair to accept that the general view of security officers in policing has been neglected. At one level there has been little attention paid to security officers by researchers in terms of their contribution to policing, as Jones and Newburn (1998, 1) observe in the opening paragraph of their study on the private security industry,

> Over the past two decades, criminologists have become increasingly preoccupied with policing. However, their gaze has been almost exclusively fixed upon that body of state officials which forms what is known as the police service.

Indeed a perusal through many books on policing will frequently find them dominated by the police with little or no reference to private security or some of the many other agencies engaged in this process. The police, by contrast, have been the subject of serious research on almost every aspect of their work (see Newburn 2003). This probably reflects the general perception of private security officers in society (which is only recently beginning to change), where they have been dismissed by policy-makers, the police and the public as of negligible importance. The low status given to private security was illustrated in 1996, when the then Home Office Minister David Maclean responded to an Opposition debate on the private security industry by castigating the then Shadow Home Secretary, Jack Straw, for bothering to raise such an issue. He said,

> ...why on earth has he selected this subject (private security) for debate? We know that Oppositions value their Opposition days and that they normally use them to discuss the burning issues of the day... This is the first Opposition day debate on law and order that they have requested *and what have they selected – the private security industry* (Author's emphasis) (*Hansard* 13th of February 1996: 874–876).

There have been a plethora of initiatives pursued on policing in recent years, but only with the Police White Paper of 2001 and the subsequent Police Reform Act 2003 has there been any recognition of the role private security could play in policing more generally (Home Office 2001). The police also frequently hold dismissive views of the importance of private security generally. For instance a study of Canadian police officers attitudes towards private security found they considered security to undertake trivial and insignificant functions. One extract from an interview with a police officer summed up this view very well, 'I wouldn't trust some security men to get a kitten out of a tree. They are incompetent. A lot of them need supervision, organization and training' (Shearing et al. 1985, 132). However, the research also found a more positive view at an individual level probably reflecting experience of security at a nodal level. Nevertheless overall Shearing et al. (1985, 151) concluded,

> Police tend to trivialize the significance of private security, and many of our respondents appeared to resent what they thought was an attempt to compare private security with police.

This research was based upon Canada, but a similar – though much smaller scale – study of police officers in North Wales came to similar conclusions (Cronin-Wojdat 2001).

A further illustration of the low regard security officers are held in by many is a guide for environmental protesters on wrecking road building (although many of the attributes would also apply in varying degrees at the two case study sites). In this guide there is a section on 'Know your enemy' and security officers are covered. It states,

Guards will be mostly male, with most of the bottom level coming straight from the dole, being paid peanuts and treated badly by their "superiors". Many may not like the job, but are victims of financial necessity. This is the level most likely to walk out, turn a blind eye to holes in security fences etc, or to leak information to protesters. Hence, they are trusted with minimal responsibility; work on sowing discontent! There will of course be a sprinkling of psychos, rambo fantasists, and people turned down by the army or police for being too aggressive, especially at the team leader level (see end of Chapter 10 for ideas on dealing with violence). The most senior guards are most likely to be army lieutenant types, and will generally avoid getting their hands dirty (Road Alert, u.d.).

Indeed there is limited empirical research on the public's perception of private security in policing in society generally, but that which does exist tends to provide a negative view. For instance a MORI survey for the Audit Commission found the public perceived a police officer on foot to provide a level of public reassurance of over +80 per cent. A marked police car provided around +70 per cent, a CCTV camera nearly +40 per cent. These was followed by a Neighbourhood Watch Sticker which gave a figure of around -5 per cent and then a security guard which gave a reassurance of only around -15 per cent. If there is consolation it is that traffic wardens were considered the least effective at over -50 per cent (Audit Commission 1996). Nevertheless the research illustrated that the public (those surveyed) considered a sticker to provide more reassurance than a security guard. Clearly evidence of how security officers are perceived as ineffective. More recent research of the extended policing family by Crawford and Lister (2004a) also rated the symbolic power of security officers in the very lowest of their four-fold categorisation.

The treatment of private security in the media also tends to highlight the low status, incompetence and even criminality of security staff. Livingstone and Hart (2003) cite links with the incompetent image and portrayal of the old 'watchmen' in the pre 1829 system of policing and they illustrate the current image with the treatment of Group 4 in the media following their appointment to transport prisoners in the East Midlands in the early 1990s. They go on to argue, 'The image of private security depicted and discussed in this article are expressive of society's scepticism and provide cultural shorthand for its communication' (2003, 169). These views have been increasingly challenged in recent years by a number of writers illustrating the growing importance of private security in policing (Kakalik and Wildhorn 1972 a, b, c, d, e; National Advisory Council on Criminal Justice Standards and Goals 1976; Cunningham and Taylor 1985; Cunningham et al. 1990; and Jones and Newburn 1998). However, it would be fair to argue that in the currency of policing more broadly in society, private security are still considered low value. However, when private security are viewed in their own nodes or 'ponds' of operation as part of a broader system of security (design, barriers etc) the evidence from this research suggests a higher value, role and importance in the roles they undertake.

'Big fish in little ponds'

The research for this book illustrated the important functions undertaken as well as the extensive powers of security officers in policing their workplace. At this point it is worth reminding ourselves of some of the key findings vis-à-vis security staff and the policing of the sites they operate within.

Legal tools

Security officers possess a wide range of legal tools that enable them to undertake their role. Chapter 3 illustrated these could be divided between 'universal legal tools' which are based upon citizens' rights to undertake arrests and use reasonable force to prevent crimes. In addition to these many security officers also draw upon 'select legal tools' depending upon their location of operation, which include tools to deny entrance, remove from property, search, as well as apply sanctions to name most. There are potentially a very wide range of tools that security officers can draw upon and the two research sites illustrated that these are not always identified as tools to be used by security officers and even when they were the extent of use amongst officers varied.

Nodes of governance

The two case study sites were identified as nodes with their own systems of governance and security. In doing so some of the challenges and risks faced by these two nodes were illustrated. This chapter was also important in demonstrating how security staff form one part of a much more complex range of strategies that are designed to secure compliance and control. Some of the characteristics of the security staff were also identified, showing the median officer at Pleasure Southquay as white, male, aged 31–40 years, holding 5 GCSEs or equivalent, having left school at 16, and completed the 5 weeks induction training of Pleasure Southquay; compared to Armed Industries where they were male, white, at least 51 years or more, had no qualifications, having left school at 16, and completed only the SITO basic training.

Knowledge of legal tools

The security officers were tested on a wide range of legal tools that they may have used. The research revealed generally a good performance, although on average of the 13 questions asked they would make one **major** and one *minor* error. Further analysis revealed, however, that most of these mistakes did not generally relate to an activity they were engaged in. More interesting was the general lack of confidence amongst the security officers interviewed. This revealed there was a significant minority who expressed a view that they 'didn't know' or were 'somewhat unsure' of their legal tools. For instance at Pleasure Souhquay around 20 per cent were 'somewhat unsure' or 'didn't know' their legal tools relating to arrest, search and the use of force. Overall the results revealed that the majority of security officers interviewed were not very confident about their understanding of their legal tools, despite a generally good performance in questions testing their knowledge.

Use of legal tools

This book in Chapters 6 and 7 considered security officers use of their 'universal' and 'select' legal tools respectively. With the former, arrest and the use of force were explored, which largely related to Pleasure Southquay. The research revealed a core group of officers that were actively involved in apprehending shoplifters as well as using force to control physical confrontations. In using the power to arrest officers largely relied upon compliance and consent amongst those being policed, where as physical confrontations were largely resolved by force. The desire amongst officers for special powers and non-lethal weapons – within this context – was also examined. The research found a clear majority against both in all categories of officers, except on the issue of non-lethal weapons where there was a very small majority of 'frontline' Pleasure Southquay officers in favour of their use. On 'select' legal tools access control, search and a variety of other property and or employment based legal tools were examined. These differed in that they largely related to the needs of the organisation and were pursued through general compliance, consent and commonsense. The chapter illustrated the extensive use of search at Armed Industries as well as some other very impressive functions such as the enforcement of the speed limit. The chapter concluded by revisiting Lukes three dimensional view of power and applying it to the two nodes, illustrating where and how security officers fit this trichotomy.

Occupational hazards

In undertaking their work security officers are faced with a variety of occupational hazards. This book elucidated some of the most significant faced at the two research sites, but which also probably apply more broadly because of the structural causes of them. First there was the challenge of serving multiple masters, which frequently have different agendas. Linked to this is the threat of loss of position on a site, which may result in a *de facto* termination of employment. Second, security officers faced a degree of isolation both in having to work alone as well as in their relationship with the public and fellow workers. Finally this book illustrated the significant amount of abuse faced by many security officers ranging from verbal abuse, threats of violence to actual assault.

Culture and orientation

Drawing from the two research sites as well as other relevant research the book identified core characteristics of the culture of security officers, as well as differences that distinguish two distinct orientations. The core traits included a desire to be doing another job or be somewhere else; a pre-occupation with the challenging working conditions faced; a strong sense of solidarity, isolation and inferiority; a degree of machismo; and a focus upon suspicion and risk. The research also revealed another trait, which could be placed upon a continuum, which at one end could be called the 'parapolice' orientation and the other, the 'watchman' orientation. This was based upon their willingness to deal with conflict and disorder, the extent of use of their legal tools and their perception of their role. The research revealed a variety of officers displaying one or other orientation in varying degrees.

Theoretical and Research Implications

Earlier in this book a number of theoretical observations were made vis-à-vis Lukes's three dimensional view of power and the security of Pleasure Southquay and Armed Industries. It was shown that at both places the primary strategy for security was based upon third dimensional strategies to secure compliance from denizens through measures that unconsciously shape their wants and desires. Security officers were largely used in terms of the second dimension of power through their mere presence to prevent denizens from pursuing the action they wanted to. Thirdly it was illustrated that the first dimension methods of verbal requests, threats, coercion etc were the last resort in the system and of varying effectiveness. These findings were based upon only two research sites. As such there is a need for more research to shed further empirical and theoretical light on these issues.

There is always a risk with case study based research that they might not be representative. Therefore it is important that further similar research is carried out upon comparable locations to assess if the findings of this research can be generalised. It would also be useful for research to be conducted on other examples of quasi-public space such as hospitals, universities, airports and private space, such as office complexes and other factories to investigate any differences amongst these. Similarly space where entrance is based upon a ticket such as a sports venue or pop concert also warrants research. A question of particular importance will be how similar the balance of the three dimensions of security strategies are and specifically where security officers fit in the overall security system.

A significant finding was the importance of the marketing department in security decision-making and their important 'third dimension' role in securing compliance. This is undoubtedly an area in need of much more research to scope the full range of strategies, their rationale, their impact and how they are developed to name some. There are also inherent contradictions in such strategies between maximising profitability and increasing the attractiveness to 'riskier' clients who compromise the former and how this is reconciled by the new 'governors' of such space.

This leads to another area this book did not have the time or space to develop in any depth, the governing structures of such places or nodes. Given the growing interest in nodal governance it is time to research further the people who ultimately control the governance of such places. Issues such as the structures of governance, the number and type of decision-makers involved, their style of governance and their relationship with denizens need to be explored.

The denizens or public that frequent such places is another area it was not possible to explore in this study. It would be useful to not only interview but also focus observations on them and their interactions with the security system. This would also further add to our understanding of the three dimensional nature of power as applied to the two case study sites in this book.

Other issues arise that also require further research. The change in arrest powers for security officers raises a wide range of potential research questions: from the level of awareness amongst officers to the implications on the ground of the changes. The knowledge of their legal tools amongst security officers was found to be generally good, but the extent to which this reflects the wider private security industry is difficult to assess. Similarly the extent of use of legal tools amongst security officers in different types of workplace would also provide further useful data. The serious abuse, both verbal and physical, received by security officers needs further investigation to assess to what extent this applies to the wider private security industry. Indeed if such levels were found to be exposed amongst occupations with a greater political influence, such as the police, serious government attention would no doubt occur.

The private security industry in England and Wales is currently orientating itself for the challenge of regulation. This has been introduced with a number of aims, one of which is to raise the standards of the industry (Home Office 1999). There has been criticism that these proposals do not go far enough and this research does illustrate some of the limitations of the proposed regulatory structure based upon the performance of security officers in this research (Button 2003). It also illustrates some of the issues that regulation is not going to address, but should.

The introduction of regulation of the private security industry in England and Wales has been justified on grounds that it will raise the standards of the private security industry. Part of this argument is based upon the introduction of mandatory training for all security officers. At present the proposals of the SIA are for three days class-room training and one day on the job. This research has illustrated that even with officers from the quality end of the market undertaking several weeks training they still make mistakes when tested on their knowledge. It is therefore difficult to imagine that the proposed mandatory standards will have any impact upon the overall performance of officers on this issue. More importantly, however, the roles being undertaken by security officers in many 'hybrid' space locations, which Pleasure Southquay is typical of many, illustrates the need for much more extensive training, focused not only upon legal tools but also the use of appropriate force. If security officers are expected to deal with disorder and to intervene in physical confrontations then they clearly need training for dealing with such scenarios. At present there is no provision in the SIAs mandatory training, other than for a very brief one day course on conflict resolution, which although helpful, will not go far enough. More broadly the roles being undertaken by the security officers raises an important debate – which is yet to be seriously considered – over what role security officers should have in 'risky' situations. With the advent of police community support officers, wardens and other examples of the growing extended police family there really needs to be a debate about what security officers are expected to deal with, given their general training and abilities.

Linked to the debate over their role in 'risky' situations comes the disturbing findings on the verbal abuse, threats of violence and assaults security officers experience. The latter may have been over-represented in Pleasure Southquay compared to the wider industry, but clearly part of the norm of a security officer's job is regular verbal abuse, occasional threats of violence and for some, the real risk of assault. This says much about the nature of our society, particularly in the NTE. However, training on how to deal with and defuse these situations would seem to be a major priority for employers.

The treatment of security officers by the public also raises the issue of whether they should be given special protection and rights. The police have a special protection in the form of a specific offence of assaulting a police officer. Given there is an active campaign for some public workers to be given such special protections (UNISON 2004), should these also apply to security officers? More controversially should more special powers and rights be given to security officers? It was illustrated that the 'frontline' security officers at Pleasure Southquay desired the right to use non-lethal weapons and how some also sought greater powers. If security officers are expected to deal with such situations, should they also be given such rights for protection?

Security officers at Pleasure Southquay (and many other comparable locations) are regularly dealing with physical confrontations that raises the risk of them using excessive force. The structures being created by the SIA to license security officers currently do not provide for an independent complaints bureau. As security officers continue to accumulate more impressive roles, legal structures to adequately hold security officers to account – as well as protect them from malicious complaints – clearly need to be created. Most significantly, however, there is no provision for the licensing of in-house security officers under the current legislation. Given the functions security officers generally undertake, as illustrated in this book, if these employees were in-house it would raise major concerns if they were not licensed and subject to the governance of the SIA. Undoubtedly the exemption of these officers from regulation is a significant folly.

Regulation also fails to address the challenge of private space being increasingly used as 'public' space. This raises fundamental legal questions about how such locations are treated and the powers that security staff derive from them. The arbitrary nature of such space is evidently being challenged, but it has not been given up yet. The extensive rights this gives landowners and their agents poses questions on whether the time has come to reconsider the legal basis of security officers' powers. This is not a new question and over two decades ago Shearing and Stenning (1981, 239) argued,

The need to re-examine these fundamental legal institutions on which the role, jurisdiction, and powers of private security are founded has, in our view, been obscured and neglected as a result of the concentration on licensing and other forms of direct regulation which has pre-occupied public authorities in so many jurisdictions.

Security officers could be even more powerful if there was the desire to make full use of their legal and other tools linked with a 'parapolice' orientation. The research has highlighted, amongst many other findings, how some security officers do not utilise their full range of legal tools, do not understand their rights relating to their legal tools, are often not confident, may rarely exercise their legal tools and might be orientated not to put themselves in situations of danger. Rigakos (2002) in his study of Intelligarde elucidated a security firm with officers that generally did make full use of their tools, understand them and were prepared to put themselves in situations of danger. This 'parapolice' culture was only found amongst a minority of the Pleasure Southquay security staff. Indeed if Figure 3.1 is revisited and the different orientations applied upon them, the prospect of a very powerful security officer is revealed.

Model of Security Officer Power	Orientation	
Basic Security Officer	Watchman	Parapolice
Semi-empowered	Watchman	Parapolice
Complete empowered	Watchman	Parapolice

Figure 10.1   Security officer orientation applied to models of security officer power

Given the legal tools available to the 'semi-empowered' and 'complete empowered' security officer combined with a 'parapolice' orientation the prospect of security officers actively undertaking exclusion and removal, searching, imposing sanctions for breaches of regulations within nodes of governance is revealed. There is nothing to stop managers encouraging security staff to pursue a 'parapolice' culture, utilising the full use of legal tools. This was only evident amongst a minority of security officers at Pleasure Southquay, but there is much more scope for this to be pursued by the employers of security. The more this is pursued, so the issues of improving the regulatory structure discussed above become more important. However, perhaps the reasons there are not more examples of the 'parapolice' orientation is the ability of organisations to rely on much more subtle strategies.

In studying the two research sites it became evident that security staff were part of a much more complex web of control of which they were only a part. The application of Lukes's (1974) three dimensional model illustrated the importance of the third dimension strategies. Indeed it was evident that both locations were largely Foucaldian 'disciplined nodes' based upon surveillance and other strategies rather than coercion. The most important controlling mechanisms were often subtle, hidden and largely lead to a 'mentality' of compliance amongst those using this space. The most significant caveat to this was the NTE where alcohol fuelled a breakdown in the social control and discipline that could often only be addressed through coercion.

The book also raised issues that impact upon social justice. There is a growing debate over the distribution of policing resources. Areas of high insecurity (which are not necessarily those of highest risk) with strong middle class communities are increasingly pushing for more policing and when not satisfied purchasing additional resources themselves (Crawford and Lister 2004a). Areas of high risk, which frequently require more policing provision than is provided by the state, and which are also usually the most socially deprived are generally less able to lobby for or purchase additional security. Security is a fundamental right and when this starts to become based upon your wealth and where you live a fundamental inequality has emerged which impacts upon many other aspects of life. An example the divisions in policing resources was illustrated particularly in relation to Pleasure Southquay where residents and corporate clients were at low risk of victimisation but protected by an extensive security infra-structure, juxtaposed to the neighbouring estate of much higher risks where security amounted to the state's bare minimum.

The second aspect of social justice is the fair access of all legitimate visitors to places of shopping and entertainment. It was shown at Pleasure Southquay that although evidence of arbitrary exclusion of groups did not occur, there was evidence of exclusion on a very informal and unsystematic basis. There also remains the potential for exclusion to be used in a much more discriminatory and divisive manner should landowners and their agents desire when utilising their controlling mechanisms. Indeed examples cited elsewhere in the book from the CIN properties case as well as other the work of McCahill (2002) and Atkinson (2003) demonstrate exclusion is occurring in many shopping malls and entertainment zones. If unchecked and regulated in some locations certain individuals (and perhaps groups) could be denied access to many desirable shopping and leisure facilities without any fair institutional process having taken place.

The controlling mechanisms therefore raise questions about the 'order' that is sought. Preventing anti-social behaviour such as urinating in public, throwing litter on the floor, excessive noise, graffiti to name some are 'common goods' that most reasonable people would not question. However, what if that 'order' begins to question whom may enter the space, and controls behaviours not usually regarded as anti-social? There is already evidence emerging of an infra-structure of surveillance targeting particular groups more than others (McCahill 2002) and of dispossessed groups being excluded (Gray and Gray 1999b and c). Evidence is also emerging of security being used to enforce the appropriate corporate image, for instance at the Sydney Olympics in 2000 security officers searched for and confiscated brands that were not official sponsors, as well as for knives and weapons (Chaundhary 2000). Shearing and Stenning (1987) have illustrated how something as innocuous as a child taking off her shoes to walk barefoot can become the interest of security. If the substantial controlling mechanisms begin to be used to pursue a more controversial agenda, given the importance such space is beginning to assume in many peoples' lives, this raises the significant prospect of a new feudalism (Shearing and Stenning 1981). As Shearing (1993, 228) has argued,

> The fear is that the reality might be pervasive and intrusive corporate governance, in which the interests of capital are more directly pursued than state-centred theories of capitalism ever dreamed could be possible; the state might wither away, but this may not mean a lessening of the hegemony of capital interests.

This 'order' that is emerging unchecked requires greater attention of researchers and policy-makers to ensure such space is governed to the same standards we would expect of public space, otherwise the fear is of a patchwork of 'Brave New Nodes'.

Bibliography

Ackroyd, S. and Crowdy, P., A. (1990), 'Can Culture be Managed? Working with 'Raw' Material: The Case of English Slaughtermen', *Personnel Review* 19:5, 3–13.

Ackroyd, S. and Thompson, P. (1999), *Organisational Misbehaviour* (London: Sage).

Adu-Boakye, K. (2002), *Private Security and Retail Crime Prevention: An Ethnographic Case Study of Retail Shops in Portsmouth* (MSc Dissertation, University of Portsmouth).

Agnew, N., M. and Pyke, S., W. (1982), *The Science Game: An Introduction to Research in the Behavioural Sciences* (Englewood Cliffs: Prentice Hall).

Alfredsson, L., Akerstedt, M., Mattsson, M and Wilborg, B. (1991), 'Self-reported Health and Well Being Amongst Night Security Guards: A Comparison with the Working Population', *Ergonomics* 34:5, 525–530.

Allen, S. (1991), *The A–Z Guide to European Manned Guarding* (London: Network Security Management).

Atkinson, R. (2003), 'Domestication by Cappuccino or a Revenge on Urban Space? Control and Empowerment in the Management of Public Spaces', *Urban Studies* 40:9, 1829–1843.

Audit Commission (1996), *Streetwise Effective Police Patrol* (London: HMSO).

Bayley, D. and Shearing, C., D. (1996) 'The Future of Policing', *Law and Society Review* 30:3, 585–606.

Baker, N. (1999) 'Searching Employees', *Croner Employment Digest* 487: 4–6.

Banton, M. (1964), *The Policeman in the Community* (London: Tavistock).

Beck, U. (1992), *Risk Society: Towards a New Modernity* (London: Sage).

Becker, T., M. (1974), 'The Place of Private Police in Society: An Area of Research for the Social Sciences', *Social Problems* 21:3, 438–453.

Bell, J. (1993), *Doing Your Research Project* (Buckingham: Open University Press).

Bickman, L. (1974), 'The Social Power of a Uniform', *Journal of Applied Social Psychology* 4:1, 47–61.

Blakely, E., J. and Snyder, M., J. (1997), *Fortress America – Gated Communities in the United States* (Washington DC: Brookings Institution Press).

Blyton, P. and Bacon, N. (1997), 'Re-Casting the Occupational Culture in Steel: Some Implications of Changing from Crews to Teams in the UK Steel Industry', *The Sociological Review* 45:1 79–101.

Bourdieu, P. (1991), *Language and Symbolic Power* (Cambridge: Polity).

Bowie, V. (2002), 'Defining Workplace Violence at Work: A New Typology', in Martin Gill et al. (eds.) *Violence at Work: Causes, Patterns and Prevention* (Cullompton: Willan).

Bowie, V., Fisher, B., S. and Cooper, C., L. (eds.) (2005), *Workplace Violence: Issues, Trends, Strategies* (Cullompton: Willan).

Braun, M., A. and Lee, D., J. (1971) Private Police Forces: Legal Powers and Limitations. *University of Chicago Law Review* 38: 555–582.

British Retail Consortium (1998), *Retail Crime Survey 1997* (London: British Retail Consortium).

British Retail Consortium (2002), *9th Retail Crime Survey 2001* (London: British Retail Consortium).

British Security Industry Association (1994), The *UK Manned Guarding Market* (Worcester: BSIA).

British Security Industry Association (1999), *Manned Security Market Survey* (Worcester: BSIA).

Broderick, J. (1973), *Police in a Time of Change* (Morristown, NJ: General Learning).

Brown, M. (1981), *Working the Street* (New York: Russell Sage).

Buchanan, D. and Huczynski, A. (2001), *Organizational Behaviour: An Introduction* (Fifth Edition. London: Prentice Hall).

Bushman, B., J. (1984) 'Perceived Symbols of Authority and their Influence on Compliance', *Journal of Applied Social Psychology* 14:6, 501–508.

Button, M. (1993), *Why Security Officers Don't Join Trade Unions. A Micro Level Analysis of Barriers to Trade Union Development in the Manned Sector of the Security Industry* (MA Dissertation, University of Warwick).

Button, M. (1998) 'Beyond the Public Gaze – The Exclusion of Private Investigators from the British Debate Over Regulating Private Security', *International Journal of the Sociology of the Law* 26:1, 1–16.

Button, M. (2002), *Private Policing* (Cullompton: Willan Publishing).

Button, M. (2003), 'Private Security Industry Law in Europe: The Case of Great Britain', in Stefan Outer and Rolf Stober (eds.) *Recht des Sicherheitsgewerbes* (Koln: Heymanns).

Button, M. (2004), "Softly, Softly', Private Security and the Policing of Corporate Space', in Roger Hopkins-Burke, (ed.) *Hard Cop, Soft Cop: Dilemmas and Debates in Contemporary Policing* (Cullompton: Willan Publishing).

Button, M. and George, B. (1994), 'Why Some Organisations Prefer In-house to Contract Security Staff', in Martin Gill (ed.) *Crime at Work: Studies in Security and Crime Prevention* (Leicester: Perpetuity Press).

Button, M. and George, B. (1998), 'Why Some Organisations Prefer Contract to In-house Security Staff', in Martin Gill (ed.) *Crime at Work: Increasing the Risk for Offenders* (Leicester: Perpetuity Press).

Button, M. and George, B. (2001), 'Government Regulation in the United Kingdom Private Security Industry: The Myth of Non-Regulation', *Security Journal* 14:3, 55–66.

Button, M. and John, T. (2002), "'Plural Policing' In Action: A Review of the Policing of Environmental Protests in England and Wales', *Policing and Society* 12: 2, 111–121.

Campbell, G. and Reingold, B. (1994), 'Private Security and Public Policing in Canada', in *Juristat Service Bulletin* (Ottawa: Canadian Centre for Justice Statistics).

Card, R., Murdoch, J. and Murdoch, S. (1998), *Law for Estate Management Students* (London: Butterworths).

Castells, M. (1989), *The Informational City: Information Technology, Economic Restructuring and the Urban Restructuring Process* (Blackwell: Oxford).

Chan, J. (1996), 'Changing Police Culture', *British Journal of Criminology* 36:1, 109–134.

Chan, J. (1997), *Changing Police Culture in a Multicultural Society* (Cambridge: Cambridge University Press).

Chaundhary, V. (2000), 'Any bombs, Knives, Pepsi? Security gets tough at the Olympics' *The Guardian* 18 September, 2000.

Choongh, S. (1997), *Policing as a Social Discipline* (Oxford: Clarendon).

Cohen, L. (1976), *Educational Research in Classrooms and Schools: A Manual of Materials and Methods* (London: Harper and Row).

Cohen, S. (1985), *Visions of Social Control* (Cambridge: Polity Press).

Collins, B., E. and Raven, B., H. (1969), 'Group Structure: Attractions, Coalitions, Communication and Power', in G. Lindzey et al. (eds.) *The Handbook of Social Psychology* (Reading, Mass: Addison-Wesley).

Crawford, A. (1997), *The Local Governance of Crime* (Oxford: Clarendon Press).

Crawford, A. (1998), *Crime Prevention and Community Safety* (Harlow: Longman).

Crawford, A. (2002), 'The Governance of Crime and Insecurity in an Anxious Age: the Trans-European and the Local' in Adam Crawford (ed.) *Crime and Insecurity The Governance of Safety in Europe* (Cullompton: Willan).

Crawford, A. and Lister, S. (2004a), *The Extended Policing Family* (York: Joseph Rowntree Foundation).

Crawford, A. and Lister, S. (2004b), 'The Patchwork Shape of Reassurance Policing in England and Wales: Integrated Local Security Quilts or Frayed, Fragmented and Fragile Tangled Webs?' *Policing: An International Journal of Police Strategies and Management* 27:3, 413–430.

Croner Employment Digest (1992), 'May I Look in Your Bag?', *Croner Employment Digest* 355: 1–3.

Cronin-Wojdat, W., P. (2001), *Investigation into the Attitudes of North Wales Police Officers Towards Private Security* (MSc Dissertation, University of Portsmouth).

Cumming, J. and Winyard, S. (1984), *Working Insecurity* (Liverpool: Low Pay Unit).

Cunningham, W., C., Strauchs, J., J. and Van Meter, C., W. (1990), *Private Security Trends 1970–2000* (Stoneham (USA): Butterworth-Heinemann).

Cunningham, W., C. and Taylor, T. (1985), *Private Security and Police in America* (Portland: Chancellor Press).

Davis, M. (1990), *City of Quartz* (London: Vintage).

De Waard, J. (1993), 'The Private Security Sector in Fifteen European Countries: Size, Rules and Legislation', *Security Journal* 4:2, 58–62.

De Waard, J. (1999), 'The Private Security Industry in International Perspective', *European Journal of Criminal Policy and Research* 7:2, 143–174.

Dickinson, D. (2003), 'Promised – Not Predicted', *The 208 Newsletter*, Summer 2003: 3.

Dixon, D. (1997), *Law in Policing: Legal Regulation and Police Practices* (Oxford: Clarendon Press).

Dowding, K. (1996), *Power* (Buckingham: Open University Press).

Draper, H. (1978), *Private Police* (Sussex: Harvester Press).

ERS Market Research (2003), *Police Federation of England and Wales Officer Safety/Arming Survey 2003 Top-Line Report* (Surbiton: Police Federation).

Feldman, D. (1986), *The Law Relating to Entry, Search and Seizure* (London: Butterworths).

Fitzpatrick, J., S. (1980), 'Adapting to Danger A Participant Observation Study of an Underground Mine', *Sociology of Work and Occupations* 7:2 131–158.

Flynn, P. (1997), *Regulating the Privatisation of Policing* (PhD Thesis, Essex University).

Foster, J. (2003) 'Police Cultures', in Tim Newburn (ed.) *Handbook of Policing* (Cullompton: Willan).

Foucault, M. (1977), *Discipline and Punish* (London: Penguin).

Franzen, M. (2001) 'Urban Order and the Preventative Restructuring of Space: The Operation of Border Controls in Micro Space', *Sociological Review* 49:2 302–318.

French, J., R., P. and Raven, B., H. (1959), 'The Basis of Social Power', in D. Cartwright (ed.) *Studies in Social Power* (Ann Arbor: University of Michigan Press).

Garland, D. (1996) 'The Limits of Sovereign State: Strategies of Crime Control in Contemporary Society', *British Journal of Criminology* 36:4, 445–71.

George, B. and Button, M. (1998), "Too Little Too Late' An Assessment of Recent Proposals for the Private Security Industry in the United Kingdom', *Security Journal* 10:1, 1–7.

George, B. and Button, M. (2000), *Private Security* (Leicester: Perpetuity Press).

Giddens, A. (1990), *The Consequences of Modernity* (Cambridge: Cambridge University Press).

Gill, M., Fisher, B., and Bowie, V. (eds.) (2002), *Violence at Work: Causes, Patterns and Prevention* (Cullompton: Willan).

Gold, R. (1969), 'Roles in Sociological Field Observations', in George McCall and J. Simmons (eds.) *Issues in Participant Observation: A Text and Reader* (Mass: Addison-Wesley).

Goodwin, M. (1996), *Local Authority – Lawful Authority? An Examination of Wandsworth Parks Police Arrests and Interaction with the Metropolitan Police on the Battersea Division* (BSc Dissertation, University of Portsmouth).

Goold, B., J. (2004), *CCTV and Policing* (Oxford: Clarendon).

Gottfried, H. and Graham, L. (1993), 'Constructing Difference: The Making of Gendered Subcultures in a Japanese Assembly Plant', *Sociology* 27:4, 611–628.

Gray, K. (1994), 'Equitable Property', *Current Legal Problems* 47:2 157–214.

Gray, K. and Gray, S., F. (1999a), *Land Law* (London: Butterworths).

Gray, K. and Gray, S., F. (1999b), 'Civil Rights, Civil Wrongs and Quasi-Public Space', *EHRLR* 1:1 46–102.

Gray, K. and Gray, S., F. (1999c), 'Private Property and Public Propriety', in J. McLean (ed.) *Property and Constitution* (Oxford: Hart Publishing).

Hagan, F. (1993), *Research Methods in Criminal Justice and Criminology* (New York: MacMillan).

Haas, J. (1977), 'Learning Real Feelings A Study of High Steel Ironworkers' Reactions to Fear and Danger', *Sociology of Work and Occupations* 4:2 147–170.

Hearn, J. (1985), 'Men's Sexuality at Work', in A. Metcalf and M. Humphries (eds.) *The Sexuality of Men* (London: Pluto Press).

Hobbs, D., Hadfield, P., Lister, S. and Winlow, S. (2003), *Bouncers: Violence and Governance in the Night-time Economy* (Oxford: Oxford University Press).

Hobbs, D., Hall, S., Winlow, S., Lister, S. and Hadfield, P. (2000), *Bouncers: The Art and Economics of Intimidation* (ESRC Research Programme Violence Final Report).

Hobbs, D., Lister, S., Hadfield, P., Winlow, S. and Hall, S. (2000), 'Receiving Shadows: Governance and Liminality in the Night-time Economy', *British Journal of Sociology* 51:4, 701–717.

Home Affairs Committee (1995), *The Private Security Industry*, Vol I and II, HC 17 I and II (London: HMSO).

Home Office (1979), *The Private Security Industry: A Discussion Paper* (London: HMSO).

Home Office (1998), *Fairer, Faster and Firmer – A Modern Approach to Immigration and Asylum*, Cm 4018 (London: The Stationery Office).

Home Office (1999), *The Government's Proposals for the Regulation of the Private Security Industry in England and Wales,* Cm 4254 (London: The Stationery Office).

Home Office (1993), *Wheelclamping on Private Land* (London: HMSO).

Home Office (2001), *Policing A New Century: A Blueprint for Reform*, Cm 5326 (London: The Stationery Office).

Hoogenboom, B. (1991), 'Grey Policing: A Theoretical Framework', *Policing and Society* 2:1, 17–30.

Hopkins, J. (1994), 'Orchestrating an Indoor City Ambient Noise Inside a Mega-Mall', *Environment and Behaviour* 26:6, 785–812.

Huggins, M., K. (2000), 'Urban Violence and Police Privatisation in Brazil: Blended Invisibility', *Social Justice* 27:2, 113–34.

Hunt Saboteurs Association (1994), *Public Order, Private Armies* (Nottingham: Hunt Saboteurs Association).

Jason-Lloyd, L. (2003), *Quasi-Policing* (London: Cavendish Publishing).

Jason-Lloyd, L. (2005) *An Introduction to Policing and Police Powers* (London: Cavendish Publishing).

Joh, E., E. (2005), 'The Paradox of Private Policing', *The Journal of Criminal Law and Criminology* 95:1, 49–132.

Johnston, L (1992), *The Rebirth of Private Policing* (London: Routledge).

Johnston, L. (2000), *Policing Britain: Risk, Security and Governance* (London: Longman).

Johnston, L. and Shearing, C., D. (2003), *Governing Security* (London: Routledge).

Jones, T. and Newburn, T. (1995), 'How Big is the Private Security Industry?', *Policing and Society* 5:2, 221–32.

Jones, T. and Newburn, T. (1998), *Private Security and Public Policing* (Oxford: Clarendon Press).

Kakalik, J. and Wildhorn, S. (1971a), *Private Police in the United States, Findings and Recommendations, Vol 1* (Washington DC: Government Printing Office).

Kakalik, J. and Wildhorn, S. (1971b), *The Private Police Industry: Its Nature and Extent, Vol 2* (Washington DC: Government Printing Office).

Kakalik, J. and Wildhorn, S. (1971c), *Current Regulation of Private Police: Regulatory Agency Experience and Views, Vol 3* (Washington DC: Government Printing Office).

Kakalik, J. and Wildhorn, S. (1971d), *The Law and Private Police, Vol 4* (Washington DC: Government Printing Office).

Kakalik, J. and Wildhorn, S. (1971e), *Special Purpose Public Police, Vol 5* (Washington DC: Government Printing Office).

Kempa, M., Stenning, P., C. and Wood, J. (2004), 'Policing Communal Spaces', *British Journal of Criminology* 44:4, 563–581.

Lees, L. (1997), 'Agegraphia, Heterotopia, and Vancouver's New Public Library', *Environment and Planning D: Society and Space* 15, 321–347.

Liberty (1995), 'Memorandum of Evidence', in House of Commons Home Affairs Committee, *The Private Security Industry*, Volume II (London: HMSO).

Lidstone, K., W. and Bevan, V. (u.d.), *Search and Seizure Under the Police and Criminal Evidence Act 1984* (Sheffield: Faculty of Law, University of Sheffield).

Lister, S. and Crawford, A. (2003), *The Patchwork Shape of Reassurance Policing in England and Wales: Integrated Local Security Quilts or Frayed, Fragmented and Fragile Tangled Webs* (In Search of Security: An International Conference on Policing and Security. Montréal, Québec, Canada. February, 2003).

Lister, S., Hobbs, D., Hall, S. and Winlow, S. (2000), 'Violence in the Night-Time Economy; Bouncers: The Reporting, Recording and Prosecution of Assaults', *Policing and Society* 10:3, 383–402.

Livingstone, K. and Hart, J. (2003), 'The Wrong Arm of the Law? Public Images of Private Security', *Policing and Society* 13:2, 159–170.

Loader, I. (1997), 'Policing and the Social: Questions of Symbolic Power', *British Journal of Sociology* 48:1, 1–18.

Loader, I. (2000), 'Plural Policing and Democratic Governance', *Social and Legal Studies* 9:3, 323–345.

Loader, I. and Walker, N. (2004), 'State of Denial? Rethinking the Governance of Security', *Punishment and Society* 6:2, 221–228.

Lukes, S. (1974), *Power: A Radical View* (London: Macmillan).

McCahill, M. (2002), *The Surveillance Web* (Cullmpton: Willan Publishing).

McKenzie, I., K. and Gallagher, G., P. (1989), *Behind the Uniform Policing in Britain and America* (Hemel Hempstead: Harvester Wheatsheaf).

McLeod, R. (2002), *Parapolice – A Revolution in the Business of Law Enforcement* (Toronto: Boheme Press).

McManus, M. (1995), *From Fate to Choice: Private Bobbies, Public Beats* (Aldershot: Avebury).

Macauley, S. (1986), 'Private Government', in Leon Lipson and Stanton Wheeler (eds.) *Law and the Social Sciences* (New York: Russell Sage Foundation).

Maguire, M. (2000), 'Researching 'Street Criminals': A Neglected Art', Roy King and Emma Wincup (eds.) *Doing Research in Crime and Justice* (Oxford: Oxford University Press).

Massey, J. (2005), *Patrols and Control in New Urban Space,* Paper presented to the British Society of Criminology Conference, Leeds, 14th July, 2005.

Maxwell, A. (2006) Civilians and the Powers of Arrest. *Professional Security*, July 2006, 51–53.

Mathews, R. (1989), 'Privatisation in Perspective', in Roger Mathews (ed.) *Privatizing Criminal Justice* (London: Sage).

Meara, H. (1974), 'Honor in Dirty Work The Case of American Meat Cutters and Turkish Butchers', *Sociology of Work and Occupations* 1:3, 259–283.

Michael, D. (2002), *'A Sense of Security? The Ideology and Accountability of Private Security Officers* (PhD Thesis, London School of Economics).

Milgram, S. (1975), *Obedience to Authority* (New York: Harper Torchbooks).

Monaghan, L., F. (2002), 'Hard Men, Shop Boys and Others: Embodying Competence in a Masculinist Occupation', *Sociological Review* 50:3, 334–355.

Mopas, M. S. and Stenning, P., C. (2001), 'Tools of the Trade: the Symbolic Power of Private Security – An Exploratory Study', *Policing and Society* 11:1, 67–97.

Moser, C. A. and Kalton, G. (1971), *Survey Methods in Social Investigation* (London: Heinemann).

Murray, C. (1996), 'The Case Against Regulation', *International Journal of Risk, Security and Crime Prevention* 1:1, 59–62.

National Advisory Committee on Criminal Standards and Goals (1976), *Private Security. Report of the Task Force on Private Security* (Washington DC: Government Printing Office).

National Association of Healthcare Security (1997), *Basic Training Manual and Study Guide.*

Newburn, T. (ed.) (2003), *Handbook of Policing* (Cullompton: Willan).

Noaks, L. (2000) 'Private Cops on the Block: A Review of the Role of Private Security in Residential Communities', *Policing and Society* 10: 143–161.

Oc, T. and Tiesdell, S. (1997), 'Opportunity Reduction Approaches to Crime Prevention', Tanner Oc and Steven Tiesdell (eds.) *Safer City Centres – Reviving the Public Realm* (London: Paul Chapman Publishing).

Phillips, E., M. and Pugh, D., S. (1994), *How to get a PhD* (Buckingham: Open University Press).

Plews, G. (2001), A Guard's Right to Bear Arms, *SMT*, October 2001: 17.

Poyser, S. (2003), *From 'Casbah' to 'Quays' – Designing Crime in or Out?* (MSc Dissertation, University of Portsmouth).

Raco, M. (2003), 'Remaking Place and Securitising Space', *Urban Studies* 9, 1869–1887

Ralph, R. (2004), *The Carrying of Handcuffs by Security Officers in the United Kingdom: An Analysis of the Training and Legal Implications* (BSc Dissertation, University of Portsmouth).

Ransley, J. (1991), *Chambers Dictionary of Political Biography* (Edinburgh: Chambers).

Rawlings, P. (2002), *Policing A Short History* (Cullompton: Willan).

Reeve, A. (1998), 'The Panopticisation of Shopping: CCTV and Leisure Consumption', in Clive Norris et al. (eds.) *Surveillance, Closed Circuit Television and Social Control* (Aldershot: Ashgate).

Reiner, R. (1978), *The Blue Coated Worker* (Cambridge: Cambridge University Press).

Reiner, R. (2000a), *The Politics of the Police* (Oxford: Oxford University Press).

Reiner, R. (2000b), 'Police Research', in Roy King and Emma Wincup (eds.) *Doing Research in Crime and Justice* (Oxford: Oxford University Press).

Rigakos, G., S. (2002), *The New Parapolice* (Toronto: University of Toronto Press).

Rigakos, G., S. and Greener, D., R. (1999), 'Bubbles of Governance: Private Policing and the Law in Canada', *Canadian Journal of Law and Society* 15:2, 145–185.

Sarre, R. (1994), 'The Legal Powers of Private Police and Security Providers', in Paul Moyle (ed.) *Private Prisons and Police – Recent Australian Trends* (Leichhardt, NSW: Pluto Press).

Sarre, R. and Prenzler, T. (1999) 'The Regulation of Private Policing: Reviewing Mechanisms of Accountability', *Crime Prevention and Community Safety: An International Journal* 1, 17–28.

Sarre, R. and Prenzler, T. (2005) *The Law of Private Security in Australia* (Pyrmont: Thomson).

Schein, E., H. (1992), *Organizational Culture and Leadership* (San Francisco: Jossey Bass Publishers).

Scott, J. (1990), *A Matter of Record* (Cambridge: Polity Press).

Scott, T., M. and McPherson, M. (1971) The Development of the Private Sector of the Criminal Justice System. *University of Chicago Law Review* 6: 267–288.

Security Industry Training Organisation (1993), *Store Detectives – The Role, Duties and Responsibilities of Store Detectives. Unit 2 The Law, Crime and Evidence* (Worcester: SITO).

Security Industry Training Organisation (1999), *The Advanced Security Officer* (Worcester: SITO).

Sharp, D. and Wilson, D. (2000), ''Household Security': Private Policing and Vigilantism in Doncaster', *Howard Journal* 39:2, 113–131.

Shearing, C., D. (1981), 'Subterranean Processes in the Maintenance of Power', *Canadian Review of Sociology and Anthropology* 18:3, 283–98.

Shearing, C., D. (1993), 'Policing: Relationships Between Public and Private Forms', in Mark Findlay et al. (eds.) *Alternative Policing Styles* (Boston: Kluwer Law and Taxation Publishers).

Shearing, C., D. (2004), 'Thoughts on Sovereignty', *Policing and Society* 14:1, 5–12.

Shearing, C, D and Stenning, P, C (1981), 'Modern Private Security: Its Growth and Implications', in Michael Tonry (ed.) *Crime and Justice An Annual Review of Research* (Chicago: University of Chicago Press).

Shearing, C, D and Stenning, P, C (1982a), *Private Security and Private Justice* (Montreal: Institute for Research on Public Policy).

Shearing, C., D. and Stenning, P., C. (1982b), 'Snowflakes or Good Pinches? Private Security's Contribution to Modern Policing', in R. Donelan (ed.) *Maintenance of Order in Society* (Ottawa: Ministry of Supply and Services).

Shearing, C., D. and Stenning, P., C. (1987), 'Say "Cheese!": The Disney Order that is not so Mickey Mouse', in Clifford Shearing and Philip Stenning (eds.) *Private Policing* (Newbury Park: Sage).

Shearing, C., D., Stenning, P., C. and Addario, S., M. (1985), 'Police Perceptions of Private Security', *Canadian Police College Journal* 9:2, 127–153.

Shearing, C. and Wood, J. (2003), 'Nodal Governance, Democracy and the New 'Denizens'', *Journal of Law and Society* 30:3, 400–19.

Sheptycki, J., W., E. (1998), 'Policing, Postmodernism and Transnationalisation', *British Journal of Criminology* 38:4, 485–503.

Silva, J., A., Gregory, B., Leong, M., D. and Weinstock, R. (1993), 'The Psychotic Patient as a Security Guard', *Journal of Forensic Sciences* 38:6, 1436–1440.

Smith, D. (1972), *Report from Engine Co. 82* (New York: Warner Books).

Smith, D. (2002), *Firefighters their Lives in their Own Words* (New York: Broadway Books).

South, N. (1985), *Private Security and Social Control: The Private Security Sector in the United Kingdom, Its Commercial Functions and Public Accountability* (PhD Thesis, Middlesex Polytechnic).

South, N. (1988), *Policing for Profit* (London: Sage).

South, N. (1989), 'Reconstructing Policing: Differentiation and Contradiction in Post-War Private and Public Policing', in Roger Mathews (ed.) *Privatizing Criminal Justice* (London: Sage).

South, N. (1993), 'Who Does Policing? Dr Nigel South: Privatisation to Vigilantism', C. Martin (ed.) *Changing Policing: Business or Service*. Report of a conference organised held at the London School of Economics on the 21st September, 1993 (London: ISTD).

South, N. (1997), 'Crime Control and 'End of Criminology'', in Peter Francis et al. (eds.) *Policing Futures The Police, Law and the Twenty-First Century* (Basingstoke: MacMillan).

Spitzer, S. and Scull, A., T. (1977), 'Privatisation and the Capitalist Development of the Police', *Social Problems* 25:1, 18–29.

Stenning, P., C. (2000), 'Powers and Accountability of the Private Police', *European Journal on Criminal Policy and Research* 8:3, 325–52.

Stenning, P., C. and Shearing, C., D. (1979), *Search and Seizure: Powers of Private Security Personnel. A Study Paper Prepared for the Law Reform Commission of Canada* (Ottawa: Law Reform Commission of Canada).

Stenning, P., C. and Shearing, C., D. (1980), 'The Quiet Revolution: The Nature, Developments and General Legal Implications of Private Security in Canada', *Criminal Law Quarterly* 22, 220–248.

Stone, R. (1994), *Textbook on Civil Liberties* (London: Blackstone).

Stone, R. (1997), *Textbook on Civil Liberties* (London: Blackstone).

Strange, S. (1996), *The Retreat of the State The Diffusion of Power in the World Economy* (Cambridge: Cambridge University Press).

Turnbull, P. (1992), 'Dock Strikes and the Demise of Dockers 'Occupational Culture', *The Sociological Review* 40, 294–318.

Upson, A. (2004), *Violence at Work: Findings from the 2002/2003 British Crime Survey* (London: Home Office).

Waddington, P., A., J., Badger, D. and Bull, R. (2006), *The Violent Workplace* (Cullompton: Willan).

Walsh, J., L. (1977), 'Career Styles and Police Behaviour', in David Bayley (ed.) *Police and Society* (Beverley Hills, CA: Sage).

Wakefield, A. (2003), *Selling Security – The Private Policing of Public Space* (Cullompton: Willan).

Wakefield, A. (2001), *The Private Policing of Public Space* (PhD thesis submitted to the University of Cambridge).

Walklate, S. (2000), 'Researching Victims', Roy King and Emma Wincup (eds.) *Doing Research in Crime and Justice* (Oxford: Oxford University Press).

Walliman, N. (2001), *Your Research Project* (London: Sage).

Weber, M. (1948), 'Politics as a Vocation', in H., H. Gerth and C., W. Mills (eds. and translators) *From Max Weber: Essays in Sociology* (London: Routledge and Keegan Paul).

Whitehead, P. (2006) Trainer: Our Powers Have Nose-dived. *Professional Security*, July 2006, 56.

Williams, D., George, B. and MacLennan, E. (1984), *Guarding Against Low Pay – The Case for Regulation of Contract Security* (London: Low Pay Unit).

Willis, P., E. (1977), *Learning to Labour – How Working Class Kids Get Working Class Jobs* (Farnborough: Saxon House).

Wilson, J., Q. and Kelling, G., L. (1982) 'Broken Windows', *The Atlantic Monthly* March 1982, 29–38.

Winlow, S. (2001), *Badfellas: Crime, Tradition and New Masculinities* (Oxford: Berg).

Wolfgang, M. (1976), 'Ethical Issues of Research in Criminology', in P. Nejelski (ed.) *Social Research in Conflict with Law and Ethics* (Cambridge, MA: Ballinger).

Wood, J. (2004), 'Cultural Change in the Governance of Security', *Policing and Society* 14:1, 31–48.

Zander, M. (2003), *The Police and Criminal Evidence Act 1984* (London: Street and Maxwell).

Zander, M. (1995), *The Police and Criminal Evidence Act 1984* (London: Street and Maxwell).

Zukin, S. (1995), *The Cultures of Cities* (Oxford: Blackwell).

Internet based references

'Equal Opportunities Commission', *2001 Census: Hours of Work in England and Wales* <http://www.eoc.org.uk/cseng/research/2001_census_hours_of_work.asp> accessed, 16 April 2004.

'Federation of Employed Door Supervisors and Security', *Welcome to the Official FEDS Union Website* < http://www.fedsunion.org.uk> accessed, 5 August 2005.

'Road Alert', *Road Raging Top Tips for Wrecking Road Building* < http://www.eco-action.org/rr/ch7.html#sec> accessed, 26 April 2004.

'UNISON', *MSPs Briefing – Protection of Emergency Workers Debate* < http://www.unison-scotland.org.uk/briefings/emergency.html> accessed, 29 April 2004.

'USDAW', *USDAW Survey Reveals High Levels of Workplace Violence and Abuse* <http://www.usdaw.org.uk/usdaw/news/1073411308_26901.html> accessed 28 February 2004.

Index

airports, security officers, search powers
35–6
'Armed Industries' corporation
access control 111–12, 114–16
cameras, prohibition 125–6
CCTV 56
general description 54
mentalities
examples 130
of governance 57
prohibited items 125–7
searches
conducted 116
procedures 117–20
security, governance 54–5
security officers
abuse of 140–9
alternative employment, seeking 158–9
arrests carried out 87–100
with consent 89–90
with force 91–5
assaults on 145
see also violence
commitment to job 155, 156–8
current employment, reasons for 158
educational qualifications 60, 180
extra special legal powers, views on
101–4
hours worked 160
isolation 138–41
knowledge
arrest powers 69, 70, 71–2
legal tools 81–2
overall level 83–4
reasonable force 79–81
search powers 73–9
length of service 156
machismo 164–5
non-lethal weapons, views 104–8
'parapolice' model 171–2
pay, views on 161, 163
personal characteristics 59–60

relationship with management 134, 135
sexist views 164–5, 166
suspicious minds 166, 167
teamwork 163
training 61
arrest powers 68
powers to use force 68
search powers 68
views on 62, 63–4, 68
turnover 156
verbal abuse of 141–3
violence, threats of 143, 145
'watchman' model 169–70
work routines 55, 56–7
working conditions 161
'works police' culture 55–6
traffic
offences 123
regulations 121–3
arrest, meaning 87–8
see also citizen's arrest
arrestable offences 34–5

breach of the peace 33, 34, 92
British Retail Consortium (BRC), retail
crime statistics 17
British Security Industry Association
(BSIA) 57
membership 58
BS 7499 standard 52, 55, 58, 60, 61

case studies see 'Armed Industries';
'Pleasure Southquay'
CCTV 51, 52, 56, 112, 114, 167
public reassurance rating 179
Channel Tunnel, security officers, search
powers 36
citizen's arrest 2, 6, 39, 71, 103
codes of practice 21
consent
police powers 8
and search powers 38–41

court security officers, special powers 36
Crime Prevention Agency, *Making Arrests* 22
culture
  definition 151
  influences on 152
  levels 151–2
  see also police culture; security officers, culture

data analysis
  NUDIST software 28
  SPSS software 26
denizen, definition 46
denizens 47, 57, 182, 183
documents
  definition 26
  research 27
door supervisors 154, 161–2
  sexist views 165

Electronic Article Surveillance Equipment (EAS) 39
ethics, in research 28–9
exclusions, of undesirables 17, 112–13, 186

Federation of Employed Door Supervisors and Security (FEDS) 161–2

governance, dimensions 46

human rights, and property rights 37–8
Hunt Saboteurs Association (HSA), violence against members 18

informed consent, research 29
Institute of Personnel and Development 21
International Professional Security Association (IPSA) 58
interviews 23–4
  tape recording 24

language
  as police strategy 9
  as security officer strategy 14
Lawtel database 22

mentalities
  creation of 129

examples 129–30
mentality, definition 47
Milgram experiments, obedience to authority 16
models, of security officers 42–3, 168–73, 185

night-time economy (NTE) 53, 93, 94, 95, 97, 109, 130, 133, 134, 139, 141, 149, 165, 184, 186
nodes
  definition 45
  of governance 45–6, 177, 180, 182–3
NUDIST software 28

obedience to authority, and security officers 16
observation
  approaches 26
  ideal types 25

panopticon 6
'Pleasure Southquay' retail/leisure complex 46–54
  access control 111, 112–14
  CCTV 51, 52, 167
  crime figures 53
  exclusions 112–13, 186
  general description 46–7
  mentalities
    cleanliness 50
    customer-friendly security officers 49
    design 50
    examples 130
    exclusivity 48, 50
    image 47–50
    reputation 49
  photography, restrictions 127
  security
    governance 50–4
    strategies 47
    success 53–4
    supervision of 52
  security officers
    abuse of 140–9
    alternative employment, seeking 158–9
    arrests carried out 87–100, 170–1
      with consent 89–90
      with force 91–100

assaults on 145–7
see also violence
coercion, threat of 53
commitment to job 158
current employment, reasons for 158
educational qualifications 60, 180
extra special legal powers, views on
        101–4
hours worked 160
isolation 138–41, 163
knowledge
    arrest powers 69, 70, 71–2
    legal tools 81–2, 180–1
    overall level 83–4
    powers to use force 70
    reasonable force 79–81
    search powers 73–9
length of service 156
machismo 165–6
management, relationship with 134–5
non-lethal weapons, views on 104–8
'parapolice' model 170–1, 185
pay, views on 161
personal characteristics 59–60
police, relationship with 49, 52, 93–4,
        98–100, 135–7
searches conducted 116, 120
sexist views 165
suspicious minds 166, 167
teamwork 162–3
training 61
    arrest powers 68
    powers to use force 68
    search powers 68
    views on 62, 63, 64, 68
troublemakers, profiling 167
turnover 156
uniforms 161, 163
verbal abuse 141–2
violence, threats of 143–4, 148
'watchman' model 169
work routines 51, 52
working conditions 161
traffic regulations 120, 124–5
police
attitude to security officers 178
research on 178
violence against 148
police culture 152–3

characteristics 153–4
    varieties 153, 167–8
police powers 7–9
    attitudes to 7
    to obtain consent 8, 9
police strategies
    search threats 9
    suspect's
        ignorance 9
        implied guilt 9
    use of language 9
policing
    private 2
    resources, social justice issues 186
power
    outcome power, definition 6
    social power, definition 6
    three dimensional model 5–6, 128–30,
        181, 182, 185
private property, trespassers, right to remove
        36
private security industry 1
    HAC inquiry 18
private space 2, 10, 120, 128
    as quasi-public space 37, 42, 182, 184
property protection
    injunctions 36
    removal of trespassers 36
property rights, and human rights 37–8

railway security officers, search powers 36
research
    on the police 178
    on security officers, lack of 177–8
research methods 21, 22–6
    anonymity guarantee 29
    data analysis 26–8
    documents 26, 27
    ethical matters 28–9
    and informed consent 29
    interviews 23–4
    observation 25–6
research questions 2
retail crime, statistics 17

search powers
    airport security officers 35–6
    Channel Tunnel security officers 36
    with consent 38–41, 73–4, 77

railway security officers 36
search threats, as police strategy 9
searches
    after arrest 41
    as employment condition 39–40
    as entry condition 38–9
    transparency requirements 40–1
security, and social control issues 186–7
security industry
    market value 57–8
    regulation 183
Security Industry Training Organisation
        (SITO)
    Advanced Security Officer course 21, 32
    basic training 61, 64
    Professional Security Officer course 21, 33
    training manuals/courses 21
security officers
    abuse of powers 17–18
    age profiles 58, 59
    airports 35–6
    arrest powers 32–5, 87–8
    culture 154–5, 168–75, 182
    educational qualifications 58
    force, use of 35
    knowledge tools 14–16
        cultural context 16
    legal powers 1–2, 6
        basis, need to examine 184–5
        sources 10
    legal tools
        citizens' legal powers 12
        employment contracts 13
        establishing 21–2
        exclusions 17
        knowledge of 65–85, 183
        in nodal context 22
        property owners' rights 12–13, 36–8
        select 35–41, 180
        special legal powers 10–12
        universal 32–5, 180
    linguistic tools 14
    marital status 58
    models 42–3, 168–73
        'watchman', v parapolice 173, 185
    numbers 58
    and obedience to authority 16
    occupational hazards 133–49, 181
    pay 58

perception
    by media 179
    by police 178
    by public 178–9
    personal characteristics 57–64
    physical tools 13–14
        identity badges 13
        uniforms 13, 14
    in public areas, special powers 36
    racial profiles 58, 59
    regulation of 18–19
    research on, neglect 177–8
    and right to ask 31–2
    role, need for debate 183–4
    trade unions 161–2
    training 60, 183
    uniformed, as authority figures 32
    use of powers 16–17
    violence, use of 18
    violence against 148
    women 58, 164–5
    working conditions 159–60
    workplace violence 140–9, 184
    see also under 'Armed Industries';
            'Pleasure Southquay'
shopping centres, trespass in 37
social control issues, and security 186–7
SPSS software, data analysis 26
store detectives 17, 32, 34, 49, 144

trade unions, security officers 161–2
training
    arrest powers 68
    courses 21
    in legal tools 67–8
    manuals 21, 22
    in powers to use force 68
    Professional Guard I 61
    search powers 68
    security officers 60
    SITO
        basic 61, 64
        Professional Security Officer course 21, 33
trespass
    forms of 36
    on private property 36
    in quasi-public space, and HRA 37
    in shopping centres 37

uniform, authority symbol 32

violence
  against
    hunt saboteurs 18
    police officers 148
    protesters 18
    security officers 148
  by security officers 18
  power to use 35
  risk of 37

Wandsworth Parks Police 8–9
wheel clamping 41
women, security officers 58, 164–5
working conditions 159–60

www.ingramcontent.com/pod-product-compliance
Ingram Content Group UK Ltd.
Pitfield, Milton Keynes, MK11 3LW, UK
UKHW020353010325
455677UK00021B/435